When should I [ ] the best airfare?

Where do I go for answers to my travel questions?

What's the best and easiest way to plan and book my trip?

frommers.travelocity.com

Frommer's, the travel guide leader, has teamed up with **Travelocity.com,** the leader in online travel, to bring you an in-depth, easy-to-use resource designed to help you plan and book your trip online.

At **frommers.travelocity.com**, you'll find free online updates about your destination from the experts at Frommer's plus the outstanding travel planning and purchasing features of Travelocity.com. Travelocity.com provides reservations capabilities for 95 percent of all airline seats sold, more than 47,000 hotels, and over 50 car rental companies. In addition, Travelocity.com offers more than 2,000 exciting vacation and cruise packages. Travelocity.com puts you in complete control of your travel planning with these and other great features:

> **Expert travel guidance from Frommer's** - over 150 writers reporting from around the world!

> **Best Fare Finder** - an interactive calendar tells you when to travel to get the best airfare

> **Fare Watcher** - we'll track airfare changes to your favorite destinations

> **Dream Maps** - a mapping feature that suggests travel opportunities based on your budget

> **Shop Safe Guarantee** - 24 hours a day / 7 days a week live customer service, and more!

Whether traveling on a tight budget, looking for a quick weekend getaway, or planning the trip of a lifetime, Frommer's guides and Travelocity.com will make your travel dreams a reality. You've bought the book, now book the trip!

P O R T A B L E

Los Angeles
1st Edition

by Stephanie Avnet Yates

IDG Books Worldwide, Inc.
An International Data Group Company
Foster City, CA • Chicago, IL • Indianapolis, IN • New York, NY

ABOUT THE AUTHOR

A native of Los Angeles and an avid traveler, antiques hound, and pop-history enthusiast, **Stephanie Avnet Yates** believes that California is best seen from behind the wheel of a little red convertible. Stephanie has authored *Frommer's Los Angeles, Frommer's San Diego,* and *Frommer's Wonderful Weekends from Los Angeles,* and cowritten *Frommer's California,* in addition to contributing to several other regional guidebooks and Web sites. Online, Stephanie can be reached directly at *savvy_girl@hotmail.com.*

IDG BOOKS WORLDWIDE, INC.

An International Data Group Company
IDG Books Worldwide, Inc.
909 Third Avenue
New York, NY 10022

Find us online at **www.frommers.com**

ISBN 0-7645-6092-1
ISSN 1528-2201

Editor: Nicole Daro
Special Thanks to Chad McNeal and Sharz Divsalar
Production Editor: Donna Wright
Photo Editor: Richard Fox
Design by Michele Laseau
Cartographer: John Decamillis
Production by IDG Books Indianapolis Production Department

SPECIAL SALES

For general information on IDG Books Worldwide's books in the U.S., please call our Consumer Customer Service department at 1-800-762-2974. For reseller information, including discounts, bulk sales, customized editions, and premium sales, please call our Reseller Customer Service department at 1-800-434-3422.

Manufactured in the United States of America

5 4 3 2 1

Contents

List of Maps

AN INVITATION TO THE READER

In researching this book I have discovered many wonderful places—hotels, restaurants, shops, and more. I'm sure you'll find others. Please tell us about them, so that I can share the information with your fellow travelers in upcoming editions. If you were disappointed with a recommendation, I'd love to know that, too. Please write to:

Frommer's Portable Los Angeles, 1st Edition
IDG Books Worldwide, Inc.
909 Third Avenue
New York, NY 10022

AN ADDITIONAL NOTE

Please be advised that travel information is subject to change at any time, and this is especially true of prices. We therefore suggest that you write or call ahead for confirmation when making your travel plans. The author, editors, and publishers cannot be held responsible for the experiences of readers while traveling. Your safety is important to us, however, so we encourage you to stay alert and be aware of your surroundings. Keep a close eye on cameras, purses, and wallets, all favorite targets of thieves and pickpockets.

WHAT THE SYMBOLS MEAN

✪ Frommer's Favorites

Our favorite places and experiences—outstanding for quality, value, or both.

The following abbreviations are used for credit cards:

AE	American Express	EC	Eurocard
CB	Carte Blanche	JCB	Japan Credit Bank
DC	Diners Club	MC	MasterCard
DISC	Discover	V	Visa
ER	EnRoute		

FIND FROMMER'S ONLINE

www.frommers.com offers up-to-the-minute listings on almost 200 cities around the globe—including the latest bargains and candid, personal articles updated daily by Arthur Frommer himself. No other Web site offers such comprehensive and timely coverage of the world of travel.

Planning a Trip to Los Angeles

*L*os Angelenos know that their city will never have the sophisticated style of Paris or the historical riches of London—but we cheerfully lay claim to living in the most fun city in the United States, maybe the world. Home to the planet's first amusement park, L.A. regularly feels like one, as the line between fantasy and reality is so often obscured. From the unattainable, anachronistic glamour of Beverly Hills to the earthy, often-scary street energy of Venice, each of the city's diverse neighborhoods is like a mini–theme park, offering its own kind of adventure. The colors of this city seem a little bit brighter—and more surreal—than they do in other cities, the angles just a little sharper. Drive down Sunset Boulevard, and you'll see what I mean: The billboards are just a bit taller, the wacky folks just a touch wackier. Everything seems larger than life. No, you're not in Kansas anymore—you're in Toon Town now.

This chapter contains practical information to help you make your travel arrangements, pick a time to visit, find local resources for specialized needs, and even access megabytes of useful information on the Internet.

1 Visitor Information

If you'd like information on the city before you go, contact the **Los Angeles Convention and Visitors Bureau,** 633 W. 5th St., Suite 600, Los Angeles, CA 90071 (☎ **213/624-7300;** www.lacvb.com).

In addition, almost every municipality and economic district in Los Angeles has a dedicated tourist bureau or chamber of commerce that will be more than happy to send you information on a particular area; see "Orientation" in chapter 2 for a complete list.

You can also find information on Los Angeles at the following Web sites:

- **www.at-la.com** is the home page of At L.A., whose exceptional search engine provides links to more than 41,000 sites in thousands of categories relating to all of Southern California.

- **www.calendarlive.com** is the entertainment division of the *Los Angeles Times*. It's an online guide to entertainment news and local listings.
- **www.digitalcity.com/losangeles** is the local outpost of the nationally popular Digital City series, offering up-to-date articles on life in L.A., including dining, shopping, and entertainment info.
- **www.losangeles.com** is the L.A. feature of Boulevards, whose national alternative Web sites emphasize travel, arts, entertainment, contemporary culture, and politics.

2 When to Go

Tourism peaks during **summer,** when coastal hotels fill to capacity, restaurant reservations can be hard to come by, and top attractions are packed to the gills with visitors and locals off from work or school. Summer can be miserable in the inland valleys, where daytime temperatures—and that famous L.A. smog—can reach stifling levels, but the beach communities almost always remain comfortable.

Moderate temperatures, fewer crowds, and sometimes lower hotel rates make travel to L.A. most pleasurable during the **winter.** The city is particularly delightful from early autumn to late spring, when the skies are less smoggy. Rain is rare in Los Angeles, but it can cause crippling flooding when it does sneak up on the unsuspecting city; precipitation is most likely from February to April, and virtually unheard of between May and November. Even in January, daytime temperature readings regularly reach into the 60s and higher—sometimes even into the 80s.

Los Angeles's Average Temperatures (°F)

	Jan	Feb	Mar	Apr	May	Jun	Jul	Aug	Sept	Oct	Nov	Dec
Avg. High	65	66	67	69	72	75	81	81	81	77	73	69
Avg. Low	46	48	49	52	54	57	60	60	59	55	51	49

LOS ANGELES AREA CALENDAR OF EVENTS

January

- **Tournament of Roses,** Pasadena. A spectacular parade down Colorado Boulevard, with lavish floats, music, and extraordinary equestrian entries, followed by the Rose Bowl Game. Call

☎ **626/449-4100** for details, or just stay home and watch it on TV (you'll have a better view). January 1.

February

- **Nissan L.A. Open Golf Tournament,** Pacific Palisades. The PGA Tour makes its only Tinseltown appearance each year at the exclusive Riviera Country Club overlooking the ocean. Expect to see stars in attendance, watching defending champion Kirk Triplett going for another L.A. win. For tickets and information, call the Los Angeles Junior Chamber of Commerce (☎ **213/482-1311**). Mid-February.

March

- **Los Angeles Marathon.** This 26.2-mile run through the streets of Los Angeles attracts thousands of participants, from world champions to the guy next door. The run starts in downtown Los Angeles. Call ☎ **310/444-5544** or visit **www.lamarathon.com** for registration or spectator information. Early March.

April

- **Toyota Grand Prix,** Long Beach. An exciting weekend of Indy-class auto racing and entertainment in and around downtown Long Beach, drawing world-class drivers from the United States and Europe, plus many celebrity contestants and spectators. Contact the Grand Prix Association at ☎ **800/752-9524** or 562/981-2600; www.longbeachgp.com. Mid-April.

May

- **Cinco de Mayo,** Los Angeles. A weeklong celebration of Mexico's jubilant Independence Day takes place throughout the city. There's a carnival atmosphere with large crowds, live music, dancing, and food. The main festivities are held at El Pueblo de Los Angeles State Historic Park, downtown; call ☎ **213/628-1274** for information. Other events are held around the city. The week surrounding May 5.

- **Venice Art Walk,** Venice Beach. Celebrating 22 years in 2001, this annual weekend event gives visitors a chance to take docent-guided tours of galleries and studios, plus a Sunday self-guided art walk through the private home studios of more than 50 emerging and well-known artists. For details, call the Venice Family Clinic, which coordinates the event (☎ **310/ 392-8630,** ext. 1), or visit its Web site at www.vfc.net. Second half of May.

June

- **Playboy Jazz Festival,** Los Angeles. Bill Cosby is the traditional master of ceremonies, presiding over the top artists at the Hollywood Bowl. Call ☎ **310/449-4070.** Mid-month.
- **Gay & Lesbian Pride Celebration,** West Hollywood. In its 31st year, this West Hollywood gathering promises to be larger than ever. Outdoor stages, disco- and western-dance tents, food, and general revelry culminate in Sunday's flamboyant parade down Santa Monica Boulevard. Call ☎ **323/658-8700.** Last weekend in June.

July

- **Beach Festival,** Huntington Beach. Two straight weeks of fun in the sun, featuring two surfing competitions—the U.S. Open of Surfing and the world-class Pro of Surfing—plus extreme sports events like inline skating, BMX biking, skateboarding, and more. Includes entertainment, food, tons of product booths and giveaways—and plenty of tanned, swimsuit-clad bodies of both sexes. Call U.S. Surfing (☎ **949/366-4584**) for more information. End of July.

August

- **African Marketplace and Cultural Fair.** African arts, crafts, food, and music are featured at this cultural-awareness event. Call ☎ **323/734-1164.** Held at Rancho La Cienega Park, 5001 Rodeo Rd.; to get there, take I-10 to the La Brea Avenue exit. Weekends, mid-August through Labor Day.

September

- **Los Angeles County Fair,** Pomona. Horse racing, arts, agricultural displays, celebrity entertainment, and carnival rides are among the attractions at one of the largest county fairs in the world. Held at the Los Angeles County Fair and Exposition Center; call ☎ **909/623-3111** or visit **www.fairplex.com** for information. Throughout September.

November

- **Doo Dah Parade,** Pasadena. An outrageous spoof of the Rose Parade, featuring such participants as the Briefcase Precision Drill Team and a kazoo-playing marching band. Call ☎ **626/449-3689.** Near Thanksgiving.
- **Hollywood Christmas Parade.** This spectacular, star-studded parade marches through the heart of Hollywood. For information, call ☎ **323/469-2337.** Sunday after Thanksgiving.

3   Tips for Travelers with Special Needs

FOR TRAVELERS WITH DISABILITIES

Los Angeles's spirit of tolerance and diversity has made it a welcoming place for travelers with disabilities. Strict construction codes make most public facilities and attractions extremely accessible (though some historic sites and older buildings simply can't accommodate drastic remodeling), and the city provides many services for those with disabilities.

A little advance planning is always useful. There are more resources out there than ever before. *A World of Options,* a 658-page book for travelers with disabilities, covers everything from biking trips to scuba outfitters. It costs $45 (less for members) and is available from **Mobility International USA,** P.O. Box 10767, Eugene, OR 97440 (☎ **541/343-1284,** voice and TDD; www.miusa.org). Annual membership for Mobility International is $35, which includes its quarterly newsletter, *Over the Rainbow.*

You can join **The Society for the Advancement of Travel for the Handicapped** (SATH), 347 5th Ave., Suite 610, New York, NY 10016 (☎ **212/447-7284,** fax 212-725-8253; www.sath.org), for $45 annually, $30 for seniors and students, to gain access to a vast network of connections in the travel industry. The Society provides information sheets on travel destinations and referrals to tour operators that specialize in travelers with disabilities. Its quarterly magazine, *Open World for Disability and Mature Travel,* is full of good information and resources. A year's subscription is $13 ($21 outside the United States).

Access-Able Travel Source offers a comprehensive online index of accessible hotels, restaurants, attractions, and disabled-service providers throughout California; log on to www.access-able.com or call ☎ **303/232-2979.**

The **Junior League of Los Angeles,** Farmers Market, 3rd and Fairfax streets, Gate 12, Los Angeles, CA 90036 (☎ **323/937-5566**), distributes *Around the Town with Ease,* a free brochure detailing the accessibility of various Los Angeles sites. There's a $2 handling fee for mail orders.

CAR RENTALS   Many of the major car-rental companies now offer hand-controlled cars for drivers with disabilities. **Avis** (☎ **800/331-1212**) can provide such a vehicle at any of its locations in the United States with 48-hour advance notice; **Hertz** (☎ **800/654-3131**) requires between 24 and 72 hours of advance reservation at most of its locations. **Wheelchair Getaways** (☎ **800/873-4973;** www.wheelchair-getaways.com) rents specialized vans with wheelchair lifts and other features for those with disabilities in more than 100 cities across the United States.

FOR GAY & LESBIAN TRAVELERS

When **West Hollywood** was incorporated in 1984 (it was formerly just a Los Angeles neighborhood), it proudly flaunted a lesbian mayor and a predominantly gay city council. WeHo, as it's come to be known, has been waving the rainbow banner ever since. While L.A.'s powerful gay community is far too vast to be contained in this 2-square-mile city, West Hollywood has the largest concentration of gay- and lesbian-oriented businesses and services. Santa Monica, Venice, Silver Lake, and Studio City are other lesbian and gay enclaves.

GUIDES & PUBLICATIONS   There are many gay-oriented publications with information and up-to-date listings, including *The Advocate,* a biweekly national magazine; *Frontiers,* a Southern California–based biweekly; and *Nightlife,* a local weekly with comprehensive entertainment listings, complete with maps. The nation's outstanding travel-specific gay periodical is *Out and About* (☎ **800/929-2268;** www.outandabout.com), hailed for its "straight" and savvy reporting on gay travel. The magazine, which aims for the more upscale traveler, profiles gay and gay-friendly places in a variety of worldwide destinations. It's been praised by everybody from *Travel & Leisure* to the *New York Times.*

The periodicals above are available at most newsstands citywide and at the following bookstores. **A Different Light Bookstore,** 8853 Santa Monica Blvd., West Hollywood (☎ **310/854-6601;** www.adlbooks.com), is L.A.'s largest and best gay-oriented bookshop. Its Web site is also enormously helpful. **Sisterhood Books,** 1351 Westwood Blvd., West Los Angeles (☎ **310/477-7300;** www.sisterhood.com) is one of the best sources for lesbian-oriented books, magazines, and newspapers; its Web site has links to many other sites of lesbian and bisexual interest.

ORGANIZATIONS   The **International Gay & Lesbian Travel Association** (IGLTA; ☎ **800/448-8550** or 954/776-2626; www.iglta.org) links travelers up with the appropriate gay-friendly service organization or tour specialist. With around 1,200 members, it offers quarterly newsletters, marketing mailings, and a membership directory that's updated quarterly.

FOR SENIORS

Nearly every attraction in Los Angeles offers a senior discount; age requirements vary. Public transportation and movie theaters also have reduced rates. Don't be shy about asking for discounts, but always carry some kind of identification, such as a driver's license, that shows your date of birth. Also, mention the fact that you're a senior citizen when you first make your travel reservations. For example, both **Amtrak** (☎ **800/USA-RAIL;** www.amtrak.com) and **Greyhound** (☎ **800/752-4841;** www. greyhound.com) offer discounts to persons over 62.

Members of the **American Association of Retired Persons (AARP),** 601 E St. NW, Washington, DC 20049 (☎ **800/ 424-3410** or 202/434-2277), get discounts not only on hotels but on airfares and car rentals too. AARP also offers members a wide range of other special benefits, including *Modern Maturity* magazine and a monthly newsletter.

Mature Outlook, P.O. Box 9390, Des Moines, IA 50306 (☎ **800/336-6330**), began as a travel organization for people over 50, though it now caters to people of all ages. Members receive a bimonthly magazine as well as discounts on hotels. Annual membership is $19.95.

The Mature Traveler, a monthly 12-page newsletter on senior-citizen travel, is a valuable resource. It's available by subscription ($30 a year) from GEM Publishing Group, Box 50400, Reno, NV, 89513-0400. GEM also publishes *The Book of Deals,* a collection of more than 1,000 senior discounts on airlines, lodging, tours, and attractions around the country; it's available for $9.95 by calling ☎ **800/460-6676.** Another helpful publication is *101 Tips for the Mature Traveler,* available from Grand Circle Travel, 347 Congress St., Suite 3A, Boston, MA 02210 (☎ **800/221-2610** or 617/350-7500; fax 617/346-6700). Also check your newsstand for the quarterly magazine *Travel 50 & Beyond.*

FOR FAMILIES

Several books on the market offer tips to help you travel with kids. *Family Travel* (Lanier Publishing International) and *How to Take Great Trips with Your Kids* (The Harvard Common Press) are full of good general advice.

Family Travel Times is published six times a year by TWYCH (Travel with Your Children; ☎ **888/822-4388** or 212/477-5524) and includes a weekly call-in service for subscribers. Subscriptions are $40 a year for quarterly editions. A free publication list and a sample issue are available by calling the above number

Families Welcome!, 92 N. Main, Ashland, OR 97520 (☎ **800/326-0724** or 541/482-6121), is a travel company specializing in worry-free vacations for families.

4 Getting There

ARRIVING BY PLANE

All major U.S. carriers serve Los Angeles International Airport (LAX). Domestic airlines flying in and out of LAX include **Alaska Airlines** (☎ 800/426-0333; www. alaskaair.com), **America West** (☎ 800/235-9292; www.americawest.com), **American Airlines** (☎ 800/433-7300; www.aa.com), **Continental Airlines** (☎ 800/525-0280; www.continental.com), **Delta Air Lines** (☎ 800/221-1212; www.delta.com), **Northwest Airlines** (☎ 800/225-2525; www.nwa.com), **TWA** (☎ 800/221-2000; www.twa.com), **United Airlines** (☎ 800/241-6522; www.ual.com), and **US Airways** (☎ 800/428-4322; www.usair.com).

Several smaller carriers are known for the excellent and comprehensive service they provide up and down the California coast. **America West** (☎ 800/235-9292; www. americawest.com), **Skywest** (☎ 800/453-9417; www.skywest.com), and **Southwest Airlines** (☎ 800/435-9792; www.southwest.com) are some of the biggest carriers offering regular service between California cities. You can often find round-trip coach fare between San Francisco and L.A. for about $198—book early, or during a sale, and you can pay as little as $79 to $89.

GETTING INTO TOWN FROM LAX

BY CAR To reach Santa Monica and other northern beach communities, exit the airport, take Sepulveda Boulevard north, and follow the signs to Calif. 1 (Pacific Coast Highway, or PCH) north.

To reach Redondo, Hermosa, Newport, and the other southern beach communities, take Sepulveda Boulevard south, then follow the signs to Calif. 1 (Pacific Coast Highway, or PCH) south.

To reach Beverly Hills or Hollywood, exit the airport via Century Boulevard, then take I-405 north to Santa Monica Boulevard east.

To reach downtown or Pasadena, exit the airport, take Sepulveda Boulevard south, then take I-105 east to I-110 north.

BY SHUTTLE   Many city hotels provide free shuttles for their guests; ask about transportation when you make reservations. The **SuperShuttle** (☎ **800/554-3146** from LAX, or 310/782-6600) offers regularly scheduled minivans from LAX to any location in the city. The set fare can range from about $10 to $50 per person, depending on your destination (you're unlikely to pay more than $35, which will get you as far as Burbank or Universal City). It's cheaper to cab it to most destinations if you're a group of three or more, but the vans are infinitely more comfortable; however, you might have to stop at other passengers' destinations before you reach your own. Reservations, while not required, are strongly advised.

BY TAXI   Taxis line up outside each terminal. Rides are metered. Expect to pay about $25 to $30 to Hollywood and downtown, $20 to $25 to Beverly Hills, $20 to Santa Monica, and $45 to Pasadena, including a $2.50 service charge for rides originating at LAX.

ARRIVING BY CAR

Los Angeles is well connected to the rest of the United States by several major highways. Among them are Interstate 5, which enters the state from the north; Interstate 10, which originates in Jacksonville, Florida, and terminates in Los Angeles; and U.S. 101, a scenic route that follows the western seaboard from Los Angeles north to the Oregon state line. If you're planning to take smaller roads, call the **California Highway Patrol** (☎ **213/953-7383**) to check road conditions before heading out.

If you're driving **from the north,** you have two choices: the quick route, along I-5 through the middle of the state, or the scenic route along the coast. Heading south along I-5, you'll pass a small town called Grapevine. This marks the start of the mountain pass with the same name. Once you've reached the southern end of the pass, you'll be in the San Fernando Valley, which is the start of Los Angeles County. To reach the beach communities and L.A.'s Westside, take I-405 south; to get to

Travel Tip

If you're planning a road trip, it's a good idea to be a member of the **American Automobile Association (AAA).** Members who carry their cards with them not only receive free roadside assistance but also have access to a wealth of free travel information (detailed maps and guidebooks). Also, many hotels and attractions throughout California offer discounts to AAA members—always inquire. Call ☎ **800/922-8228** or your local branch for membership information.

Hollywood, take Calif. 170 south to U.S. 101 south (this route is called the Hollywood Freeway the entire way); the I-5 will take you along the eastern edge of downtown and into Orange County.

If you're taking the scenic coastal route from the north, take U.S. 101 to I-405 or I-5, or stay on U.S. 101, following the instructions as listed above to your final destination.

If you're approaching **from the east,** you'll be coming in on I-10. For Orange County, take Calif. 57 south. I-10 continues through downtown and terminates at the beach. If you're heading to the Westside, take I-405 north. To get to the beaches, take Calif. 1 (PCH) north or south, depending on your destination.

From the south, head north on I-5. At the southern end of Orange County, I-405 splits off to the west; take this road to the Westside and beach communities. Stay on I-5 to reach downtown and Hollywood.

Here are some handy **driving times** if you're on one of those see-the-U.S.A. car trips: From Phoenix, it's about 350 miles, or 6 hours (okay, 7, if you drive the speed limit) to Los Angeles via I-10. Las Vegas is 265 miles northeast of Los Angeles (about a 4- or 5-hr. drive). San Francisco is 390 miles north of Los Angeles on I-5 (between 6 and 7 hrs.), and San Diego is 115 miles (about 2 hrs.) south.

Getting to Know Los Angeles

*T*he freeways crisscrossing the Los Angeles metropolitan area are your lifelines to the sights, but it will take you a little time to master the maze. Even locals sometimes have trouble making their way around this sprawling city. This chapter will help you get familiar with the setup of the city and will start you on the road to negotiating it like a native.

1 Orientation

VISITOR INFORMATION CENTERS

The **Los Angeles Convention and Visitors Bureau,** 633 W. 5th St., Suite 600, Los Angeles, CA 90071 (☎ **213/624-7300;** www.lacvb.com), is the city's main source for information. The bureau also staffs a **Visitors Information Center** at 685 S. Figueroa St., downtown between Wilshire Boulevard and 7th Street; it's open Monday through Friday from 8am to 5pm and Saturday from 8:30am to 5pm.

Many Los Angeles–area communities also have their own information centers, and often they maintain detailed and colorful Web sites. **Beverly Hills Visitors Bureau,** 239 S. Beverly Dr., Beverly Hills, CA 90212 (☎ **800/345-2210** or 310/271-8174; www.bhvb.org), is open Monday through Friday from 9am to 5pm.

Visitor Information Center Hollywood, Janes House, 6541 Hollywood Blvd., Hollywood, CA 90028 (☎ **213/236-2331**), is open Monday through Saturday from 9am to 5pm.

Santa Monica Convention and Visitors Bureau, 2219 Main St., Santa Monica, CA 90405 (☎ **310/393-7593;** www. santamonica.com), is the best source for information about Santa Monica. The Santa Monica Visitors Bureau Palisades Park is located near the Santa Monica Pier, at 1400 Ocean Ave. (between Santa Monica Boulevard and Broadway), and is open daily from 10am to 5pm.

West Hollywood Convention and Visitors Bureau, 8687 Melrose Ave., M-26, West Hollywood, CA 90096 (☎ **800/ 368-6020** or 310/289-2525; fax 310/289-2529; www. visitwesthollywood.com), is open Monday through Friday from 8am to 6pm.

OTHER INFORMATION SOURCES

Local tourist boards are terrific for unbiased information regarding attractions and special events, but they often fail to keep a finger on the pulse of what's really happening, especially with regard to dining, culture, and nightlife. Several city-oriented newspapers and magazines offer up-to-date info on current happenings. *L.A. Weekly* (www.laweekly.com), a free weekly listings magazine, is packed with information on current events around town. It's available from sidewalk news racks and in many stores and restaurants around the city; it also has a lively Web site.

The *Los Angeles Times* **"Calendar"** section of the Sunday paper, an excellent guide to the world of entertainment in and around L.A., includes listings of what's doing and where to do it. The *Times* also maintains a comprehensive Web site at **www. calendarlive.com**; once there you'll find departments with names like "Southland Scenes," "Tourist Tips," "Family & Kids," and "Recreation & Fitness." Information is culled from the newspaper's many departments and is always up-to-date. If you'd like to check out L.A.'s most immediate news, the *Times's* main Web site is **www.latimes.com**.

Los Angeles Magazine (www.lamag.com) is a stylish city-based monthly full of real news and pure gossip, plus guides to L.A.'s art, music, and food scenes. Its calendar of events, which has been getting better lately, gives an excellent overview of goings-on at museums, art galleries, musical venues, and other places. The magazine is available at newsstands around town and in select other major U.S. cities; you can also access stories and listings from the current issue on the Internet. Serious cyberhounds should visit **At L.A.'s** Web site at **www.at-la.com**; the site's exceptionally precise search engine (one of the author's favorite tools) provides links to more than 23,000 sites relating to the L.A. area.

CITY LAYOUT

Los Angeles is not a single compact city, but a sprawling suburbia comprising dozens of disparate communities. Most of the city's communities are located between mountains and ocean, on the flatlands of a huge basin. Even if you've never visited L.A. before, you'll recognize the names of many of these areas: Hollywood, Beverly Hills, Santa Monica, Malibu. Ocean breezes push the city's infamous smog inland, toward dozens of less well-known residential communities, and through mountain passes into the suburban sprawl of the San Fernando and San Gabriel valleys.

Downtown Los Angeles—which isn't where most tourists go— is in the center of the basin, about 12 miles east of the Pacific Ocean. Most visitors will spend the bulk of their time either on the coast or on the city's Westside (see "Neighborhoods in Brief," below, for complete details on all of the city's sectors).

MAIN ARTERIES & STREETS

L.A.'s extensive system of toll-free, high-speed freeways connects the city's patchwork of communities. The system works well to get you where you need to be, although rush-hour traffic can sometimes be bumper-to-bumper. Here's an overview:

U.S. 101, called the "Ventura Freeway" in the San Fernando Valley and the "Hollywood Freeway" in the city, runs across L.A. in a roughly northwest–southeast direction, from the San Fernando Valley to the center of downtown.

Calif. 134 continues as the "Ventura Freeway" after U.S. 101 turns into the city and becomes the Hollywood Freeway. This branch of the Ventura Freeway continues directly east, through the valley towns of Burbank and Glendale, to I-210 (the "Foothill Freeway"), which will take you through Pasadena and out toward the eastern edge of Los Angeles County.

I-5, otherwise known as the "Golden State Freeway" north of I-10 and the "Santa Ana Freeway" south of I-10, bisects downtown on its way from San Francisco to San Diego.

I-10, labeled the "Santa Monica Freeway" west of I-5 and the "San Bernardino Freeway" east of I-5, is the city's major east–west freeway, connecting the San Gabriel Valley with downtown and Santa Monica.

I-405, also known as the "San Diego Freeway," runs north–south through L.A.'s Westside, connecting the San Fernando Valley with LAX and the southern beach areas.

I-105, Los Angeles's newest freeway—called the "Century Freeway"—extends from LAX east to I-605.

I-110, commonly known as the "Harbor Freeway," starts in Pasadena as Calif. 110 (the "Pasadena Freeway"); it becomes an

The Neighborhoods in Brief

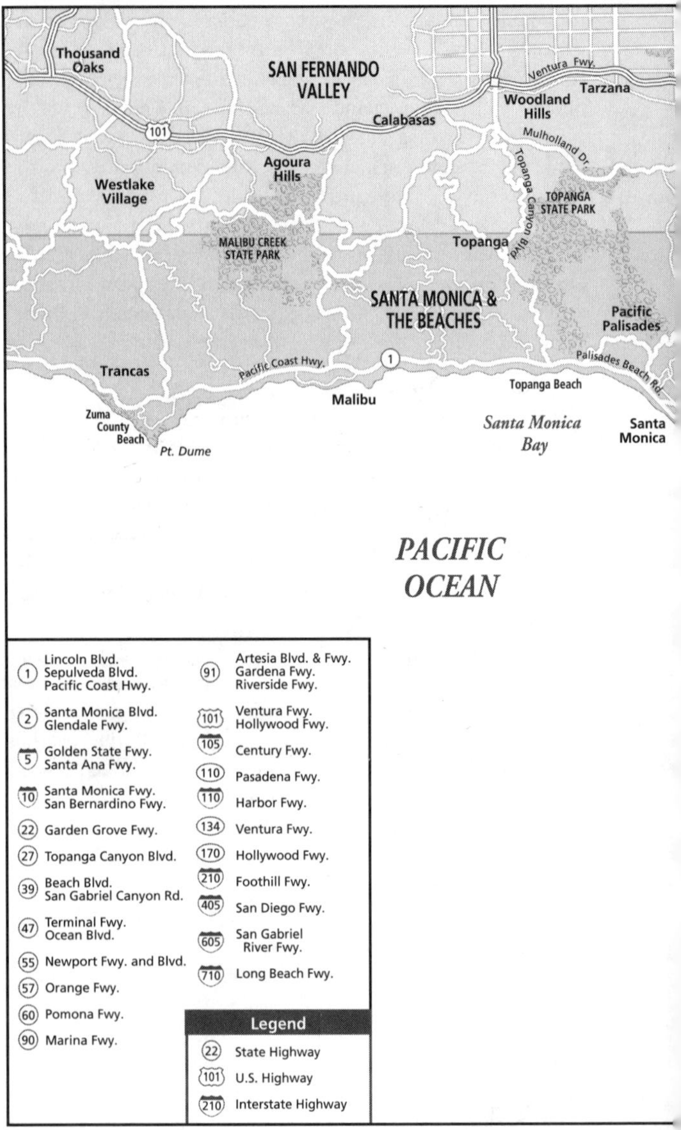
Thousand Oaks
SAN FERNANDO VALLEY
Ventura Fwy.
Tarzana
Woodland Hills
Calabasas
101
Mulholland Dr.
Agoura Hills
Westlake Village
Topanga Canyon Blvd.
TOPANGA STATE PARK
MALIBU CREEK STATE PARK
Topanga
SANTA MONICA & THE BEACHES
Pacific Palisades
Trancas
Pacific Coast Hwy.
1
Palisades Beach Rd.
Topanga Beach
Malibu
Zuma County Beach
Pt. Dume
Santa Monica Bay
Santa Monica
PACIFIC OCEAN
1 Lincoln Blvd. Sepulveda Blvd. Pacific Coast Hwy.
2 Santa Monica Blvd. Glendale Fwy.
5 Golden State Fwy. Santa Ana Fwy.
10 Santa Monica Fwy. San Bernardino Fwy.
22 Garden Grove Fwy.
27 Topanga Canyon Blvd.
39 Beach Blvd. San Gabriel Canyon Rd.
47 Terminal Fwy. Ocean Blvd.
55 Newport Fwy. and Blvd.
57 Orange Fwy.
60 Pomona Fwy.
90 Marina Fwy.
91 Artesia Blvd. & Fwy. Gardena Fwy. Riverside Fwy.
101 Ventura Fwy. Hollywood Fwy.
105 Century Fwy.
110 Pasadena Fwy.
110 Harbor Fwy.
134 Ventura Fwy.
170 Hollywood Fwy.
210 Foothill Fwy.
405 San Diego Fwy.
605 San Gabriel River Fwy.
710 Long Beach Fwy.
Legend
22 State Highway
101 U.S. Highway
210 Interstate Highway

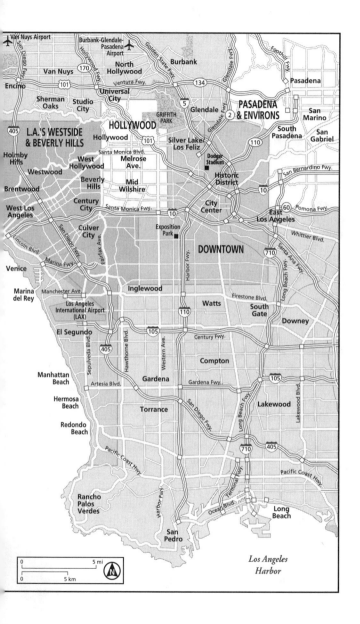

interstate in downtown Los Angeles and runs directly south, where it dead-ends in San Pedro. The section that is now the Pasadena Freeway was Los Angeles's first freeway, known as the Arroyo Seco when it opened in 1940.

I-710, aka the "Long Beach Freeway," runs in a north–south direction through East Los Angeles and dead-ends at Long Beach.

I-605, the "San Gabriel River Freeway," runs roughly parallel to the I-710 farther east, through the cities of Hawthorne and Lynwood and into the San Gabriel Valley.

Calif. 1—called "Highway 1," the "Pacific Coast Highway," or simply "PCH"—is really more of a scenic parkway than a freeway. It skirts the ocean, linking all of L.A.'s beach communities, from Malibu to the Orange Coast.

The freeways are complemented by a complex web of surface streets. From north to south, the major east–west thoroughfares connecting downtown to the beaches are **Sunset Boulevard, Santa Monica Boulevard, Wilshire Boulevard,** and **Olympic, Pico,** and **Venice boulevards.** The section of Sunset Boulevard that runs between Crescent Heights Boulevard and Doheny Drive is the famed **Sunset Strip.**

NEIGHBORHOODS IN BRIEF

Los Angeles is a very confusing city, with fluid neighborhood lines and labels. The best way to grasp the city is to break it into six regions: Santa Monica and the beaches, L.A.'s Westside and Beverly Hills, Hollywood, Downtown, the San Fernando Valley, and Pasadena and environs. Each region encompasses a more-or-less distinctive patchwork of city neighborhoods and independently incorporated communities.

Throughout the book, I'll discuss the regions in the order of their natural geographical progression from west to east (except for the San Fernando Valley, which is roughly north of the city's other major regions, separated from them by the Hollywood Hills). Most visitors arrive at Los Angeles International Airport (LAX), which is located on the coast just south of L.A.'s primary beach communities. Unless you're coming to L.A. on business, you're likely to concentrate your visit in the city's western districts, since that's where the majority of attractions, restaurants, and shops are; many visitors never make it as far east as Downtown.

Santa Monica & the Beaches

These are my favorite L.A. communities. The 60-mile beachfront stretching from Malibu to the Palos Verdes Peninsula has milder weather and less smog than the inland communities, and traffic is nominally lighter—except on summer weekends, of course. The towns along the coast all have a distinct mood and charm. They're listed below from north to south.

Malibu, at the northern border of Los Angeles County, 25 miles from downtown, was once a privately owned ranch—purchased in 1857 for 10¢ an acre. Today its particularly wide beaches, sparsely populated hills, and relative remoteness from the inner city make it extremely popular with rich recluses. Indeed, the resident lists of Malibu Colony and nearby Broad Beach—oceanfront strips of closely packed mansions—read like a Who's Who in Hollywood. With plenty of green space and dramatic rocky outcroppings, Malibu's rural beauty is unsurpassed in L.A.

Pretty **Santa Monica,** Los Angeles's premier beach community, is known for its long ocean pier, artsy atmosphere, and somewhat-wacky residents. It's also noted for its particularly acute homeless problem. The Third Street Promenade, a pedestrian-only outdoor mall lined with great shops and restaurants, is one of the country's most successful revitalization projects.

Venice, a planned community in the spirit of its Italian fore-bear, was constructed with a series of narrow canals connected by quaint one-lane bridges. The area had become infested with grime and crime over the years, but gentrification is now in full swing, bringing scores of great restaurants and boutiques and rising property values for the quaint canal-side homes and apartment duplexes. Some of L.A.'s most innovative and interesting architecture lines funky Main Street. Without question, Venice is best known for its Ocean Front Walk, a nonstop circus of skaters, vendors, and poseurs of all ages, colors, types, and sizes.

Marina del Rey, just south of Venice, is a somewhat-quieter, more upscale community best known for its small-craft harbor, one of the largest of its kind in the world.

Manhattan, Hermosa, and **Redondo beaches** are laid-back, mainly residential neighborhoods with modest homes (except for oceanfront real estate), mild weather, and residents happy to have fled the L.A. hubbub. There are excellent beaches for volleyball players, surfers, and sun worshippers here, but when it comes to cultural activities, pickings can be slim. The restaurant scene, while limited, has been improving steadily.

L.A.'s Westside & Beverly Hills

The Westside, an imprecise, misshapen L sandwiched between Hollywood and the city's coastal communities, includes some of Los Angeles's most prestigious neighborhoods, virtually all with names you're sure to recognize:

Beverly Hills is roughly bounded by Olympic Boulevard on the south, Robertson Boulevard on the east, and the districts of Westwood and Century City on the west; it extends into the hills to the north. Politically distinct from the rest of Los Angeles, this famous enclave is best known for its palm tree–lined streets of palatial homes and high-priced shops. But it's not all glitz and glamour; the healthy mix of filthy rich, wanna-bes, and tourists that people downtown Beverly Hills creates a unique—and sometimes bizarre—atmosphere.

West Hollywood is a key-shaped community whose epicenter is the intersection of Santa Monica and La Cienega boulevards. It's bounded on the west by Doheny Drive and on the south roughly by Melrose Avenue. The tip of the key extends east for several blocks north and south of Santa Monica Boulevard as far as La Brea Avenue, but West Hollywood is primarily located to the west of Fairfax Avenue. Nestled between Beverly Hills and Hollywood, this politically independent town can feel either tony or tawdry, depending on which end of the city you're in. In addition to being home to some of the area's best restaurants, shops, and art galleries, West Hollywood is the center of L.A.'s gay community.

Bel Air and **Holmby Hills,** located in the hills north of Westwood and west of the Beverly Hills city limits, are wealthy residential areas that feature prominently on most maps to the stars' homes.

Brentwood, the world-famous backdrop to the O.J. Simpson melodrama, is really just a tiny, quiet, relatively upscale neighborhood with the typical L.A. mix of homes, restaurants, and strip malls. It's west of I-405 and north of Santa Monica and West Los Angeles. The Getty Center looms over Brentwood from its hilltop perch next to I-405.

Westwood, an urban village that the University of California at Los Angeles (UCLA) calls home, is bounded by I-405, Santa Monica Boulevard, Sunset Boulevard, and Beverly Hills. This area used to be a hot destination for a night on the town, but it has lost much of its appeal thanks to overcrowding, general rudeness, and even street violence. There's still a high concentration of movie theaters here, but we're all waiting for Westwood to regain its old charm.

Century City is a compact, busy, rather-bland high-rise area sandwiched between West Los Angeles and Beverly Hills. It was once the back lot of 20th Century Fox studios. The primary draws here are the Shubert Theater and the Century City Marketplace, a pleasant open-air mall. Century City's three main thoroughfares are Century Park East, Avenue of the Stars, and Century Park West; the area is bounded on the north by Santa Monica Boulevard and on the south by Pico Boulevard.

West Los Angeles is a label that generally applies to everything that isn't one of the other Westside neighborhoods. It's basically the area south of Santa Monica Boulevard, north of Venice Boulevard, east of Santa Monica and Venice, and west and south of Century City.

Hollywood

Yes, they still come. Young hopefuls with stars in their eyes are attracted to this town like moths fluttering in the glare of neon lights. But Hollywood is now much more a state of mind than a glamour center. Many of the neighborhood's former movie studios have moved to more spacious venues in Burbank, on the Westside, and in other parts of the city. Hollywood Boulevard has become one of the city's seediest strips. The area is now just a less-than-admirable part of the whole of Los Angeles, but the legend of the neighborhood as the movie capital of the world endures.

For our purposes, the label "Hollywood" extends beyond the worn central area of Hollywood itself to the surrounding neighborhoods. It generally encompasses everything between Western Avenue to the east and Fairfax Avenue to the west and from the Hollywood Hills south.

Seedy **Hollywood,** which centers around Hollywood and Sunset boulevards, is the historic heart of L.A.'s movie industry. It's home to several important attractions, such as the Walk of Fame and Mann's Chinese Theatre.

Melrose Avenue, a scruffy but fun neighborhood, is the city's funkiest shopping district.

The stretch of Wilshire Boulevard that runs through the southern part of Hollywood is known as the **Mid-Wilshire** district, or

Miracle Mile. It's lined with contemporary apartment houses and office buildings. The stretch of the boulevard just east of Fairfax Avenue, now known as Museum Row, is home to almost a dozen museums, including the Los Angeles County Museum of Art, the La Brea Tar Pits, and that shrine to L.A. car culture, the Petersen Automotive Museum.

Griffith Park, up Western Avenue in the northernmost reaches of Hollywood, is one of the country's largest urban parks. It's home to the Los Angeles Zoo and the famous Griffith Observatory.

Downtown

Roughly bounded by the U.S. 101, I-110, I-10, and I-5 freeways, L.A.'s downtown is home to a tight cluster of high-rise offices, the El Pueblo de Los Angeles Historic District, and the neighborhoods of Koreatown, Chinatown, and Little Tokyo. The construction of skyscrapers—bolstered by earthquake-proof technology—transformed downtown Los Angeles into the business center of the city. Despite the relatively recent construction of numerous cultural centers (such as the Music Center and the Museum of Contemporary Art) and a few hip restaurants, Downtown isn't the hub that it would be in most cities. The Westside, Hollywood, and the beach communities are all more popular.

For our purposes, the residential neighborhoods of Silver Lake and Los Feliz, Exposition Park (home to Los Angeles Memorial Coliseum, the L.A. Sports Arena, and several downtown museums), and East and South-Central L.A., the city's famous barrios, all fall under the Downtown umbrella.

El Pueblo de Los Angeles Historic District, a 44-acre ode to the city's early years, is worth a visit. Neither Chinatown nor Little Tokyo is on the scale of its San Francisco equivalent and, quite honestly, neither is worth going out of your way for.

Silver Lake, a residential neighborhood located just north of downtown, and adjacent **Los Feliz,** just to the west, are arty areas with ethnic cafes, theaters, graffiti, and art galleries—all in equally plentiful proportions.

Exposition Park, just south and west of downtown, is home to the Los Angeles Memorial Coliseum and the L.A. Sports Arena. The park also contains the Natural History Museum of Los Angeles County, the California African American Museum, and the California Science Center Center. The University of Southern California is next door.

East and **South-Central L.A.,** just east and south of downtown, are home to the city's large barrios. This is where the 1992 L.A. Riots were centered; it was here, at Florence and Normandie avenues, that a news station's reporter, hovering above in a helicopter, videotaped Reginald Denny being pulled from the cab of his truck and beaten by several young men. These neighborhoods are, without question, quite unique, though they contain few tourist sites (the Watts Towers being a notable exception).

The San Fernando Valley

The San Fernando Valley, known locally as "The Valley," was nationally popularized in the 1980s by the notorious mall-loving "Valley Girl" stereotype. Snuggled between the Santa Monica and the San Gabriel mountain ranges, most of the Valley is residential and commercial and off the beaten track for tourists. But some of its attractions are bound to draw you over the hill. **Universal City,** located west of Griffith Park between U.S. 101 and Calif. 134, is home to Universal Studios and the trippy shopping and entertainment complex known as CityWalk. And you may make a trip to **Burbank,** just west of these other suburbs and north of Universal City, to see one of your favorite TV shows being filmed at NBC or Warner Brothers Studios. There are also a few good restaurants and shops along Ventura Boulevard, in and around Studio City.

Glendale is a largely residential community north of downtown, sandwiched between the Valley and Pasadena. Here you'll find Forest Lawn, the city's best cemetery for sightseeing.

Pasadena & Environs

Best known to the world as the site of the Tournament of Roses Parade each New Year's Day, **Pasadena** was mercifully spared from the tear-down epidemic that swept L.A., so it has a refreshing old-time feel. Once upon a time, Pasadena was every Angeleno's best-kept secret—a quiet community whose slow and careful regentrification meant excellent, unique restaurants and boutique shopping without the crowds, in a revitalized downtown respectful of its old brick and stone commercial buildings. Although the area's natural and architectural beauty still shines through—so much so that Pasadena remains Hollywood's favorite backyard location for countless movies and TV shows—Old Town has become a pedestrian mall similar to Santa Monica's Third Street Promenade, complete with huge crowds, predictable mid-range chain eateries, and standard mall-issue stores. It still gets my vote as a scenic alternative to the congestion of central L.A., but it has lost much of its small-town charm.

Pasadena is also home to the famous California Institute of Technology (Caltech), which boasts 22 Nobel Prize winners among its alumni. The Caltech-operated Jet Propulsion Laboratory was the birthplace of America's space program, and Caltech scientists are the first to report earthquake activity worldwide.

The residential neighborhoods in Pasadena and its adjacent communities—**Arcadia, La Cañada, San Marino,** and **South Pasadena**—are renowned for well-preserved historic homes, ranging from humble bungalows to lavish mansions. These areas feature public gardens, designated historic neighborhoods, house museums, and bed-and-breakfast inns.

2 Getting Around

BY CAR

Need we tell you that Los Angeles is a car city? You're really going to need one to get around. An elaborate network of well-maintained freeways connects this incredible urban sprawl, but you'll have to learn how to make sense of the system and cultivate some patience for dealing with the traffic. The golden rule of driving in Los Angeles is this: Always allow more time to get to your destination than you think you'll need, especially during morning and evening rush hours. For an explanation of the city layout and details on the freeway system, see "Orientation," above.

RENTALS

Los Angeles is one of the cheaper places in America to rent a car. Major national car-rental companies usually rent Geo Metros, Ford Escorts, and the like for about $35 per day and $120 per week with unlimited mileage.

All the major car-rental agencies have offices at the airport and in the larger hotels. If you're thinking of splurging, however, the place to call is **Budget Rent-a-Car of Beverly Hills,** 9815 Wilshire Blvd., Beverly Hills (☎ **310/274-9173**), which rents Mercedes, BMWs, and Porsches for up to $450 per day.

SAVING MONEY ON A RENTAL CAR   Car-rental rates vary even more than airline fares. The price you pay will depend on the size of the car, where and when you pick it up and drop it off, the length of the rental period, where and how far you drive it, whether you purchase insurance, and a host of other factors. A few key questions could save you hundreds of dollars:

- Are weekend rates lower than weekday rates? Ask if the rate is the same for pickup Friday morning, for instance, as it is for Thursday night.
- Does the agency assess a drop-off charge if you don't return the car to the same location where you picked it up?
- Are special promotional rates available? If you see an advertised price in your local newspaper, be sure to ask for that specific rate; otherwise, you may be charged the standard cost. Terms change constantly.
- Are discounts available for members of AARP, AAA, frequent flyer programs, or trade unions? If you belong to any of these organizations, you may be entitled to discounts of up to 30%.
- How much tax will be added to the rental bill? Local tax? State use tax?
- How much does the rental company charge to refill your gas tank if you return with the tank less than full? Though most rental companies claim these prices are "competitive," fuel is almost always cheaper in town. Try to allow enough time to refuel the car yourself before returning it. Some companies offer "refueling packages," in which you pay for an entire tank of gas up front. The price is usually fairly competitive with local gas prices, but you don't get credit for any gas remaining in the tank. If a stop at a gas station on the way to the airport will make you miss your plane, then by all means take advantage of the fuel purchase option; otherwise, skip it.

DEMYSTIFYING RENTER'S INSURANCE   Before you drive off in a rental car, be sure you're insured. Hasty assumptions about your personal auto insurance or a rental agency's additional coverage could end up costing you tens of thousands of dollars—even if you are involved in an accident that was clearly the fault of another driver.

If you already hold a **private auto insurance** policy in the United States, you are most likely covered for loss of or damage to a rental car and liability in case of injury to any other party involved in an accident. Be sure to find out whether you are covered in the area you are visiting, whether your policy extends to all persons who will be driving the rental car, how much liability is covered in case an outside party is injured in an accident, and whether the type of vehicle you are renting is included under your contract. (Rental trucks, sport utility vehicles, and luxury vehicles or sports cars may not be covered.)

Most **major credit cards** provide some degree of coverage as well—provided they were used to pay for the rental. Terms vary widely, however, so be sure to call your credit-card company directly before you rent. The credit card will usually cover damage or theft of a rental car for the full cost of the vehicle, minus a deductible. If you already have auto insurance, your credit card will provide secondary coverage—which basically covers your deductible.

Credit cards will not cover liability, or the cost of injury to an outside party and/or damage to an outside party's vehicle. If you do not hold an insurance policy, you may want to consider purchasing additional liability insurance from your rental company. Be sure to check the terms, however: Some rental agencies cover liability only if the renter is not at fault.

The basic insurance coverage offered by most car-rental companies, known as the **Loss/Damage Waiver (LDW)** or **Collision Damage Waiver (CDW),** can cost as much as $20 per day. It usually covers the full value of the vehicle with no deductible if an outside party causes an accident or other damage to the rental car. In all states but California, you will probably be covered in case of theft as well. Liability coverage varies according to the company policy and state law, but the minimum is usually at least $15,000. If you are at fault in an accident, however, you will be covered for the full replacement value of the car but not for liability. In California, you can buy additional liability coverage for such cases. Most rental companies will require a police report in order to process any claims you file, but your private insurer will not be notified of the accident.

Be sure to communicate any special needs in advance to the reservations agent. Most companies offer infant/child seats and vehicles equipped for drivers with disabilities. And many are now offering portable cell phones with their cars—it's a good idea to consider this option. In addition to being invaluable for summoning help in case of an accident, they're also useful for calling for directions when you're lost and for getting roadside assistance in the event of mechanical difficulties.

Parking

Explaining the parking situation in Los Angeles is like explaining the English language—there are more exceptions than rules. In some areas, every establishment has a convenient free lot or ample street parking; other areas are pretty manageable, as long as you have a quick eye and are willing to take a few turns around the block; but there are some frustrating parts of town (particularly around restaurants after 7:30pm) where you'll have to give in and use valet parking. Whether there's valet parking depends more on the congestion of the area than on the elegance of the establishment these days; the size of an establishment's lot often simply won't allow for self-parking.

Restaurants and nightclubs sometimes provide a complimentary valet service, but more often they charge between $2.50 and $5. Some areas, like Santa Monica and Beverly Hills, offer self-park lots and garages convenient to the neighborhood action; costs range from $2 to $10. Most of the hotels listed in this book offer off-street parking, for which they charge up to $20 per day.

Driving

You may turn right at a red light after stopping unless a sign says otherwise. Likewise, you can turn left on a red light from a one-way street onto another one-way street after coming to a full stop. Keep in mind that pedestrians in Los Angeles have the right-of-way at all times, so stop for people who have stepped off the curb. Also, California has a seat-belt law for both drivers and passengers, so buckle up before you venture out.

Many Southern California freeways have designated **carpool lanes,** also known as High Occupancy Vehicle (HOV) lanes or

---

One-Stop Transportation Shopping

Gotta get somewhere? You can get your bearings by calling ☎ **800/COMMUTE,** an automated system that'll connect you to information on bus and rail transit schedules, freeway/highway information, bicycle and ride-share agencies, and more. Online, point your browser to **www.smart-traveler.com**, which provides links to the above information. Both of these systems were designed primarily to help L.A.'s commuters navigate the city and environs, but they have plenty to offer visitors as well.

"white diamond" lanes (after the large diamonds painted on the blacktop along the lane). Some require two passengers, others three. Most on-ramps are metered during even light congestion to regulate the flow of traffic onto the freeway; cars in HOV lanes can pass the signal without stopping. Although there are tales of drivers sitting life-sized mannequins next to them in order to beat the system, don't consider ignoring the stoplights for any reason if you're not part of a carpool—fines begin at $271.

BY PUBLIC TRANSPORTATION

I've heard rumors about visitors to Los Angeles who have toured the city entirely by public transportation, but they can't be more than that—rumors. It's hard to believe that anyone can comprehensively tour Auto Land without a car. Still, if you're in the city for only a short time, are on a very tight budget, or don't expect to be moving around a lot, public transport might be for you.

The city's trains and buses are operated by the **Los Angeles County Metropolitan Transit Authority** (MTA; ☎ **213/ 626-4455;** www.mta.net), and MTA brochures and schedules are available at every area visitor center.

BY BUS

Spread-out sights, sluggish service, and frequent transfers make extensive touring by bus impractical. For short hops and occasional jaunts, however, buses are both economical and environmentally correct. However, it isn't recommended to ride buses late at night.

The basic bus fare is $1.35 for all local lines, with transfers costing 25¢. Express buses, which travel along the freeways, and buses on intercounty routes charge higher fares; phone for information.

The **Downtown Area Short Hop (DASH)** shuttle system operates buses throughout downtown and the west side of L.A. Service runs every 5 to 20 minutes, depending on the time of day, and costs just 25¢. Contact the MTA (☎ **213/626-4455;** www. mta.net) for schedules and route information.

BY RAIL & SUBWAY

The **MetroRail** system is a sore subject around town. For years the MTA has been digging up the city's streets, sucking away huge amounts of tax money, and pushing exhaust vents up through peaceful parkland—and for what? Let's face it, L.A. will never have New York's subway or San Francisco's BART. Today, the system is still in its infancy, mainly popular with commuters from outlying suburbs. Here's an overview of what's currently in place:

The **Metro Blue Line,** an above-ground rail system, connects downtown Los Angeles with Long Beach. Trains operate daily from 6am to 9pm; the fare is $1.35.

The **Metro Red Line,** L.A.'s first subway, has been growing since 1993 and opened a highly publicized Hollywood extension in 1999. The line begins at Union Station, the city's main train depot, and travels west underneath Wilshire Boulevard, looping north into Hollywood. The fare is $1.35; discount tokens are available at Metro service centers and many area convenience stores. The Red Line will be extended into the San Fernando Valley (with a convenient Universal City stop) by late 2000.

The **Metro Green Line,** opened in 1995, runs for 20 miles along the center of the new I-105, the Glenn Anderson (Century) Freeway, and connects Norwalk in eastern Los Angeles County to LAX. A connection with the Blue Line offers visitors access from LAX to downtown L.A. or Long Beach. The fare is $1.35.

Call the **MTA** (☎ **213/626-4455;** www.mta.net) for information on all Metro lines, including construction updates and details on purchasing discount tokens or passes.

BY TAXI

Distances are long in Los Angeles, and cab fares are high; even a short trip can cost $10 or more. Taxis charge $1.90 at the flag drop, plus $1.60 per mile. A service charge is added to fares originating at LAX.

Except in the heart of downtown, passing cabs will usually not pull over when hailed. Cab stands are located at airports, at downtown's Union Station, and at major hotels. To ensure a ride, order a taxi in advance from **Checker Cab** (☎ **323/654-8400**), **L.A. Taxi** (☎ **213/627-7000**), or **United Taxi** (☎ **213/483-7604**).

FAST FACTS: LOS ANGELES

American Express   In addition to those at 327 N. Beverly Dr., Beverly Hills (☎ **310/274-8277**), and at 8493 W. 3rd St., Los Angeles (☎ **310/659-1682**), offices are located throughout the city. To locate one nearest you, call ☎ **800/221-7282.**

Area Codes   Those areas west of La Cienega Boulevard, including Beverly Hills and the city's beach communities, use the **310** area code. Portions of Los Angeles county east and south of the city, including Long Beach, are in the **562** area. The San Fernando Valley has the **818** area code, while points east—including parts of Burbank, Glendale, and Pasadena— use the newly created **626** code. The downtown business area uses **213.** All other numbers, including Griffith Park, Hollywood, and parts of West Hollywood (east of La Cienega Boulevard) now use the new area code **323.** If it's all too much to remember, just call directory assistance at ☎ **411.**

Baby-Sitters   If you're staying at one of the larger hotels, the concierge can usually recommend a reliable baby-sitter. If not, contact the **Baby-Sitters Guild** in Glendale (☎ **818/552-2229**) or **Sitters Unlimited** (☎ **800/328-1191**).

Dentists   For a recommendation in the area, call the **Dental Referral Service** (☎ **800/422-8338**).

Doctors   Contact the **Uni-Health Information and Referral Hotline** (☎ **800/922-0000**) for a free, confidential physician referral.

Emergencies   For police, fire, or highway patrol, or in case of life-threatening medical emergencies, dial ☎ **911.**

Hospital   The centrally located (and world-famous) **Cedars-Sinai Medical Center,** 8700 Beverly Blvd., Los Angeles (☎ **310/855-5000**), has a 24-hour emergency room staffed by some of the country's finest MDs.

Liquor Laws   Liquor and grocery stores can sell packaged alcoholic beverages between 6am and 2am. Most restaurants, nightclubs, and bars are licensed to serve alcoholic drinks during the same hours. The legal age for purchase and consumption is 21; proof of age is required.

Newspapers/Magazines   See "Other Information Sources" above. **World Book & News Co.,** at 1652 N. Cahuenga Blvd., near Hollywood and Vine and Mann's Chinese Theatre, stocks lots of out-of-town and foreign papers and magazines. No one minds if you browse through the magazines, but you'll be reprimanded for thumbing through the newspapers. It's open 24 hours.

Pharmacies   **Horton & Converse** has locations around L.A., including 2001 Santa Monica Blvd., Santa Monica (☎ **310/**

829-3401); 9201 Sunset Blvd., Beverly Hills (☎ **323/ 272-0488**); and 11600 Wilshire Blvd., West Los Angeles (☎ **310/478-0801**). Hours vary, but the West L.A. location is open until 2am.

Police   In an emergency, dial ☎ **911.** For nonemergency police matters, call ☎ **213/485-2121;** in Beverly Hills, dial ☎ **310/550-4951.**

Post Office   Call ☎ **800/ASK-USPS** to find the one closest to you.

Taxes   The combined Los Angeles County and California state sales taxes amount to 8.25%; hotel taxes add 12% to 17% to room tariffs.

Taxis   See "Getting Around," above.

Time Zone   Los Angeles is in the Pacific time zone, which is 8 hours behind Greenwich mean time and 3 hours behind Eastern time. Call ☎ **853-1212** for the correct time (operates in all local area codes).

Weather   Call **Los Angeles Weather Information** (☎ **213/ 554-1212**) for the daily forecast. For beach conditions, call the **Zuma Beach Lifeguard** recorded information (☎ **310/ 457-9701**).

3

Accommodations

*I*n sprawling Los Angeles, location is everything. Choosing the right neighborhood as a base can make or break your vacation. If you plan to while away a few days at the beach but base yourself downtown, for example, you're going to lose a lot of valuable relaxation time on the freeway. For business travelers, choosing a location is easy: Pick a hotel near your work—don't commute if you don't have to. For vacationers, though, the decision about where to stay is a more difficult one. Take into consideration where you want to spend your time before you commit yourself to a base (check out the "Neighborhoods in Brief" section, in chapter 2, for information). But wherever you stay, count on doing a good deal of driving—no hotel in Los Angeles is convenient to everything.

1 Santa Monica & the Beaches

Southern California means only one thing to some people— the beach. If you're nodding your head, don't consider staying anywhere but here. Not only will you avoid the traffic crush as everyone from the valleys flocks to the seaside on clear, sunny days, but you also can soak up the laid-back, often-funky, vibe that only beach communities have. Only a few blocks inland, Santa Monica becomes as chic and sophisticated as the Westside, so shopping and dining are right at your doorstep, too.

LAX is also near the coast, so I'm including accommodations near the airport in this section as well.

Save Money on Your Hotel Room

In our hotel descriptions, we list a hotel's "rack rate"—its official published rate. You can almost always do better—sometimes simply by asking, "Is that your best rate?" Don't be afraid to bargain a little, and always ask about seasonal discounts and package deals.

A Note on Rates and Extra Charges

The prices given in this book do not include state and city **hotel taxes,** which run from 12% to a whopping 17%. Be aware that most hotels in densely populated parts of the city make additional charges for **parking** (with in-and-out privileges, except where noted). Also, some provide a **free airport shuttle;** so before you take a taxi, check to see what your hotel can offer.

VERY EXPENSIVE

✪ **Hotel Oceana.** 849 Ocean Ave., Santa Monica, CA 90403. ☎ **800/ 777-0758** or 310/393-0486. Fax 310/458-1182. www.hoteloceana.com. 63 units. A/C TV TEL. $325 studio suite; $345–$700 1- or 2-bedroom suite. Rates include continental breakfast. AE, CB, DC, DISC, MC, V. Valet parking $17.50.

Excellently located in a residential neighborhood right on Ocean Avenue, this all-suite hotel sits side-by-side with low-rise (but high-rent) apartment/condos, several blocks from the Santa Monica hubbub. The lobby, which is capped by an enormous skylight, is light and airy, and completely covered with Jean Cocteau–inspired floor-to-ceiling murals. With their bright Matisse-style colors and cushy IKEA-ish furniture, the completely renovated suites are colorful and current, offering comfy robes and Neutrogena bath products. Their enormous size makes them terrific for families or intimate groups—kids will enjoy Sega Genesis games and VCRs. Ocean-view suites feature balconies and two-person whirlpool tubs. In-room lunch and dinner service is provided by Wolfgang Puck Cafe, but since all suites come with fully equipped kitchens, cooking for yourself is another option. Everything about the Oceana is fresh, welcoming, and noninstitutional; it's no wonder advertising execs make this their choice for long-term stays.

Amenities: Outdoor heated pool, exercise room, concierge, room service (from 11am to 10pm), continental breakfast in suite, dry-cleaning/laundry service, self-service Laundromat, newspaper delivery.

Loews Santa Monica Beach Hotel. 1700 Ocean Ave. (south of Colorado Blvd.), Santa Monica, CA 90401. ☎ **800/223-0888** or 310/458-6700. Fax 310/458-6761. 341 units. A/C TV TEL. $275–$515 double; from $590 suite. AE, CB, DC, EC, MC, V. Valet parking $18; self-parking $15. Pets accepted with $500 refundable deposit; $10-per-day cleaning fee.

Accommodations in
Santa Monica & the Beaches

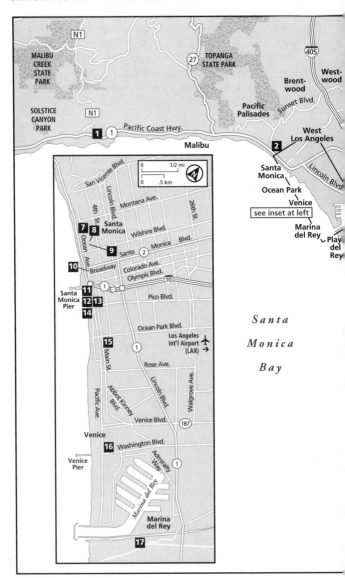

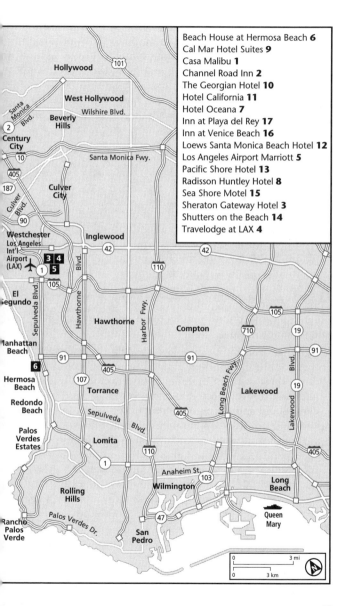

Beach House at Hermosa Beach **6**
Cal Mar Hotel Suites **9**
Casa Malibu **1**
Channel Road Inn **2**
The Georgian Hotel **10**
Hotel California **11**
Hotel Oceana **7**
Inn at Playa del Rey **17**
Inn at Venice Beach **16**
Loews Santa Monica Beach Hotel **12**
Los Angeles Airport Marriott **5**
Pacific Shore Hotel **13**
Radisson Huntley Hotel **8**
Sea Shore Motel **15**
Sheraton Gateway Hotel **3**
Shutters on the Beach **14**
Travelodge at LAX **4**

If it weren't for Shutters, this would be the finest hotel in Santa Monica. Loews isn't exactly beachfront; it's on a hill less than a block away, but the unobstructed ocean views are fabulous. While the standard rooms seem a bit, well, standard for Loews's luxury rates, in return you get great location and the outstanding service of a very friendly staff. A dramatic, multistory glass-and-steel atrium lobby gives way to amply sized rooms outfitted with the latest luxury amenities. This popular hotel doesn't need our recommendation to stir up business; it's become something of a darling for industry functions and is booked to capacity in the summer months. By the end of 2001, complete renovations will bring an updated casual elegance to public areas and guest rooms.

Dining: Fine dining is in the Provençal-flavored restaurant Lavande; there is also a more casual restaurant and poolside snack service.

Amenities: Outdoor heated pool and whirlpool, fitness center, full-service spa, concierge, 24-hour room service, nightly turn-down, bike and skate rental, summer kids' program, baby-sitting, pet services, business center, VCRs on request.

✪ **Shutters on the Beach.** 1 Pico Blvd., Santa Monica, CA 90405. ☎ **800/ 334-9000** or 310/458-0030. Fax 310/458-4589. www.shuttersonthebeach.com. 198 units. A/C MINIBAR TV TEL. $355–$595 double; from $750 suite. AE, DC, DISC, EC, MC, V. Valet parking $20.

Light and luxurious Shutters enjoys one of the city's most prized locations: directly on the beach, a block from Santa Monica Pier. Guest rooms are located either in a tower or in cottage-like structures on the beach. The beach-cottage rooms are clearly more desirable and no more expensive than those in the towers. The views and sounds of the ocean are the most outstanding qualities of the rooms, some of which have fireplaces and whirlpool tubs; all have VCRs and floor-to-ceiling windows that open. Showers come with waterproof radios, biodegradable bathing supplies, and toy duckies. Despite this welcome whimsy, there's a relaxed and elegant atmosphere throughout the hotel, which is filled with contemporary art. The small swimming pool on an elevated deck and the sunny lobby lounge overlooking the sand are two great places for spotting the celebrities who swear by Shutters as an alternative hangout to smoggy Hollywood.

Dining/Diversions: One Pico, the hotel's premier restaurant, is very well regarded. The best meals at the more casual Pedals are prepared on the wood-burning grill. The overdesigned Handle Bar offers good happy-hour specials.

Amenities: Outdoor heated pool and whirlpool, exercise room, sauna, concierge, 24-hour room service, overnight laundry, nightly turndown, in-room massage, beach equipment rental, bicycle rental.

EXPENSIVE

✪ **Beach House at Hermosa Beach.** 1300 The Strand, Hermosa Beach, CA 90254. ☎ **888/895-4559** or 310/374-3001. Fax 310/372-2115. www. beach-house.com. 96 units. A/C TV TEL. $199–$299 double. Midweek rates and packages available. Rates include continental breakfast. AE, DC, DISC, JCB, MC, V. Valet parking $17. From LAX take Sepulveda Blvd. south to Pier Ave.; turn right on Pier, then right again on Hermosa Ave, then left on 14th St.; the hotel is on the left.

Every possible need is addressed at this luxurious, romantic new hotel, which is more akin to the historic Surf & Sand beach club (which once stood on this spot) than the flophouse motels farther down the Strand. Sporting a Cape Cod style with white wood accents and stylish beige furnishings, most of the rooms have at least a partial ocean view; the very best are just inches away from the beach. No detail has been overlooked; each room is equipped with a queen sleeper sofa, a complete microkitchen (plus dishes and flatware for four), an elevated king-bed sleeping niche, plush down comforters and flannel robes, and a mood-enhancing stereo/CD player. The bathroom is a study in relaxation, with clean white tile and chrome lines, extra deep soaking tub, and pampering Aveda products. In the morning, a generous continental breakfast is laid out downstairs, with to-go trays if you prefer to have it on the beach or your private balcony. Despite the summertime carnival atmosphere of The Strand, the Beach House keeps serene with double-paned windows and walls designed to keep out the noise.

✪ **Channel Road Inn.** 219 W. Channel Rd., Santa Monica, CA 90402. ☎ **310/459-1920.** Fax 310/454-9920. www.channelroadinn.com. 14 units. TV TEL. $150–$265 double; $315 suite. AE, MC, V. All rates include full breakfast and afternoon tea, wine, and hors d'oeuvres. Midweek rates available. Free parking.

When it was built in 1910, this charming colonial revival house was located in downtown Santa Monica; later it was moved to its current location on West Channel Road, just 1 block from the beach. All rooms are fitted with pine furnishings and a smattering of antiques. Some have four-poster beds covered with hand-sewn Amish quilts; some enjoy ocean views; two have fireplaces; and two more boast whirlpool bathtubs. Pampering touches include a romantic hillside hot tub, bathrobes, hair dryers, VCRs (videos are provided downstairs), and bicycles for guests' use. There's an impressive Batchelder fireplace in the living room.

The Georgian Hotel. 1415 Ocean Ave. (between Santa Monica Blvd. and Broadway), Santa Monica, CA 90401. ☎ **800/538-8147** or 310/395-9945. Fax 310/451-3374. www.georgianhotel.com. 84 units. MINIBAR TV TEL. Summer $225–$275 double, from $340 suite; off-season $210–$260 double. Rates include continental breakfast. Packages available. AE, CB, DC, MC, V. Valet parking $15. Small pets accepted with $250 refundable deposit and $100 fee.

This gracious eight-story art deco *grande dame* was established in 1933 as the Lady Windermere. The "Lady" was frequented by Hollywood elite who often patronized the infamous nightclubs lining PCH below; in fact, it even had its own speakeasy, rumored to have been established by mobster Bugsy Siegel—guests now enjoy breakfast in the historic room. Today, the elegantly tasteful Georgian building features Classical Revival architecture juxtaposed with bold pastels (à la Miami Beach's hotels of the same era), and every comfort is considered, from in-room robes and Starbucks coffee to comfy wicker chaises on the front veranda. Most rooms have a partial or full ocean view; the hotel is perched with an unobstructed coastal vista.

Amenities: Concierge, room service, complimentary shoe shine and daily newspaper, laundry/dry cleaning, twice-daily maid service.

Inn at Playa del Rey. 435 Culver Blvd., Playa del Rey, CA 90293. ☎ **310/574-1920.** Fax 310/574-9920. www.innatplayadelrey.com. 21 units. TV TEL. $150–$215 double; $325 suite. Midweek discounts available. Rates include full breakfast, afternoon wine and cheese. AE, DISC, MC, V. Free parking. From LAX, take Sepulveda Blvd. north, veering left onto Lincoln Blvd. Turn left at Jefferson Blvd., which turns into Culver Blvd.

Though only 5 minutes from LAX, this pampering B&B is as much a sanctuary as the protected Ballona wetlands just outside the back door. From the street, the contemporary Inn looks like a set of condos; but inside, it glows with its true character. Fresh salty breezes and the quiet chirping of waterfowl fill a cozy fireplace lounge whose long veranda overlooks peaceful marshland. Hiking trails wind through the wildlife preserve, and a wooden observation platform 50 yards out is ideal for contemplation, bird watching, or spying on sailboats that pass to and fro along the

⓲ Family-Friendly Hotels

The L.A. area's highest concentration of family-friendly accommodations—those that make families with kids their primary concern—are found close to Disneyland (see "A Side Trip to Disneyland," in chapter 5). There are, however, a number of L.A. hotels that welcome kids with open arms.

Loews Santa Monica Beach Hotel *(see p. 31)* offers comprehensive children's programs throughout the summer. More like a resort than any other L.A. hotel, Loews boasts an unbeatable location: it's right by the beach and the boardwalk. It also offers baby-sitting services, so you can enjoy a kid-free evening on the town.

Hotel Oceana *(see p. 31)* is a spacious all-suite hotel overlooking the beach at Santa Monica. Kids will love the brightly colored walls and cushy furniture, and all suites come with Nintendo video games.

Inn at Venice Beach *(see p. 40)* is a great choice for ocean-loving families because of its location and value. The 3-block walk to the beach is lined with snack bars, surf shops, and bike and skate rentals; the resident ducks of the Venice canals are equally close, as are the attractions of Marina del Rey. The under-12 set is welcomed free of charge, and everyone starts the day with complimentary breakfast.

Sheraton Universal Hotel *(see p. 65)* enjoys a terrifically kid-friendly location, adjacent to Universal Studios and the fun CityWalk mall. Baby-sitting services are available, and there's a large game room on the premises.

Hollywood Hills Magic Hotel *(see p. 59)* is a good affordable choice for families. It offers roomy apartment-style suites and a location near Hollywood Boulevard's attractions.

channel. Guest rooms are spotlessly clean and decorated in a classy and casual beach chic that evokes Nantucket, Santa Barbara, or Palm Beach. Only the best furniture, the snuggliest comforters, and the plushest towels are used. Most rooms have whirlpool tubs, fireplaces, and decks. Bicycles are provided for enjoying a nearby beach bike path, and the inn also has an outdoor hot tub.

Radisson Huntley Hotel. 1111 2nd St. (north of Wilshire Blvd.), Santa Monica, CA 90403. ☎ **800/333-3333** or 310/394-5454. Fax 310/458-9776. www. radisson.com/santamonicaca. 219 units. A/C MINIBAR TV TEL. High season (Feb–Oct) $239–$259 double; low season $189–$229 double. Ask about "Super-saver" rates and/or B&B packages. AE, CB, DC, DISC, EC, MC, V. Valet parking $12.

This hotel, in one of Santa Monica's tallest buildings (18 floors), offers reliable, quality accommodations with a style and attitude one notch above the average mid-range chain—that's because this Radisson is privately owned. Even though the hotel caters primarily to corporate clients, leisure travelers will love its location, close to the Third Street Promenade and just 2 blocks from the beach. Guest rooms all boast either ocean or mountain views, and feature Nintendo games, bathrobes, freshly updated decor, and bathrooms with Italian marble floors. Toppers, the rooftop Mexican restaurant, has a great view, serves very good margaritas, and hosts live entertainment nightly. There's also a classy coffee shop serving American standards. *Fun tip:* Take a thrilling ride in the oceanside glass elevator (acrophobes, though, will find the lobby elevators more comfortable).

MODERATE

Cal Mar Hotel Suites. 220 California Ave., Santa Monica, CA 90403. ☎ **800/776-6007** or 310/395-5555. Fax 310/451-1111. 36 units. TV TEL. June–Aug and holidays $154–$169 double; off-season $104–$119 double. Extra person $10. Children under 10 stay free. AE, MC, V. Free parking.

Tucked away in a beautiful residential neighborhood 2 blocks from the ocean, these former garden apartments are lovingly

---

The Lowdown on In-Room Amenities

The times they are a-changin'—and hotels in Los Angeles are rushing to keep up with the demanding standards of savvy travelers in *every* price range. Lots of in-room goodies that seemed luxurious just a few years ago are commonplace today, so we decided not to waste the space listing them for every hotel. At each of the places in the "Very Expensive," "Expensive," and "Moderate" categories, you may generally assume your room will be equipped with **alarm clock, in-room safe, coffeemaker, hair dryer, iron and board, voice mail,** and **dataport.** A few "Inexpensive" hotels also offer some or all of these comforts, but in that price category it pays to ask when reserving if you have specific requirements.

cared for and deliver a lot of bang for your vacation buck. Each is a suite with separate bedroom, living room, and full-size kitchen; most are spacious enough to accommodate three to four people in comfort. The building was constructed in the 1950s with an eye for quality (attractive tilework, large closets). It wraps around a garden courtyard with heated swimming pool and plenty of chaise longues; there's also a laundry room on the premises. While the furnishings aren't luxurious—they may remind you of a college-era dorm or apartment—every need is provided for, and it's easy to be comfortable here for stays of a week or more. The staff is attentive and courteous, which helps account for the high rate of return clientele.

✪ **Casa Malibu.** 22752 Pacific Coast Hwy. (about $^1/_4$ mile south of Malibu Pier), Malibu, CA 90265. ☎ **800/831-0858** or 310/456-2219. Fax 310/456-5418. E-mail: casamalibu@earthlink.net. 21 units. TV TEL. $99–$139 double with garden view; $169 double with ocean view; $199–$229 beachfront double; $229–$349 suite. Rates include continental breakfast. Extra person $15. AE, MC, V. Free parking.

This modest, two-story motel on the beach is left over from the heyday of Malibu's Golden Age. The Casa Malibu doesn't try to play the sleek resort game—and we're delighted! Wrapped around a palm-studded inner courtyard with well-tended flower beds and cuppa d'oro vines climbing the walls, the 21 rooms are comfortable, charming, and thoughtfully outfitted. Casa Malibu sports a traditional "California beach cottage" look that's cozy and timeless. Each room features top-quality bedding, bathrobes, coffeemakers, and refrigerators; some have fireplaces, kitchenettes, and/or private balconies. The upstairs Catalina Suite (Lana Turner's old hideout) has the best view, while the Malibu Suite offers state-of-the-art pampering. Past the garden is a handsome brick sundeck directly over the sand (it's shielded from the wind). Wooden stairs lead to the hotel's private beach, which is raked smooth each morning. The blue Pacific provides a mesmerizing backdrop here, from breakfast—fresh coffee and pastries from Wolfgang Puck's nearby Granita restaurant—to the waves that lull you to sleep each night. Book well ahead for summer—this one's a favorite of locals and visitors alike.

The Hotel California. 1670 Ocean Ave. (south of Colorado Ave.), Santa Monica, CA 90401. ☎ **800/537-8483** or 310/393-2363. Fax 310/393-1063. www.hotelca.com. 26 units. TV TEL. Summer $150–$185 double, $200–$350 suite; off-season $125–$155 double, $175–$325 suite. AE, MC, V. Free parking.

New management has completely remade this former backpackers' flophouse into a clean and welcoming beachfront inn, one that reflects the owner's love of surfing and California beach nostalgia. With an enviable location—literally next door to the behemoth Loews—this place embodies the beachfront ambience we all want from Santa Monica. The Hotel California offers small but comfortable rooms with brand-new furnishings. You'll find fresh woodwork on doors, floors, and decks; retiled bathrooms; all-new fixtures; and lovingly tended landscaping. Privately owned cottages line your path down to the beach. The suites and some rooms have a partially obstructed ocean view; all units have new beds with down comforters, ceiling fans, nice bathroom amenities, and a small refrigerator. You can go check your e-mail via DSL hookup in the front office, and pick up a complimentary fresh-brewed cup o' joe while you're there.

Pacific Shore Hotel. 1819 Ocean Ave. (at Pico Blvd.), Santa Monica, CA 90401. ☎ **800/622-8711** or 310/451-8711. Fax 310/394-6657. www. pacificshorehotel.com. 168 units. A/C TV TEL. Summer $145–$200 double. Off-season and midweek discounts available. AE, DC, DISC, EC, JCB, MC, V. Parking $5.50.

This rectangular, eight-story glass-and-concrete monolith, located about a block from the beach, is a good choice for those who want to be in the heart of Santa Monica. The rooms are decent and well priced, and the hotel provides extras like a minigym and free area shuttle service. Great sunsets can be seen from the ocean-facing rooms on the high floors, but you'll have to look over busy Ocean Avenue and the roofs of Shutters on the Beach. Consider the discount city-view rooms, which gaze out over the hotel's charming garden, complete with heated pool. A bar and full-service restaurant are located off the lobby.

INEXPENSIVE

Inn at Venice Beach. 327 Washington Blvd., Marina del Rey, CA 90291. ☎ **800/828-0688** or 310/821-2557. Fax 310/827-0289. www. innatvenicebeach.com. 43 units. A/C TV. $95–$105 double; $135 suite. Extra person $10. Rates include continental breakfast. Children under 12 stay free in parents' room. AE, CB, DC, DISC, EC, JCB, MC, V. No cash or checks accepted. Free parking.

A charming, friendly, well-located inn with affordable rates that even include breakfast—it sounds too good to be true, but the Inn at Venice Beach is all that and more. Each room has a small balcony and a refrigerator and features such thoughtful touches as hair dryers, complimentary weekday newspapers, free movies, and separate vanity areas. Since the hotel is just 3 blocks from the ocean on the border between Venice and Marina del Rey, there's an endless parade out front of people exploring the marina, the beach, or the nearby canals on foot, bike, or in-line skates (rentals are 2 blocks away; inquire at the front desk). Breakfast is served in a cobblestone outdoor courtyard shielded from the noisy boulevard. About the only thing missing is a swimming pool, but the staff will cheerfully lend you beach towels for an ocean dip. Suites, which have high-ceilinged living rooms and spacious sleeping lofts with queen-size beds, are the best deal here.

Sea Shore Motel. 2637 Main St. (south of Ocean Park Blvd.), Santa Monica, CA 90405. ☎ **310/392-2787.** Fax 310/392-5167. www.seashoremotel.com. 20 units. TV TEL. $80–$95 double; $100 suite. Extra person $5. Midweek discounts available. Children under 12 stay free in parents' room. AE, CB, DC, DISC, MC, V. Free parking. Pets accepted for $10 fee per night.

Most denizens of Santa Monica's trendy Main Street area don't even know about this small, family-run motel in the heart of dining and shopping action. A recent total upgrade of the property (furnishings, fixtures, exterior) has brought it up to standard; rooms are unremarkable, arranged around a parking courtyard, but the management is caring and conscientious, installing conveniences like refrigerators, voice mail, and attractive terra-cotta floor tiles. A stylish little deli is attached, selling morning muffins and sandwiches and homemade soup at lunchtime. The beach is a short walk away, and the businesses on Main Street are among the city's chicest; the Sea Shore makes a terrific bargain base for exploring this part of town.

ACCOMMODATIONS NEAR LAX

Whether you have a long layover, have an early flight, or just are an aviation buff, these hotels will put you within earshot (literally, sometimes) of the airport.

Los Angeles Airport Marriott. Century Blvd. (at Airport Blvd.), Los Angeles, CA 90045. ☎ **800/228-9290** or 310/641-5700. Fax 310/337-5358. 1,029 units. A/C TV TEL. $109–$150 double; from $375 suite. AE, CB, DC, DISC, EC, MC, V. Weekend and off-season rates available. Valet parking $12; self-parking $9.

This is no cutting-edge hotel but it's a good airport choice, designed for travelers on the fly. Rooms are decorated in standard chain-hotel style; some have balconies. There's a laundry room, and ironing boards, irons, and hair dryers are available. Amenities include a giant outdoor heated pool, a swim-up bar, a whirlpool, a garden sundeck, a business center, room service, concierge, a complimentary airport shuttle, and a car-rental desk. There are also two serviceable restaurants, a coffee shop, and a bar.

Sheraton Gateway Hotel. 6101 W. Century Blvd. (near Sepulveda Blvd.), Los Angeles, CA 90045. ☎ **800/325-3535** or 310/642-1111. Fax 310/410-1267. 804 units. A/C MINIBAR TV TEL. $135–$175 double; from $300 suite. AE, CB, DC, DISC, JCB, MC, V. Valet parking $14; self-parking $8.

This 15-story hotel is so close to the Los Angeles Airport it literally overlooks the runway. Rooms have a California look, with comfortable furnishings and triple-pane windows that block out even the loudest takeoffs. There is a large, heated outdoor pool, an exercise room with Universal equipment, a whirlpool, and three 24-hour restaurants. The hotel also offers 24-hour room service, a rarity in this price range.

Travelodge at LAX. 5547 W. Century Blvd., Los Angeles, CA 90045. ☎ **800/421-3939** or 310/649-4000. Fax 310/649-0311. 147 units. A/C TV TEL. $69–$89 double. Extra person $8; children under 18 stay free. Lower rates off-season. AE, CB, DC, DISC, JCB, MC, V. Free parking.

The lobby is nondescript and the rooms are standard at this chain motel, but there's a surprisingly beautiful tropical garden surrounding the pool area. Some units have terraces. Services include free airport transportation, baby-sitting, 24-hour room service (a rarity for a budget-priced hotel), and a car-rental desk. A Denny's is attached.

2 L.A.'s Westside & Beverly Hills

The city's most competitive accommodations are found in these centrally located communities, but traffic congestion is an ever-present ill, and your car can sometimes seem more a liability than a convenience. Dining, shopping, and nightlife are at their best on the Westside, which is often the favorite locale of visiting celebs.

VERY EXPENSIVE

✪ **Beverly Hills Hotel & Bungalows.** 9641 Sunset Blvd. (at Rodeo Dr.), Beverly Hills, CA 90210. ☎ **800/283-8885** or 310/276-2251. Fax 310/281-2905. www.thebeverlyhillshotel.com. 234 units. A/C TV TEL. $335–$390 double; from $545 bungalow; from $685 suite. AE, DC, JCB, MC, V. Parking $18. Pets under 30 lb. accepted in bungalows only.

Behind the famous facade of the "Pink Palace" (pictured on the Eagles's *Hotel California*) lies the kind of hotel where legends are made, and many were: This was center stage for both deal- and star-making in Hollywood's golden days. Today, plenty of current stars and industry hotshots can be found lazing around the pool, which Katharine Hepburn once dove into fully clothed. Following a $100 million restoration, the hotel's grand lobby and impeccably landscaped grounds still retain their over-the-top glory, while guest rooms now boast every state-of-the-art luxury the first-class traveler demands. Bathrooms are outfitted with double Grecian marble sinks, TVs, and telephones for sink-side deal making. The best original touches have been retained as well, like a butler at your service with the touch of a button. The bungalows are more luxurious than ever—and who knows who you'll have as a neighbor?

Dining/Diversions: The iconic Polo Lounge is back, with its original atmosphere and traditional comfort fare, like Dutch apple pancakes or the signature guacamole. The adjacent Polo Grill takes up the nouvelle torch, specializing in California cuisine. The famous Fountain Coffee Shop has also returned, while the Tea Lounge is a new addition.

Amenities: Large outdoor heated pool and whirlpool, fitness room, VCRs with video delivery, concierge, 24-hour room service, dry cleaning, laundry service, nightly turndown, massage, airport limo service, car-rental desk, beauty salon.

Four Seasons Hotel. 300 S. Doheny Dr. (at Burton Way), Los Angeles, CA 90048. ☎ **800/332-3442**, 800/268-6282 in Canada, or 310/273-2222. Fax 310/859-3824. 285 units. A/C MINIBAR TV TEL. $370–$470 double; from $600 suite. AE, DC, EC, MC, V. Valet parking $19; free self-parking. Pets welcomed with snack bone and personalized bowl (no charge).

This 16-story hotel attracts a mix of A-list jet-setters loyal to the Four Seasons brand, and the L.A. showbiz crowd who cherish the hotel as an après-event gathering place. The small lobby is anchored by an always-stunning floral extravaganza, and lovely gardens will help you forget you're in the heart of the city. Four Seasons operates terrific hotels, with a concierge that's famously well connected and impeccable service that really goes the distance; there are complimentary cell phones for every room, so you can always answer your calls—at the pool or on the town. Newly added in 2000 was the guests-only full-service spa. Guest

Accommodations & Dining in
L.A.'s Westside & Beverly Hills

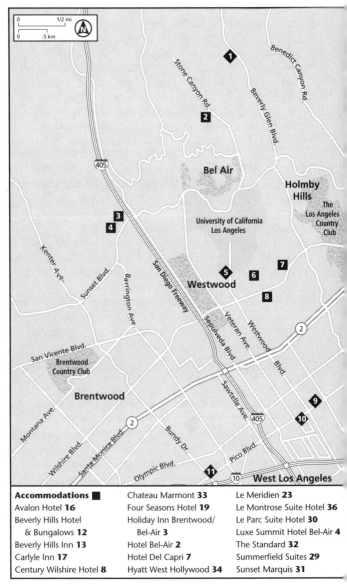

Accommodations ■

Avalon Hotel **16**

Beverly Hills Hotel
& Bungalows **12**

Beverly Hills Inn **13**

Carlyle Inn **17**

Century Wilshire Hotel **8**

Chateau Marmont **33**

Four Seasons Hotel **19**

Holiday Inn Brentwood/
Bel-Air **3**

Hotel Bel-Air **2**

Hotel Del Capri **7**

Hyatt West Hollywood **34**

Le Meridien **23**

Le Montrose Suite Hotel **36**

Le Parc Suite Hotel **30**

Luxe Summit Hotel Bel-Air **4**

The Standard **32**

Summerfield Suites **29**

Sunset Marquis **31**

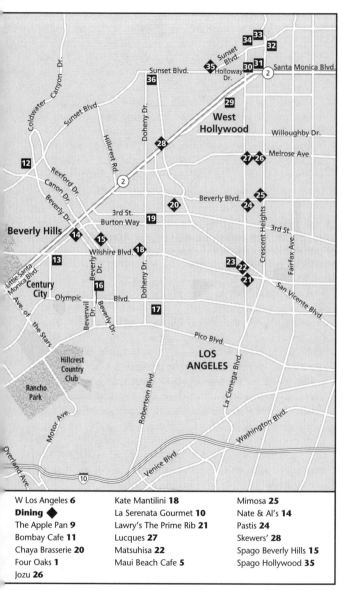

W Los Angeles **6**	Kate Mantilini **18**	Mimosa **25**
Dining ◆	La Serenata Gourmet **10**	Nate & Al's **14**
The Apple Pan **9**	Lawry's The Prime Rib **21**	Pastis **24**
Bombay Cafe **11**	Lucques **27**	Skewers' **28**
Chaya Brasserie **20**	Matsuhisa **22**	Spago Beverly Hills **15**
Four Oaks **1**	Maui Beach Cafe **5**	Spago Hollywood **35**
Jozu **26**		

rooms are sumptuously furnished in premium quality: Bulgari bathing products, bathroom TVs, and oversized private balconies. Room rates rise with the elevator, so bargain hunters sacrifice the view; ask for a corner room to get extra space at no extra cost. While colloquially known as the "Four Seasons Beverly Hills," the hotel is actually in a nice but primarily residential neighborhood adjacent to BH.

Dining: The Gardens is a terrific California-French restaurant that's often overlooked by locals; service and food are first-rate, and Sunday brunch is worth leaving your room for.

Amenities: Large outdoor heated pool (with private cabanas at no charge), open-air exercise room (personal trainers available), whirlpool, concierge, 24-hour room service, overnight laundry, complimentary shoe shine, nightly turndown, car-rental desk, florist.

✪ **Hotel Bel-Air.** 701 Stone Canyon Rd. (north of Sunset Blvd.), Bel Air, CA 90077. ☎ **800/648-4097** or 310/472-1211. Fax 310/476-5890. 92 units. A/C MINIBAR TV TEL. $380–$500 double; from $625 suite. AE, DC, DISC, JCB, MC, V. Parking $13.50. Pets accepted with $250 deposit ($200 refundable upon checkout).

Make the Hotel Bel-Air your address if you want to impress. This mission-style hotel is truly one of the finest—and most beautiful—hotels in southern California. It regularly wins praise for its attentive service and luxurious rooms. The parklike grounds—lush with ancient trees, fragrant flowers, and a swan-dotted pond—are magical, and the welcoming, richly traditional public rooms are filled with fine antiques. The guest villas are decorated in Mediterranean style with compulsive attention to detail. The rooms and garden suites are equally stunning; all have two phones, a VCR, and a CD player. Some units have wood-burning fireplaces. This hotel is a natural for honeymooners and other celebrants, but families might be put off by the Bel-Air's relative formality, which is geared more to the jet set and business professionals.

Dining/Diversions: It's worth having dinner at the restaurant. Even if you don't stay here, you might consider brunch or lunch on the hotel's outdoor woodsy terrace, or drinks at the cozy bar.

Amenities: Outdoor heated pool, health club, sundeck, nature trails, concierge, 24-hour room service, nightly turndown, valet parking, welcome tea upon arrival.

✪ **Le Meridien.** 465 S. La Cienega Blvd., Los Angeles, CA 90048. ☎ **800/ 645-5687** or 310/247-0400. Fax 310/247-0315. www.lemeridienbh.com. 300 units. A/C TV TEL. $315–$440 double; from $600 suite. AE, CB, DC, DISC, JCB, MC, V. Valet parking $18; free self-parking. Pets accepted with $100 fee (covers 4-night stay).

Finally—a hotel designed for business travelers where the primary goal isn't mimicking every other business hotel. Le Meridien refers to its interior decor as "Pacific Rim" ("Organic Pacific Rim" for the suites, which use all-organic textiles), but "well thought out" seems just as appropriate. Thanks to amenities such as in-room fax machines, three two-line phones, and large counter/desk space, the rooms function equally well as sleeping quarters and workspaces. All things electrical (lights, TV, climate control) are operated by a bedside remote, and the subdued black marble bathrooms hold elegant Hermés products; after a long day on the job, the huge Japanese soaking tubs are perfect for unwinding. Shoji screens replace curtains, allowing light to filter through or blocking it out entirely.

Dining/Diversions: Pangaea restaurant blends French and American dishes with Asian influences and offers a 14-piece, big-band brunch. There's also a cocktail lounge with nightly entertainment.

Amenities: Heated pool, 24-hour health club, massage, sauna, concierge, 24-hour room service, same-day dry cleaning and laundry, nightly turndown, business center.

✪ **Le Montrose Suite Hotel.** 900 Hammond St., West Hollywood, CA 90069. ☎ **800/776-0666** or 310/855-1115. Fax 310/657-9192. www.lemontrose.com. 132 units. A/C TV TEL. $260–$290 queen suite, $300–$380 king suite with kitchen. AE, CB, DC, EC, MC, V. Parking $16. Pets allowed with $75 fee.

For location, quality, and price, this is one of L.A.'s best values. Nestled on a quiet residential street just 2 blocks from the bustling Strip, this all-suite hotel features large one-bedroom apartments that feel more like upscale condos than standard hotel rooms. Each has a large bedroom, kitchenette or kitchen, and bathroom, as well as a sizable sunken living room complete with gas fireplace, fax machine, and Nintendo games. You have to go up to the roof for anything resembling a view, but once you're up there, you can swim in the pool or play on the lighted tennis court. This place is already popular among music-industry clientele; let's hope that when it catches on, prices will stay reasonable, and reservations won't be hard to come by.

Dining: The Library Restaurant serves continental meals all day. Light bites are served poolside.

Amenities: Outdoor heated pool, whirlpool, sundeck, lighted tennis court, exercise room with sauna, laundry room, concierge, 24-hour room service, nightly turndown, complimentary bicycles, currency exchange.

Sunset Marquis Hotel & Villas. 1200 N. Alta Loma Rd. (at Sunset Blvd.), West Hollywood, CA 90069. ☎ **800/858-9758** or 310/657-1333. Fax 310/652-5300. 114 units. TV TEL. $280–$360 junior or 1-bedroom suite; $550 2-bedroom suite; from $600 villa. AE, CB, DC, MC, V. Valet or self-parking $14.

This is the ultimate music-industry hotel, regularly hosting the biggest names in rock. Sometimes they even record in the Mediterranean-style hotel's basement studios and retire afterward to the lobby bar, where their session can be piped in directly. The hotel is located a short walk from rowdy Sunset Strip, but it feels a world away, with its lush gardens, koi ponds, exotic birds, and tropical foliage. The standard suites are done in traditional motel style; they're not particularly special, just overpriced. Each comes with a sitting area and a good-size refrigerator. The private villas take hospitality to a totally different level—they even have their own baby grand pianos and butlers. This is where Mick stays.

Dining/Diversions: The Whiskey is one of L.A.'s most exclusive bars; the likes of Axl Rose and Robert Plant turn it into a celebrity fest Wednesday through Saturday nights. Unless you're staying at the hotel, though, you'll never get in. There's also a California-style restaurant on-site.

Amenities: Two outdoor heated swimming pools, small exercise room, health spa offering beauty treatments, whirlpool, sauna, sundeck, concierge, room service (24 hr.), 24-hour business and message center, access to the hotel's 48-track/112-channel automated studio, dry cleaning, laundry service, in-room massage.

W Los Angeles. 930 Hilgard Ave., Los Angeles, CA 90024-3033. ☎ **800/421-2317** or 310/208-8765. Fax 310/824-0355. 257 units. A/C MINIBAR TV TEL. $259–$469 1-bedroom suite; from $1,200 2-bedroom suite. AAA, AARP, and weekend discounts available. AE, DC, DISC, JCB, MC, V. Valet parking $21.

This 15-story, all-suite hotel near UCLA underwent a dramatic transformation in 2000 under new owners, W Hotels, whose properties have been described as "Pottery Barns you can sleep in." Hidden behind a severe concrete exterior, this hotel has always attracted behind-the-scenes industry types drawn by its ample amenities; each suite now boasts multiline cordless phones, CD stereo, VCR, bathrobes, Aveda bathing products, and luxury bedding with down comforters. Like the all-black-clad staff, the building is dressed to impress; get past the high-concept waterfall stairway entrance and you encounter a coolly dark and modern "living room" (lobby) with geometric, yet, surprisingly comfy furniture. Hallways and suites are impeccably furnished to appeal to the business traveler; framed black-and-white architectural prints connect to the city outside, and everything in the room (from bed linens to the bed itself) is available for purchase. Two acres of landscaped gardens surround the heated outdoor pool, and there's a full-service spa that'll even do massage in your poolside cabana—now that's luxury!

Dining/Diversions: Mojo restaurant blends seamlessly with the open lobby, serving Latin-inspired cuisine and colorful cocktails to über-stylish industry types.

Amenities: Two outdoor heated pools, whirlpool, fitness center, concierge, 24-hour room service, in-room Internet access, dry cleaning, laundry service, nightly turndown.

EXPENSIVE

✪ **Carlyle Inn.** 1119 S. Robertson Blvd. (south of Olympic Blvd.), Los Angeles, CA 90035. ☎ **800/322-7595** or 310/275-4445. Fax 310/859-0496. www.carlyle-inn.com. 32 units. A/C MINIBAR TV TEL. $148–$209 double; $225 suite. Rates include full breakfast and weekday hors d'oeuvres. AE, DC, DISC, JCB, MC, V. Parking $8.

Hidden on an uneventful stretch of Robertson Boulevard just south of Beverly Hills, this four-story inn is one of the best-priced finds in L.A. Despite the property's small size and unlikely location, architects have managed to create a multistory interior courtyard, which almost every room faces. Well-planned, contemporary interiors are fitted with recessed lighting, art deco wall lamps, pine furnishings, and well-framed, classical architectural monoprints. Other amenities include VCRs and bathrobes. The hotel's primary drawback is that it lacks views; curtains must remain drawn at all times to maintain any sense of privacy. The suites are only slightly larger than standard rooms.

✪ **Chateau Marmont.** 8221 Sunset Blvd. (between La Cienega and Crescent Heights blvds.), West Hollywood, CA 90046. ☎ **800/CHATEAU** or 323/656-1010. Fax 323/655-5311. 63 units. A/C MINIBAR TV TEL. $220–$280 double; from $335 suite; from $650 bungalow. AE, CB, DC, EC, MC, V. Valet parking $19. Pets accepted with $100 fee.

The Norman-style Chateau Marmont, perched in a curve of the Sunset Strip, is a landmark from 1920s-era Hollywood; step inside and you expect to find John Barrymore or Errol Flynn holding inebriated court in the baronial living room. Greta Garbo regularly checked in as "Harriet Brown," Jim Morrison was only one of many to call this home in later years. This historical monument built its reputation on exclusivity and privacy—which was shattered when John Belushi overdosed in Bungalow No. 2. Chateau Marmont is popular because it's close to the Hollywood action and a luxurious world away at the same time. The standard rooms have views of the city and the Hollywood Hills; some have kitchenettes. The suites are large and most come with cloth-canopied balconies. The poolside Cape Cod–style bungalows—large, secluded, and cozy, with full kitchens—are some of the most coveted in town. Accustomed to the demands of showbiz big shots, the hotel provides a wide array of amenities, including 24-hour room service, same-day laundry and dry-cleaning service, in-room CD players, free use of a cell phone, and a fitness room.

Holiday Inn Brentwood/Bel-Air. 170 N.Church Lane (at intersection of Sunset Blvd. and I-405), Los Angeles, CA 90049. ☎ **800/HOLIDAY** or 310/476-6411. Fax 310/472-1157. www.hibrentwood.com. 211 units. A/C TV TEL. $169–$189 double; from $275 suite. AAA and AARP discounts, breakfast package $10 extra per room; also ask for the "Great Rate," often as low as $99. AE, DC, DISC, MC, V. Valet parking $10; self-parking $8.

It's become an L.A. landmark, the last of a vanishing breed of circular hotels from the 1960s and 1970s; this Holiday Inn is perched beside the city's busiest freeway a short hop from the popular Getty Center and centrally located between the beaches, Beverly Hills, and the San Fernando Valley. Completely refurbished in 2000, each pie-shaped room (the hotel is round, remember?) boasts a private balcony and double-paned glass to keep the freeway noise out; little extras like Nintendo games, in-room bottled water, and Bath & Body Works products add panache to otherwise-unremarkable chain-style rooms. Popular with older travelers and especially museum groups, the Holiday Inn provides complimentary shuttle service to the Getty Center uphill.

Dining/Diversions: You'll enjoy a million-dollar 360-degree view from the hotel's unadvertised top-floor Brentwood Terrace restaurant, which serves a casual, please-all cuisine. *Money-saving* *tip:* Kids 12 and under eat free from a special menu. The adjoining cocktail lounge features live piano nightly.

Amenities: Heated outdoor pool, whirlpool, exercise room, room service (6am to 11pm), coin-op laundry.

Hyatt West Hollywood. 8401 Sunset Blvd. (2 blocks east of La Cienega Blvd.), West Hollywood, CA 90069. ☎ **800/233-1234** or 323/656-1234. Fax 323/650-7024. 262 units. A/C TV TEL. $195–$230 double; $255–$450 suite. Special weekend and AAA rates available. AE, CB, DC, DISC, EC, MC, V. Valet parking $20; self-parking $15.

A few years ago, this 13-story Sunset Strip hotel completed extensive renovations that erased any last remnants of its former debauched life as the rock 'n' roll "Riot Hyatt." It doesn't even look like other Hyatts, since the management eschewed the standard corporate decor and contracted locally; the end result is a stylish cross between the clean black-and-white geometrics of a 1930s movie set and a Scandinavian birch-and-ebony aesthetic. Rooms all have beautiful city or hillside views (about half have balconies), but stay away from front-facing rooms on the lower floors—too close to noisy Sunset Boulevard. The Hyatt woos both business and leisure travelers, providing secure access to guest floors and ergonomic desk chairs in each room; in-room minifridges are an extra $5 a day. Auto-club members take note: Special AAA rates are as low as $149.

Dining/Diversions: The casual Silver Screen Bistro is a notch above a good diner. There is also a sports bar and a lobby coffee/pastry cart.

Amenities: Rooftop heated pool, concierge, room service (from 6am to midnight), same-day laundry service, business center, tour desk.

Le Parc Suite Hotel. 733 N. West Knoll Dr., West Hollywood, CA 90069. ☎ **800/5-SUITES** or 310/855-8888. Fax 310/659-7812. www.leparcsuites. com. 154 units. A/C MINIBAR TV TEL. $260–$400 suite. AE, CB, DC, JCB, MC, V. Parking $16. Pets accepted with $75 cleaning fee.

Situated on a quiet residential street, Le Parc is a high-quality, all-suite hotel with a pleasantly mixed clientele. Designers stay here because it's a few minutes' walk to the Pacific Design Center, patients and medical consultants check in because it's close to Cedars-Sinai, and tourists enjoy being near the Farmers Market and Museum Row. The nicely furnished, apartment-like units each have a kitchenette, dining area, living room with fireplace, and balcony. What this hotel lacks in cachet, it more than makes up for in value—despite climbing rack rates, rooms were available at press time for as little as $165.

Dining/Diversions: Cafe Le Parc, which is open from 6:30am to 11pm, features a full bar.

Amenities: Outdoor heated pool, rooftop night-lit tennis court, basketball hoop, health club with sauna and whirlpool, concierge, room service (from 6:30am to 11pm), dry-cleaning/laundry service, VCRs and video rentals, newspaper delivery, in-room massage, twice-daily maid service, baby-sitting, valet parking, courtesy car, bathrobes, ironing board and iron, self-service laundry, business center, car-rental desk.

Summerfield Suites. 1000 Westmount Dr. (1 block west of La Cienega Blvd.), West Hollywood, CA 90069. ☎ **800/833-4353** or 310/657-7400. Fax 310/854-6744. 109 units. A/C TV TEL. $150–$315 suite. All rates include full breakfast. AE, CB, DC, DISC, JCB, MC, V. Parking $16. Pets accepted with $250 refundable deposit, plus $75 cleaning fee and $10 daily charge.

This all-suite property in a residential West Hollywood neighborhood looks and feels much like a high-quality apartment building. A relatively unassuming interior and quiet public areas are hallmarks of value—less flash for less cash. Likewise, accommodations are detailed and plush without being excessive in either size or style. Most of the pastel-colored suites have sunken living rooms, gas fireplaces, contemporary furnishings, and petite balconies overlooking Hollywood or Beverly Hills. All have kitchenettes and pretty good original art.

Dining/Diversions: There's a California-style cafe with an adjacent bar.

Amenities: Rooftop heated pool, small exercise room with cardio machines, rooftop whirlpool, sauna, sundeck, concierge, room service (from 7am to 11pm), laundry service, dry cleaning, grocery shopping.

MODERATE

✪ **Avalon Hotel.** 9400 W. Olympic Blvd. (at Beverly Dr.), Beverly Hills, CA 90212. ☎ **800/535-4715** or 310/277-5221. Fax 310/277-4928. 88 units. A/C MINIBAR TV TEL. $189–$235 double, suites from $300. AE, DC, MC, V. Valet parking $14.

A new trend in L.A. is retro-stylish boutique hotels that sport luxury amenities but appeal to a savvy, financially challenged traveler—and this mid-century classic in the heart of Beverly Hills leads the pack. With furnishings that make every room look like a *Metropolitan Home* photo spread, in-room amenities you can *really* use, and nearly unheard-of low rates, the Avalon began attracting a very chic, low-key clientele as soon as it opened in 1999. It took enormous creativity to transform the former Beverly-Carlton (seen on *I Love Lucy* and once home to Marilyn Monroe and Mae West) into this showplace; though the simple 1950s lines of the structure are enhanced but unchanged, high-style period furniture—Eames cabinets, Haywood-Wakefield chairs, Noguchi lamps—kicks the fashion quotient up several notches. Fax machines, CD players, PC hookups, terry bathrobes, stocked fridges, and top-of-the-line bedding are standard in every room; some also have private balconies or kitchenettes. The hotel's kidney-shaped pool is modernized with simple, Zen-style plantings and edgy (but plush) chaises. There's a friendly poolside cafe off the lobby, and the staff is ready to see to your needs, including free shuttle service to Beverly Hills shopping and dining.

Beverly Hills Inn. 125 S. Spalding Dr., Beverly Hills, CA 90212. ☎ **800/ 463-4466** or 310/278-0303. Fax 310/278-1728. 46 units. A/C TV TEL. $145–$160 double; from $195 suite. Rates include full breakfast, plus afternoon fruit and cheese. AE, DC, EC, MC, V. Free parking.

The secret to a Beverly Hills lifestyle is knowing how to put on a good appearance—any face-lifted, tummy-tucked socialite will tell you that. So go ahead and brag about your Beverly Hills address to your friends; they'll never know what a bargain you got. You can honestly say you have a quiet, newly decorated room outfitted with thoughtful touches—like a bathrobe for strolling down to the small but lushly landscaped garden swimming pool. Popular with Asian business travelers, this hotel is impeccably furnished in a bland but vaguely tropical motif. Most rooms have views of either the pool or the quiet, tree-lined street out front. When you're ready to face the world, you'll find yourself ideally located just a block from Rodeo Drive shopping and dining and an easy walk from Century City. Breakfast is served in the aptly named Garden Hideaway Room (which serves afternoon snacks and also has a full bar). All in all, one of the best deals going in a high-rent neighborhood.

Century Wilshire Hotel. 10776 Wilshire Blvd. (between Malcolm and Selby aves.), Los Angeles, CA 90024. ☎ **800/421-7223** (outside CA) or 310/474-4506. Fax 310/474-2535. www.centurywilshirehotel.com. 99 units. A/C TV TEL. High season (May–Oct) $135–$165 double, from $250 suite; low season $115–$145 double, from $195 suite. Rates include continental breakfast. Weekly rates available. AE, DC, DISC, MC, V. Free parking.

For the money, it's hard to do better in Westwood. The guest rooms in this converted three-story apartment building are large (with abundant closet space), sparsely decorated, and well located, near UCLA, the Getty Center, and Beverly Hills. Most have kitchenettes and some have French doors that open onto balconies; furnishings, however, are a mishmash of style and condition. The hotel surrounds a quiet green courtyard, with a hidden, quiet swimming pool with brand-new surfacing and lounge furniture. Breakfast is served each morning either inside or out in the courtyard.

Luxe Summit Hotel Bel-Air. 11461 Sunset Blvd., Los Angeles, CA 90049. ☎ **800/HOTEL-411** or 310/476-6571. Fax 310/471-6310. www.luxehotels. com. 161 units. A/C MINIBAR TV TEL. $175–$249 double; $225–$289 suite. Extra person $30. AE, CB, DC, DISC, EC, JCB, MC, V. Valet parking $15.

Hidden away on 8 garden acres just a stone's throw from the Getty Center and busy Interstate 405, this hotel is composed of two levels. The lobby and public areas—plus some rooms—are in the main building. The most secluded guest rooms—and the delightful Romanesque swimming pool—are uphill on the Garden level. Guest rooms here are huge, each sporting stylish Gap-inspired fabrics in a sand-and-khaki color scheme; most have a large balcony or patio. Furnishings are brand new (in 2000) and give a clean, modern feel to this low-rise property. This is a place that appeals equally to business clientele, who appreciate the meeting spaces and in-room amenities, and to leisure travelers, who can relax in the green setting while being minutes away from Beverly Hills, Brentwood, Westwood Village, and Century City. In fact, hourly shuttle service is provided to the Getty Center, with a daily shuttle to Rodeo Drive shopping. Facilities and services include an indoor/outdoor restaurant, a single unlit tennis court, complimentary Sunday morning yoga, room service, laundry/dry cleaning, and a day spa with warm Japanese ambience.

INEXPENSIVE

✪ **Hotel Del Capri.** 10587 Wilshire Blvd. (at Westholme Ave.), Los Angeles, CA 90024. ☎ **800/444-6835** or 310/474-3511. Fax 310/470-9999. www. hoteldelcapri.com. 77 units. A/C TV TEL. $90–$120 double; from $135 suite. Extra person $10. Rates include continental breakfast. AE, CB, DC, EC, MC, V. Free parking. Pets accepted for additional fee equal to 1 night's stay.

The Del Capri is one of the best values in trendy Westwood. This well-located and fairly priced hotel is popular with tourists, business travelers, parents visiting their UCLA offspring, and performing artists in for the duration of a show. There are two parts to the property: a four-story building on the boulevard and a charming two-story motel with white louver shutters and delightful flowering vines. All guest room furnishings are clean and well-cared for, though the decidedly 1980s decor won't be winning any style awards. Bathrooms are small and basic; the most notable room feature is electrically adjustable beds—a decidedly novel touch. The more expensive rooms are slightly larger and have whirlpool bathtubs and an extra phone in the bathroom; most of the suites have kitchenettes. A freshly retiled swimming pool sits in the courtyard garden. The hotel provides free shuttle service to nearby shopping and attractions in Westwood, Beverly Hills, and Century City.

✪ **The Standard.** 8300 Sunset Blvd. (at Sweetzer), West Hollywood, CA 90069. ☎ **323/650-9090.** Fax 323/650-2820. 140 units. A/C MINIBAR TV TEL. $95–$215 double; from $650 suite. AE, CB, DC, MC, V. Valet parking $15.

There's something different about the Standard; you'll notice it right away. Shag carpeting on the lobby *ceiling,* blue astroturf surrounding the swimming pool, scantily clad performance artists and DJs entertaining alongside the check-in desk—this place is definitely left of center. Designed by hotelier André Balazs to appeal to the "shag-a-delic" under-35 crowd, the Standard is sometimes silly, sometimes brilliant, but always provocative (and always crowded!). Constructed from the fine bones of a vintage 1962 Sunset Strip hotel, this newcomer boasts comfortably sized rooms outfitted with silver beanbag chairs, Andy Warhol curtains, private balconies, cordless phones, CD players, T1 data lines, and minibars that hold everything from sake to condoms to animal crackers. A 24-hour restaurant downstairs features a menu composed by Jean-Georges Vongerichten from Balazs's successful Mercer in New York City; next to it sits a branch of Seattle-based Rudy's barbershop (with resident tattoo artist). Look past the retro clutter and often-raucous party scene, though, and you'll find a level of service more often associated with hotels costing twice—or three times—as much.

3   Hollywood

Many newcomers are surprised that the "Hollywood" often considered synonymous with Los Angeles is smaller and less attractive than expected. The area is highly tourist-oriented—other

Hollywood Area Accommodations & Dining

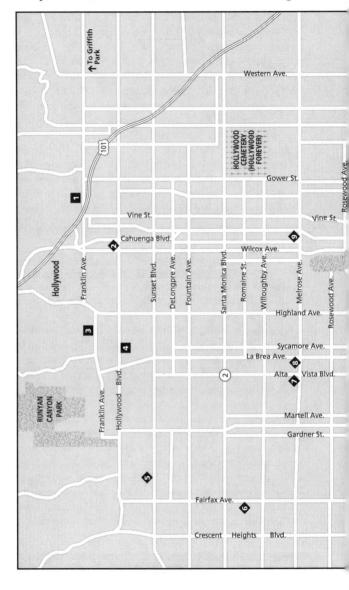

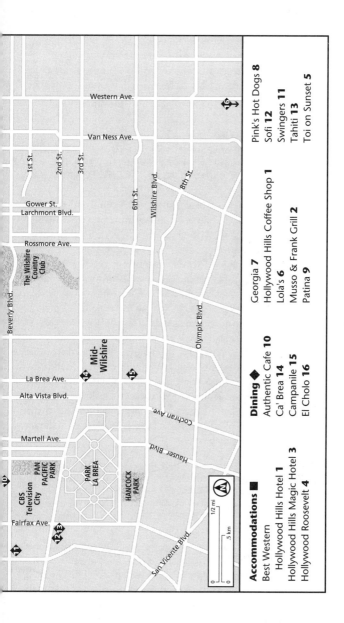

Accommodations ■
Best Western
Hollywood Hills Hotel **1**
Hollywood Hills Magic Hotel **3**
Hollywood Roosevelt **4**

Dining ◆
Authentic Cafe **10**
Ca' Brea **14**
Campanile **15**
El Cholo **16**

Georgia **7**
Hollywood Hills Coffee Shop **1**
Lola's **6**
Musso & Frank Grill **2**
Patina **9**

Pink's Hot Dogs **8**
Sofi **12**
Swingers **11**
Tahiti **13**
Toi on Sunset **5**

significant revenue sources are unmentionable in polite company. Though hotels here are often a bargain and offer generous package rates, the surroundings might be a bit crowded and loud for some. Hollywood is, however, close via freeway to Universal City and the San Fernando Valley.

MODERATE

✪ **Hollywood Roosevelt.** 7000 Hollywood Blvd., Hollywood, CA 90028. ☎ **800/950-7667** or 323/466-7000. Fax 323/469-7006. www. hollywoodroosevelt.com. 330 units. A/C MINIBAR TV TEL. $159–$219 double; from $299 suite. Discounts available. AE, CB, DC, DISC, EC, MC, V. Valet parking $12.

This 12-story movie-city landmark is located on a slightly seedy, very touristy part of Hollywood Boulevard, across from Mann's Chinese Theatre and just down the street from the Walk of Fame. The Roosevelt was one of the city's grandest hotels when it opened its doors in 1927, and it was home to the first Academy Awards ceremony. The exquisitely restored two-story lobby features a Hollywood minimuseum. The rooms, while freshly renovated, are typical of chain hotels, far less appealing—in both size and decor—than the public areas. A few, however, are charming with their original 1920s-style bathrooms. The suites are named after stars who stayed in them during the glory days; some have grand verandas, while others are rumored to be haunted by the ghosts of Marilyn Monroe and Montgomery Clift. Higher floors have unbeatable skyline views. David Hockney decorated the famous Olympic-size pool. The Cinegrill supper club draws locals with a zany cabaret show and guest chanteuses from Eartha Kitt to Cybill Shepherd.

INEXPENSIVE

Best Western Hollywood Hills Hotel. 6141 Franklin Ave. (between Vine and Gower sts.), Hollywood, CA 90028. ☎ **800/287-1700** in CA only, or 323/464-5181. Fax 323/962-0536. 82 units. A/C TV TEL. $79–$89 double. Senior and auto-club discounts available. DC, DISC, MC, V. Free parking. Pets accepted with $20 fee per stay.

Location is a big selling point for this chain representative, just off U.S. 101 (the Hollywood Freeway) and within walking distance of the famed Hollywood and Vine intersection. The walls showcase images from the golden age of movies, and the front desk offers an endless variety of arranged tours, ranging from the Hollywood Walk of Fame to Six Flags Magic Mountain. Check out the package deals for extra value. Rooms are plain and clean but lack much warmth—outer walls are painted cinder block, and closets are hidden behind institutional metal accordion doors. On the plus side, however, all rooms come with a refrigerator and free movies, and those in back have an attractive view of the neighboring hillside. There's also a gleaming blue-tiled, heated outdoor pool, and one of the city's most trendy retro-eateries, the Hollywood Hills Coffee Shop (see "Hollywood," in chapter 4, for complete restaurant listing) off the lobby.

Hollywood Hills Magic Hotel. 7025 Franklin Ave. (between La Brea and Highland), Hollywood, CA 90028. ☎ **800/741-4915** or 323/851-0800. Fax 323/874-5246. www.magichotel.com. 49 units. A/C TV TEL. $75 double; $99–$149 suite. Extra person $5. Off-season and other discounts available. AE, DC, DISC, JCB, MC, V. Free secured underground parking.

You'll love being located near all of Hollywood Boulevard's tourist attractions, and you may also be surprised by this bargain's spacious comfort. Named for the Magic Castle, the landmark illusionist club just uphill, the hotel was once an apartment building, and it hasn't lost that private feeling of being insulated from the street's frenzy. The rooms are situated around a swimming-pool courtyard. Most are apartment-style suites; all are spacious and boast kitchens with microwave and coffeemaker. Several units also have balconies overlooking the large heated pool. This place is ideal for families or long-term stays. Extras like hair dryers and irons and ironing boards are free for the asking. Self-service laundry is also available.

4 Downtown

Mainly popular among businesspeople and convention attendees, downtown is often overlooked by the leisure traveler. While L.A.'s downtown isn't the cultural hub it is in many other cities, you might want to locate here if you plan to take in some shows at the Music Center or want to take advantage of generous weekend rates offered by most hotels. Every freeway passes through downtown, so it's a breeze to head off to other parts of the city—except during weekday rush hour, that is.

VERY EXPENSIVE

Hotel Inter-Continental Los Angeles. 251 S. Olive St., Los Angeles, CA 90012. ☎ **213/617-3300.** Fax 213/617-3399. www.los-angeles.interconti.com. 434 units. A/C TV TEL. $295–$315 double; from $600 suite. Weekend rates and packages available. AE, DC, DISC, EC, MC, V. Valet parking $22.

Downtown Area Accommodations & Dining

Accommodations ■

Hotel Inter-Continental Los Angeles **6**
Kawada Hotel **5**
Regal Biltmore **8**
Wilshire Grand Hotel **10**
Wyndham Checkers Hotel **9**

Dining ◆

Cha Cha Cha **12**
Ciudad **7**
The Original Pantry Cafe **11**
Philippe The Original **2**
R23 **4**
Traxx **3**
Water Grill **10**
Yang Chow **1**

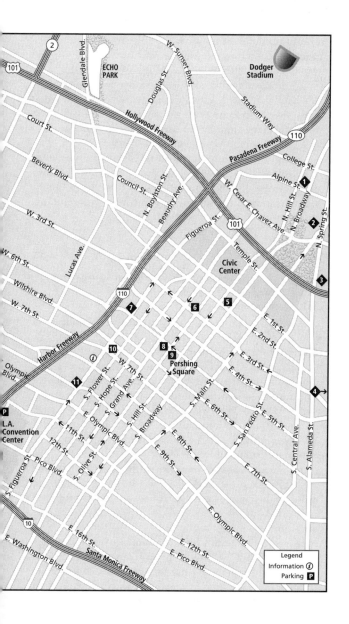

This member of the internationally prestigious Inter-Continental chain is adjacent to the Museum of Contemporary Art and within walking distance of the Music Center. It's the best-managed property in the neighborhood, run by a doting, eager-to-please staff. Conservatively styled, amenity-packed rooms boast floor-to-ceiling views and oversized bathrooms with separate dressing areas. Public areas are decorated with works of art on loan from the Museum of Contemporary Art.

Dining: The hotel's restaurant offers California cuisine all day.

Amenities: Large outdoor heated pool, small health club, sundeck, concierge, 24-hour room service, dry cleaning, laundry service, newspaper delivery, nightly turndown, express checkout on club floor, business center, valet parking.

EXPENSIVE

Regal Biltmore. 506 S. Grand Ave. (between 5th and 6th sts.), Los Angeles, CA 90071. ☎ **800/245-8673** or 213/624-1011. Fax 213/612-1545. www. thebiltmore.com. 683 units. A/C TV TEL. $225–$245 double; from $370 suite. Super breakfast and weekend discount packages available. AE, CB, DC, DISC, EC, MC, V. Parking $18.

Built in 1923, the historic and opulent Biltmore is considered the grande dame of L.A. hotels. During the 1930s and 1940s, the Academy Awards were held in the spectacular Crystal Ballroom— the first sketch of the Oscar statuette was scrawled on a linen napkin here—and the hotel was the top choice for presidents and the elite. You've seen the Biltmore in many movies, including *The Fabulous Baker Boys, Beverly Hills Cop,* and Barbra Streisand's *A Star Is Born;* the Crystal Ballroom appeared upside-down in *The Poseidon Adventure.* The 11-story hotel sparkles with Italian marble and traditional French-reproduction furnishings, but the overall elegance has been compromised by an ugly office tower that was added in the mid-1980s. Still, the sense of refinement and graciousness endures, with a vaulted, hand-painted lobby ceiling and attentively decorated—though small—rooms with marble bathrooms.

Dining/Diversions: Bernard's features high-quality continental cuisine. Smeraldi's serves homemade pastas and lighter California fare. The lunch-only Sai Sai serves sushi, tempura, and traditional Japanese kaiseki. Afternoon tea and evening cocktails are served in the lobby's stately Rendezvous Court; a full bar is also available in the Grand Avenue Sports Bar.

Amenities: Health club with original 1923 inlaid pool (extra charge), concierge, 24-hour room service, dry cleaning, laundry service, newspaper delivery, nightly turndown, business center.

✪ **Wyndham Checkers Hotel.** 535 S. Grand Ave., Los Angeles, CA 90071. ☎ **800/996-3426** or 213/624-0000. Fax 213/626-9906. 188 units. A/C TV TEL. $199–$259 double; from $500 suite. Weekend specials, often as low as $99. AE, DC, DISC, EC, MC, V. Valet parking $21. Pets accepted with $20 cleaning fee.

The atmosphere at the Wyndham Checkers, a boutique version of the Biltmore across the street, is as removed from "Hollywood" as a top L.A. hotel can get. Built in 1927, the hotel is protected by the City Cultural Heritage Commission as a Historic Cultural Monument. Plenty of polished brass throughout complements the neutral sand-colored decor; both conspire to accentuate the splendid architectural features left intact despite a complete update of the facility. Your room is a pristine temple, warmly radiant and immaculately outfitted. Spacious marble bathrooms feature bathrobes and Bath & Body Works products. Checkers is a European-styled hotel, without a lot of flashy amenities—but first-class all the way. Public areas include a wood-paneled library, a classy bar stocked with fine cigars, and corridors punctuated with Asian antiquities.

Dining: Checkers Restaurant is one of downtown's finest dining rooms (and has a Saturday-Sunday brunch worth fasting for).

Amenities: Rooftop spa, heated lap pool, whirlpool, concierge, 24-hour room service, dry cleaning, laundry service, nightly turndown.

MODERATE

The Wilshire Grand Hotel & Centre. 930 Wilshire Blvd. (at Figueroa St.), Los Angeles, CA 90071. ☎ **888/843-2888** or 213/688-7777. Fax 213/612-3987. www.thewilshiregrand.com. 900 units. A/C MINIBAR TV TEL. $169–$219 double; from $400 suite. AE, CB, DC, DISC, EC, MC, V. Valet parking $20.

At press time, this former Omni hotel had just been purchased by private owners, who plan to dispel any chain-hotel vestiges with extensive renovations throughout 2000. The hotel is centrally located, near downtown shopping, theater, dining, and the STAPLES Center sports stadium. Currently being completely redone, guest rooms will have plenty of comfort amenities and business features; the best ones have city views or overlook the oval swimming pool. The premium Executive Level (on the 15th and 16th floors) offers separate check-in facilities, a dedicated concierge, premium in-room amenities, and complimentary continental breakfast and afternoon cocktails. The hotel features five dining choices, including the northern Italian Cardini restaurant. Amenities include a large outdoor heated pool, 24-hour fitness center, concierge, 24-hour room service, dry cleaning, laundry service, and car-rental desk.

INEXPENSIVE

Kawada Hotel. 200 S. Hill St. (at Second St.), Los Angeles, CA 90012. ☎ **800/ 752-9232** or 213/621-4455. Fax 213/687-4455. www.kawadahotel.com. 116 units. A/C TV TEL. $95–$129 double. Weekend discounts available. AE, DC, DISC, EC, MC, V. Parking $6.60.

This pretty, well-kept, and efficiently managed hotel is a pleasant oasis in the otherwise-gritty heart of downtown, conveniently located near the Civic Center, the Museum of Contemporary Art, and Union Station. Behind the clean, three-story redbrick exterior are more than a hundred pristine rooms, all with handy kitchenettes and simple furnishings. The rooms aren't large but they're extremely functional, each outfitted with a VCR (movies are available free of charge) and two phones. Nonsmoking rooms are available. The hotel's lobby-level restaurant Epicentre features an eclectic international menu all day.

5 The San Fernando Valley

Universal City is on this side of the hill and most hotels do a booming business with travelers visiting Universal Studios and other showbiz attractions in the area. The Valley is a more peaceful setting than other Los Angeles neighborhoods. You can often find great off-season hotel deals here.

EXPENSIVE

Beverly Garland Holiday Inn. 4222 Vineland Ave., North Hollywood, CA 91602. ☎ **800/BEVERLY** or 818/980-8000. Fax 818/766-5230. www. beverlygarland.com. 255 units. A/C TV TEL. $169 double; from $199 suite. Discounts available; also ask about "Great Rates." AE, JCB, MC, V. Free parking.

Don't get confused by the name—this hotel is named for its owner, the actress Beverly Garland (of *My Three Sons* fame), not Beverly Hills. Grassy areas and greenery abound at this North Hollywood Holiday Inn, a virtual oasis in the concrete jungle that is most of L.A. The mission-influenced buildings that make up the hotel are a bit dated, but if you grew up with *Brady Bunch* reruns, this only adds to the charm—it looks like something

Mike Brady would have designed. Southwestern-themed fabrics complement the natural-pine furnishings in the recently renovated guest rooms; unfortunately, the painted cinder-block walls give off something of a college-dorm feel. All rooms feature balconies. Facilities include a pool, a sauna, and two tennis courts. The Paradise Restaurant serves Polynesian-influenced cuisine throughout the day. A complimentary shuttle to Universal is available.

Hilton Universal City. 555 Universal Terrace Pkwy., Universal City, CA 91608. ☎ **800/HILTONS** or 818/506-2500. Fax 818/509-2031. www.universalcity. hilton.com. 483 units. A/C TV TEL. $175–$225 double; from $275 suite. Weekend discounts available. AE, CB, DC, DISC, MC, V. Valet parking $14; self-parking $10.

Although this shiny 24-story hotel sits right outside the Universal Studios theme park, there's more of a conservative–business-traveler feel here than the raucous family-with-young-children vibe you might expect. A light-filled glass lobby leads to a seemingly endless series of conference and banquet rooms, the hotel's bread and butter. Rooms are tastefully decorated, are constantly refurbished, and have exceptional views of the surrounding area (even if the modern, mirror-surfaced windows don't actually open). The polished brass and upscale attitude make this a more adult property than the Sheraton next door (an outdoor elevator connects the two hotels). Regular shuttles provide free service to the theme park and CityWalk. For the best deals, see what national promotions Hilton is offering.

Dining: Cafe Sierra serves California cuisine all day, as well as Sunday brunch.

Amenities: Heated pool and whirlpool, free access to health club, concierge, 24-hour room service, dry cleaning, laundry service.

MODERATE

✪ **Sheraton Universal.** 333 Universal Terrace Pkwy., Universal City, CA 91608. ☎ **800/325-3535** or 818/980-1212. Fax 818/985-4980. 436 units. A/C MINIBAR TV TEL. $139–$190 double; from $325 suite. Ask about the "Universal Getaway" package, which includes parking and theme-park admission. AE, CB, DC, DISC, EC, JCB, MC, V. Valet parking $14; self-parking $11.

Despite the addition of the sleekly modern Hilton just uphill, the 21-story Sheraton is still considered "the" Universal City hotel of choice for tourists, businesspeople, and industry folks visiting the studios' production offices. It has a spacious 1960s feel, with updated styling and amenities; although the Sheraton does its share of convention/event business, the hotel feels more leisurely than the Hilton next door (an outdoor elevator connects the two properties). Choose a Lanai room for balconies that overlook the lushly planted pool area, or a Tower room for stunning views and solitude; all are equipped with Nintendo games and pay-movie channels. The hotel is very close to the Hollywood Bowl, and you can practically roll out of bed and into the theme park (via continuous shuttle). An extra $35 per night buys a Club Level room; which comes with extra in-room personal and business amenities, plus breakfast and afternoon hors d'oeuvres.

Dining/Diversions: The hotel's restaurant serves California cuisine, but the many restaurants and night spots of Universal City and CityWalk are a quick tram ride away.

Amenities: Outdoor pool and whirlpool, health club, game rooms, concierge, room service (from 6am to midnight), dry cleaning/laundry service, twice-daily maid service, express checkout, valet parking, gift shop.

Sportsmen's Lodge. 12825 Ventura Blvd. (east of Coldwater Canyon), Studio City, CA 91604. ☎ **800/821-8511** or 818/769-4700. Fax 818/769-4798. www.slhotel.com. 191 units. A/C TV TEL. $122–$172 double; from $170 suite. AE, DC, DISC, EC, MC, V. Free parking.

It's been a long time since this part of Studio City was wilderness enough to justify the lodge's name. This sprawling motel has been enlarged and upgraded since those days. The most recent improvements—sprucing up the worn room furnishings—were made within the past 3 years. You might take advantage of the new pool cabana bar and forget all about busy Ventura Boulevard beyond this garden setting. The guest rooms are large and comfortable but not luxurious; all have balconies or patios, and refrigerators are available. There are a well-equipped exercise room and a variety of shops and service desks, and both golf and bowling are nearby. A hunting-lodge motif bar and grill is on the property, adjoining a fine-dining room that serves only weekend dinner and brunch in stunning glass-enclosed surroundings. Don't miss the beautiful black and white swans frolicking out back in the koi-filled ponds.

6   Pasadena & Environs

Pretty Pasadena, on the east side of downtown, is well preserved and architecturally rich. It's close via freeway to both Hollywood and the Valley, though quite a distance from the beach communities and the Westside. There are some charming and historic hotels here, and the dining and shopping scene stands on its own.

VERY EXPENSIVE

✪ **The Ritz-Carlton, Huntington Hotel & Spa.** 1401 S. Oak Knoll Ave., Pasadena, CA 91109. ☎ **800/241-3333** or 626/568-3900. Fax 626/568-3700. 392 units. A/C MINIBAR TV TEL. $310–$495 double; from $495 suite or cottage. Discount packages always available. AE, DC, MC, V. Valet parking $20. From I-210, take Lake Ave. south, continuing as it becomes S. Oak Knoll.

Built in 1906, the opulent Huntington Hotel was one of America's grandest hotels—but not earthquake-proof! It was razed and then meticulously re-created on the same spot in the 1980s; the astonishing authenticity (including reinstallation of many decorative features) even fools patrons from the resort's early days. This Spanish-Mediterranean beauty sits on 23 meticulously landscaped acres that seem a world apart from downtown Los Angeles, though the hotel is only about 20 minutes away. Each oversize guest room is dressed in conservatively elegant Ritz-Carlton style, with marble bathrooms, thick carpets, and terry robes.

Dining: Local seniors love to celebrate in the Georgian Room, where continental meals are prepared by a classically trained French chef. The less formal Grill serves traditional fare in a comfortable, clublike setting. The Cafe serves all day, either indoors or out; it's best on Sunday for champagne brunch. High tea is served daily in the Lobby Lounge.

Amenities: Olympic-size heated outdoor pool, secluded whirlpool, sundeck, three lighted tennis courts, concierge, room service (24 hr.), nightly turndown, bicycle rental, pro shop, full-service spa/salon, exercise room, shopping promenade, all-day kids' programs.

MODERATE

The Artists' Inn Bed-and-Breakfast. 1038 Magnolia St., South Pasadena, CA 91030. ☎ **888/799-5668** or 626/799-5668. Fax 626/799-3678. www.artistsinns.com. 9 units. A/C. $110–$205 double. Rates include full breakfast and afternoon tea. Extra person $20. AE, MC, V.

This Victorian-style inn, an unpretentious yellow-shingled home pleasantly furnished with wicker throughout, was built in 1895 as a farmhouse, and recently expanded to include a neighboring 1909 home. Each of the nine rooms is decorated to reflect the style of a particular artist or period, including impressionist, Fauve, and van Gogh. Only the three annex suites have deluxe amenities—whirlpool tubs, minibars, coffeemakers, phones, and TVs—but every room is thoughtfully arranged, with fresh roses (from the front garden), hair dryers, port wine, and chocolates. The inn is on a quiet residential street 5 minutes from the heart of downtown.

Bissell House. 201 Orange Grove Ave. (at Columbia St.), South Pasadena, CA 91030. ☎ **800/441-3530** or 626/441-3535. Fax 626/441-3671. www. bissellhouse.com. 5 units. A/C. $125–$200 double. Rates include full breakfast on weekends, expanded continental breakfast weekdays, plus afternoon snacks and all-day beverages. AE, MC, V.

Hidden behind tall hedges that carefully isolate it from busy Orange Grove Avenue, this 1887 gingerbread Victorian is furnished with antiques and offers a delightful taste of life on what was once Pasadena's "Millionaire's Row." All rooms have private bathrooms with both shower and tub (one an antique clawfoot, one a private whirlpool). on The beautifully landscaped grounds feature a pool and whirlpool, and a downstairs library offers a telephone and fax machine for guests' use.

4

Dining

The hottest trend in L.A. dining is French bistro fare; even when served in the most pretentious of surroundings, it's always characterized as "simple," "classic," "traditional," or even "earthy." *Provençal* is the hottest buzzword in town, and foodies who've just recently mastered carpaccio, arugula, and tiramisu are now busy acquainting themselves with daube, brandade, and flageolet. The front-runners at press time include elegant Lavande, in Loews Santa Monica Beach Hotel, and Beverly Boulevard neighbors Mimosa and Pastis.

While it's been said that Provençal is the "new" Northern Italian, L.A.'s omnipresent contingent of trattorias shows no sign of dissipating any time soon. In fact, Italian food seems more popular than ever, with new restaurants opening all the time.

If you're looking for L.A.'s theme restaurants, you'll find the **Hard Rock Cafe** at two locations: the Beverly Center, 8600 Beverly Blvd. (at San Vicente Boulevard), Los Angeles (☎ **310/276-7605**); and Universal CityWalk, Universal Center Drive exit off U.S. 101 (☎ **818/622-7625**). **Planet Hollywood** is located at 9560 Wilshire Blvd. (west of Rodeo Drive), Beverly Hills (☎ **310/275-7828**).

The city's restaurants are categorized below first by area, then by price (*E* is expensive, *M* is moderate, and *I* is inexpensive). Keep in mind that many of the restaurants listed as "expensive" are moderately priced at lunch.

1 Restaurants by Cuisine

AMERICAN (TRADITIONAL)

Blueberry (Santa Monica, *I*)

Du-par's Restaurant & Bakery (San Fernando Valley, *I*)

Good Stuff (Manhattan Beach, *I*)

Hollywood Hills Coffee Shop (Hollywood, *I*)

Kate Mantilini (Westside, *M*)

Musso & Frank Grill (Hollywood, *M*)

The Original Pantry Cafe
(Downtown, *I*)
Sidewalk Cafe (The
Beaches, *I*)
Swingers (Hollywood, *I*)

NEW AMERICAN & AMERICAN ECLECTIC

JiRaffe (Santa Monica, *E*)
Joe's (The Beaches, *M*)
Lola's (Hollywood, *M*)
The Raymond (Pasadena, *E*)

BREAKFAST

Blueberry (Santa Monica, *I*)
Campanile (Hollywood, *E*)
Cava (Westside, *M*)
Cha Cha Cha
(Downtown, *M*)
Du-par's (San Fernando
Valley, *I*)
Hollywood Hills Coffee
Shop (Hollywood, *I*)
Jerry's Famous Deli (San
Fernando Valley, *M*)
Kate Mantilini
(Westside, *M*)
Kay 'n Dave's Cantina
(Santa Monica, *I*)
Nate & Al's (Beverly Hills, *I*)
The Original Pantry Cafe
(Downtown, *I*)
Philippe the Original
(Downtown, *I*)
Sidewalk Cafe
(The Beaches, *I*)
Swingers (Hollywood, *I*)

CALIFORNIA

Four Oaks (Westside, *E*)
Granita (The Beaches, *E*)

Jozu (Westside, *E*)
Michael's (Santa Monica, *E*)
Old Town Bakery &
Restaurant (Pasadena, *I*)
Röckenwagner (Santa
Monica, *E*)
Spago Beverly Hills (Beverly
Hills, *E*)
Tahiti (Hollywood, *M*)
Traxx (Downtown, *M*)

CALIFORNIA-FRENCH

Patina (Hollywood, *E*)
Paul's Cafe (San Fernando
Valley, *M*)
Pinot Bistro (San Fernando
Valley, *E*)

CALIFORNIA-MEDITERRANEAN

Campanile (Hollywood, *E*)

CARIBBEAN/CUBAN

Cha Cha Cha
(Downtown, *M*)

CHINESE

Yang Chow Restaurant
(Downtown, *M*)
Yujean Kang's Gourmet
Chinese Cuisine
(Pasadena, *M*)

CONTINENTAL

Musso & Frank Grill
(Hollywood, *M*)
The Raymond
(Pasadena, *E*)

DELICATESSEN

Jerry's Famous Deli (San
Fernando Valley, *M*)
Nate & Al's (Westside, *I*)

Key to Abbreviations: *VE*=Very Expensive; *E*=Expensive; *M*=Moderate; *I*=Inexpensive

FRANCO-CHINESE
Chinois on Main (Santa Monica, *E*)

FRANCO-JAPANESE
Chaya Brasserie (Westside, *M*)

FRANCO-MEDITERRANEAN
Lucques (West Hollywood, *E*)

FRENCH (PROVENÇAL)
Lavande (Santa Monica, *E*)
Mimosa (L.A.'s Westside & Beverly Hills, *E*)
Pastis (L.A.'s Westside & Beverly Hills, *M*)

GREEK
Cafe Santorini (Pasadena, *M*)
Sofi (Hollywood, *M*)

HEALTH FOOD/VEGETARIAN
Inn of the Seventh Ray (The Beaches, *M*)

INDIAN
Bombay Cafe (Westside, *M*)

INTERNATIONAL
Good Stuff (Manhattan Beach, *I*)

NORTHERN ITALIAN
Ca' Brea (Hollywood, *M*)
Valentino (Santa Monica, *E*)

TRADITIONAL ITALIAN
Miceli's (San Fernando Valley, *M*)

JAPANESE/SUSHI
Matsuhisa (Westside, *E*)
R23 (Downtown, *M*)

LATIN
Ciudad (Downtown, *M*)

MEXICAN
Border Grill (Santa Monica, *M*)
Casa Vega (San Fernando Valley, *M*)
El Cholo (Hollywood, *I*)
Kay 'n Dave's Cantina (Santa Monica, *I*)
La Serenata Gourmet (Westside, *M*)

MIDDLE EASTERN
Skewers' (Westside, *I*)

PACIFIC RIM
Jozu (Westside, *E*)
Maui Beach Cafe (Westside, *M*)
Tahiti (Hollywood, *M*)

SANDWICHES/BURGERS/ HOT DOGS
The Apple Pan (Westside, *I*)
Jody Maroni's Sausage Kingdom (The Beaches, *I*)
Philippe the Original (Downtown, *I*)
Pink's Hot Dogs (Hollywood, *I*)

SEAFOOD
Granita (The Beaches, *E*)
Maui Beach Cafe (Westside, *M*)
Water Grill (Downtown, *E*)

Key to Abbreviations: *VE*=Very Expensive; *E*=Expensive; *M*=Moderate; *I*=Inexpensive

SOUTHERN

Georgia
(Hollywood, *M*)

SOUTHWESTERN

Authentic Cafe
(Hollywood, *M*)

STEAKS

Lawry's The Prime Rib
(Westside, *E*)

THAI

Toi on Sunset
(Hollywood, *I*)

2 Santa Monica & the Beaches

EXPENSIVE

✪ **Chinois on Main.** 2709 Main St. (south of Pico Blvd.), Santa Monica. ☎ **310/392-9025.** Reservations required. Main courses $23–$29. AE, DC, MC, V. Wed–Fri 11:30am–2pm; daily 6–10:30pm. Valet parking $5. FRANCO-CHINESE.

Widely regarded as Wolfgang Puck's best restaurant, this Franco-Chinese eatery bustles nightly with locals and visitors who are wowed by the eatery's reputation and rarely disappointed by the food. Groundbreaking in its time, the restaurant still relies on the same quirky East-meets-West mélange of ingredients and technique. The menu is just about equally split between Chinois's signature dishes and new creations by head chef Makoto Tanaka. The most famous of the former are Cantonese duck in a sweet-tangy plum sauce, and farm-raised whole catfish that's perfectly deep fried and dramatically presented. Terrific newer dishes include lobster and sea bass sautéed together and flavored with porcini oil and ponzu sauce, and rare roasted loin of venison served in a ginger-spiced port and sun-dried cherries sauce. Chef Tanaka will gladly prepare, on request, grilled squab on panfried noodles. This off-menu dish comes with a rich garlic-ginger sauce and sautéed shiitake and oyster mushrooms; it's said to be a favorite of regulars Luther Vandross and Shirley MacLaine. The dining room, designed by Puck's wife, Barbara Lazaroff, is as visually colorful as it is acoustically loud.

Granita. In the Malibu Colony Plaza, 23725 W. Malibu Rd. (at Webb Way), Malibu. ☎ **310/456-0488.** Reservations required. Main courses $19–$32. AE, CB, DC, DISC, MC, V. Daily 6–10pm; Sat–Sun 11am–2pm. Free parking. CALIFORNIA/MEDITERRANEAN.

Longtime Granita/Spago staffer Jennifer Naylor now wears the toque at this, one of Wolfgang Puck's earlier Spago cousins, situated in Malibu just blocks from the star-studded "Colony."

Although the restaurant's over-the-top decor—a surreal eruption of oceanic kaleidoscopic art augmented by equally colorful fish swimming in lighted aquariums—is a bit dated, lovers of seafood don't seem to mind, judging by the ringing phones, crowded bar, and satisfied diners. Naylor's strength is interpreting the ever-changing selection of fresh seafood at her disposal; the preparations are both Puck-ish (eclectic California blendings) and reflective of Naylor's Italian training. Look for seared scallops and prawns served over an orzo-mascarpone-porcini mix, or black bass grilled with fennel, citrus reduction, and premium olive oil. Besides fish, the menu always features duck (choice of confit with celery-root gnocchi, or the splendid Cantonese style with blood orange–ginger glaze) and other inventive meat and poultry dishes. Gourmet pizzas are here too, perfect for light meals or sharing. The appetizers are delectable, expensive, and richly filling.

JiRaffe. 502 Santa Monica Blvd. (corner of 5th St.), Santa Monica. ☎ **310/ 917-6671.** Reservations recommended. Main courses $19–$26. AE, DC, MC, V. Tues–Fri noon–2pm and 6–11pm; Sat 5:30–11pm; Sun 5:30–9pm. Valet parking $4.50. AMERICAN/FRENCH.

"JiRaffe"—it isn't a long-necked zoo creature, but a blending of names from the two chefs responsible for this overnight sensation. Josiah Citrin has since left partner Raphael Lunetta to carry on alone at this crowded, upscale bistro in restaurant-hungry Santa Monica. The deafening din of conversation here is usually praise for JiRaffe's artistic treatment of whitefish (spiced and served with sugar snap peas, glazed carrots, and ginger-carrot sauce), roasted rabbit, crispy salmon, or pork chop (grilled with wild rice, smoked bacon, apple chutney, and cider sauce). JiRaffe also wins culinary points for highlighting oft-ignored vegetables like salsify, Swiss chard, and fennel, as well as complex appetizers that are more like miniature main dishes.

Lavande. In Loews Santa Monica Beach Hotel, 1700 Ocean Ave. ☎ **310/ 576-3181.** Reservations recommended. Main courses $20–$30, 6-course tasting menu $50. AE, CB, DC, MC, V. Mon–Sat noon–2:30pm and 6–10pm; Sun 11:30am–3pm. Valet parking $3 with validation. FRENCH PROVENÇAL.

For the past couple of years, southern French bistros have been quietly invading the L.A. dining scene, but the opening of Lavande heralded Provençal cuisine's true arrival. Chef Alain Giraud, doesn't shy from the spotlight, and his culinary show-manship is evident as he adapts French everyday food to this chic

Dining in Santa Monica & the Beaches

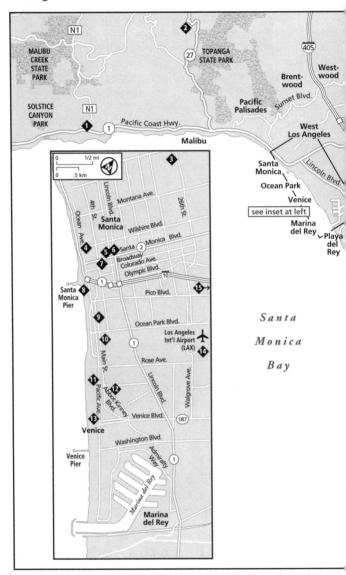

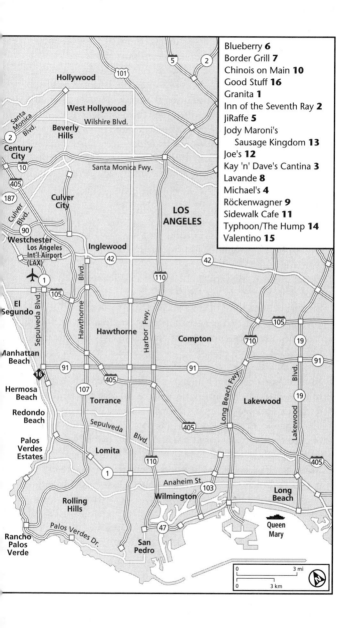

Blueberry **6**
Border Grill **7**
Chinois on Main **10**
Good Stuff **16**
Granita **1**
Inn of the Seventh Ray **2**
JiRaffe **5**
Jody Maroni's
    Sausage Kingdom **13**
Joe's **12**
Kay 'n' Dave's Cantina **3**
Lavande **8**
Michael's **4**
Röckenwagner **9**
Sidewalk Cafe **11**
Typhoon/The Hump **14**
Valentino **15**

and *cher* ("expensive") hotel dining room. Classic country fish soup is served the traditional way, with croutons and *rouille* (a saffron-pepper sauce), but ladled ceremonially from a silver tureen; and veal *daube* is the stew you expect, with the surprise refinement of carefully pitted green and black olives. In addition to enjoying splendid waterfront and ocean views, Lavande's sophisticated space is elegantly appointed with Provençal pottery and dried lavender bouquets; this traditional French herb flavors everything here from squab with honey-lavender glaze to the lavender ice cream in Lavande's signature dessert, *vacherin glace* (finished with whipped cream and crunchy meringue teardrops). Guests even depart with tiny lavender sachets.

✪ **Michael's.** 1147 3rd St. (north of Wilshire Blvd.), Santa Monica. ☎ **310/ 451-0843.** Reservations recommended. Main courses $16–$22 lunch, $24–$31 dinner. AE, DISC, MC, V. Tues–Fri 11:30am–2:30pm and 6–10:30pm; Sat 6–10:30pm. CALIFORNIA.

Owner Michael McCarty, L.A.'s answer to Alice Waters, is considered by many to be the father of California cuisine. Since the opening of Michael's in 1979 (when McCarty was only 25), several top L.A. restaurants have caught up to it, but this fetching Santa Monica restaurant remains one of the city's best, though Michael has handed executive chef responsibilities to Sam Yoon, whose impressive pedigree includes stints at L.A.'s and San Francisco's most renowned restaurants. The dining room is filled with contemporary art by Michael's wife, Kim McCarty, and the restaurant's beloved garden is a relaxed setting for always-inventive menu choices like Baqueta sea bass with a chanterelle mushroom ragout and fresh Provençal herbs, seared Hawaiian ahi accented with braised enoki mushrooms and earthy-tangy sesame wasabi ponzu sauce, or grilled pork chop sweetened with sweet potato purée and anise-pinot noir sauce. Don't miss Michael's famous warm mushroom salad, tossed with crumbled goat cheese, watercress, caramelized onion, and mustard-sage vinaigrette. *Note:* Michael's automatically adds a 15% service charge to the check.

✪ **Röckenwagner.** 2435 Main St. (north of Ocean Park Blvd.), Santa Monica. ☎ **310/399-6504.** Reservations recommended. Main courses $18–$26 dinner, $10–$18 lunch/brunch. AE, CB, DC, MC, V. Mon–Wed and Fri 6–10pm; Thurs 11:30am–2:30pm and 6–10pm; Sat 10am–3pm and 5:30–11pm; Sun 10am–3pm and 5:30–10pm. Free parking. CALIFORNIA.

Set in Frank Gehry's starkly modern Edgemar complex (itself a work of art), chef Hans Röckenwagner's eponymous restaurant continues the motif by presenting edible sculpture amid a gallery-like decor. Although it sits in the midst of a popular shopping area, the space manages to be refreshingly quiet. Röckenwagner takes his art—and his food—very seriously, once orchestrating an entire menu around German white asparagus at the height of its short season. The delightfully unpretentious staff serves deliciously pretentious dishes fusing Pacific Rim ingredients with traditional European preparations; a good example is the langoustine ravioli with mangoes in port-wine reduction and curry oil. The menu tastes as good as it reads, and desserts are to die for. Don't overlook the lunch bargains here, nor the unique European-style breakfast of bread and cheese.

✪ **Valentino.** 3115 Pico Blvd. (west of Bundy Dr.), Santa Monica. ☎ **310/ 829-4313.** Reservations required. Main courses $14–$28. AE, DC, MC, V. Mon–Thurs 5:30–10:30pm; Fri 11:30am–2:30pm and 5:30–11pm; Sat 5:30–11pm. Valet parking $4. NORTHERN ITALIAN.

Valentino is a good choice if you're splurging on just one special dinner. Charming owner Piero Selvaggio oversees two other restaurants, but his distinctive touch still pervades this 25-year-old flagship. This elegant spot continues to maintain its position as *Wine Spectator* magazine's top wine cellar, and former *New York Times* food critic Ruth Reichl calls this the best Italian restaurant in the United States. The creations of Selvaggio and his brilliant young chef, Angelo Auriana, make dinners here lengthy multicourse affairs (often involving several bottles of wine). You might begin with a crisp pinot grigio paired with caviar-filled cannolli, or crespelle, thin little pancakes with fresh porcini mushrooms and a rich melt of fontina cheese. A rich barolo is the perfect accompaniment to rosemary-infused roasted rabbit; the fantastically fragrant risotto with white truffles is one of the most magnificent dishes we've ever had. Jackets are all but required in the elegant dining room.

MODERATE

✪ **Border Grill.** 1445 4th St. (between Broadway and Santa Monica Blvd.), Santa Monica. ☎ **310/451-1655.** www.bordergrill.com. Reservations recommended. Main courses $10–$21. AE, DC, DISC, MC, V. Mon 5–10pm; Tues–Thurs 11:30am–10pm; Fri–Sat 11:30am–11pm; Sun 11:30am–10pm. MEXICAN.

Come Fly with Me . . . Two Great Meals with a View

Pilot-turned-restaurateur Brian Vidor must have endured too many snack-bar egg-salad sandwiches in his flying days, because he works hard to make his two dinner-only restaurants (alongside Santa Monica Airport's runway) culinary masterpieces. First came **Typhoon,** 3221 Donald Douglas Loop S. (☎ **310/390-6565**), a pan-Asian spot where Taiwanese spicy crickets punctuate a menu filled with less exotic fare from throughout southeast Asia; the well-stocked bar even offers a Chinese herb-infused vodka reputed to have aphrodisiac qualities. Upstairs is **The Hump** (☎ **310/313-0977**), bearing the nickname pilots have for the Himalayas. Feeling like an outpost at some airfield in the tropics, this small Japanese restaurant boasts pedigreed sushi master Hiro Nishimura, who presents ultrafresh fish artistically prepared. Despite the odd location, word-of-mouth guarantees a wait any night of the week.

Before Mary Sue Milliken and Susan Feniger spiced up cable TV as "Too Hot Tamales," they started this restaurant over in West Hollywood. Now Border Grill has moved to a boldly painted, cavernous (read: loud) space in Santa Monica, and the gals aren't in the kitchen here very much at all (though cookbooks and paraphernalia from their Food Network show are displayed prominently for sale). But their influence on the inspired menu is enough to maintain the cantina's enormous popularity with folks who swear by the authentic flavor of Yucatán fish tacos, rock shrimp with ancho chilies, and meaty *ropa vieja,* the traditional Latin stew. The best meatless dish is *mulitas de hongos,* a layering of portobello mushrooms, poblano chilies, black beans, cheese, and guacamole, spiced up with roasted garlic and seared red chard. Distracting desserts are displayed prominently near the entrance, so you may spend the meal fantasizing about the yummy coconut flan or key lime pie.

Inn of the Seventh Ray. 128 Old Topanga Canyon Rd. (on Calif. 27), Topanga Canyon. ☎ **310/455-1311.** Reservations required. Main courses $16–$25. AE, DC, DISC, MC, V. Mon–Fri 11:30am–3pm; Sat 10:30am–3pm; Sun 9:30am–3pm; daily 6–10pm. Free parking. HEALTH FOOD.

Topanga Canyon has long been the home of leftover hippies and L.A.'s New Agers; it's a mountainous, sparsely populated area that's also undeniably beautiful, even spiritual. This restaurant, a former church, is in the middle of the aura. No one comes here for the food; they come for a romantic dining experience, far from the bright lights of the city. About half of the seating is outdoors, at tables overlooking a creek and endless tangles of untamed vines and shrubs. Inside, the dining room is rustic, with a sloped roof and a glass wall offering mountain views. Everything is prepared from scratch, and foods are organic and chemical- and preservative-free. The fish are caught in deep water far offshore and served the same day; you can even order unpasteurized wines. Ten main dishes are available daily, and all are served with hors d'oeuvres, soup or salad, and vegetables. There are light dishes, like Five Secret Rays, consisting of lightly steamed vegetables served with lemon-tahini and caraway cheese sauces, but you'll also find a New York steak cut from naturally fed beef.

Joe's. 1023 Abbot Kinney Blvd., Venice. ☎ **310/399-5811.** Reservations recommended. Main courses $8–$10 lunch, $15–$18 dinner. AE, MC, V. Tues–Fri 11:30am–2:30pm and 6–11pm; Sat–Sun 11am–3pm and 6–11pm. Free street parking. AMERICAN ECLECTIC.

This is one of West L.A.'s best dining bargains. Chef/owner Joe Miller excels in simple New American cuisine, particularly grilled fish and roasted meats accented with piquant herbs. Set in a tiny, quirky storefront, the humble room is a blank palette that belies Joe's popularity. The best tables are tucked away on the enclosed back patio. Lunch is a hidden treasure for those with a champagne palate but a seltzer pocketbook. Topping out at $10, all lunches include salad, one of Miller's exquisite soups, and especially prompt service. Beer and wine are served, except during weekday lunchtime (regulation, due to the elementary school across the street).

INEXPENSIVE

Blueberry. 510 Santa Monica Blvd. (at 5th St.), Santa Monica. ☎ **310/394-7766.** Main courses $4.50–$8. AE, MC, V. Daily 8am–3pm. Metered street parking. AMERICAN/BREAKFAST.

This Santa Monica cafe is popular among shoppers and locals from the surrounding laid-back beach community. It serves only breakfast and lunch—Blueberry's owner devotes the dinner hour to the über-trendy Rix around the corner. The setting is 1930s American farmhouse. From the blue bandana seat cushions to vintage music and print ads, from picket-fence railings to overalls-clad waitstaff, this place truly does evoke a Depression-era small-town diner. The food is a "square deal" too, starting with a basket of crispy-edged minimuffins (blueberry, of course) when you're seated, and including hearty egg dishes, waffles, and pancakes, plus generous lunch salads and sandwiches. But I'll bet Ma Kettle never used goat cheese or pancetta in *her* omelets. The menu is up-to-date and served with plenty of fresh-brewed gourmet-roasted coffee. Blueberry is tiny, with just a few tables on the main floor and cozy loft, so expect a wait during peak times.

Good Stuff. 1300 Highland Ave. (at 13th St.), Manhattan Beach. ☎ **310/545-4775.** www.eatgoodstuff.com. Most menu items under $10. AE, DC, DISC, MC, V. Daily 7am–10pm (subject to dinner closure during winter). Free parking. AMERICAN/INTERNATIONAL.

A mainstay of local casual dining, this popular crowd-pleaser suits beachgoers, lunch-breakers, families, couples, and more—there's something for everyone. Inside the gray clapboard corner restaurant you'll find brightly painted marine-themed murals, lifeguard memorabilia, and picture windows to let in the sunshine. On nice days the outdoor patio fills first; its glass railings ensure a good view of bustling downtown MB's human parade. Cheerful servers positively bounce through the restaurant, clad in casual sport togs and ferrying generous platters of food that's fresh, carefully prepared, and very affordable. The mile-long menu runs the gamut, featuring standouts like Santa Fe chicken omelet, cinnamon swirl French toast, a superb homemade veggie burger, burritos and Mexican favorites, enormous main-course salads, steaming hot pastas, and a selection of dinner-only entrees. Nightly bargain "get stuffed" dinners are sized for satisfaction—the seafood stew, for example, is guaranteed to be filling or your second bowl's on the house.

Other South Bay locations include Hermosa Beach, 1286 The Strand (☎ 310/374-2334), and Redondo Beach's Riviera Village, 1617 Pacific Coast Hwy. (☎ 310/316-0262).

✪ **Jody Maroni's Sausage Kingdom.** 2011 Ocean Front Walk (north of Venice Blvd.), Venice. ☎ **310/822-5639.** www.maroni.com. Sandwiches $4–$6. No credit cards. Daily 10am–sunset. SANDWICHES/SAUSAGES.

Your cardiologist might not approve, but Jody Maroni's all-natural, preservative-free "haut dogs" are some of the best wieners served anywhere. The grungy walk-up (or in-line skate-up) counter looks fairly foreboding—you wouldn't know there was gourmet fare behind that aging hot-dog–stand facade, from which at least 14 different grilled-sausage sandwiches are served up. Bypass the traditional hot Italian and try the Toulouse garlic, Bombay curried lamb, all-chicken apple, or orange-garlic-cumin. Each is served on a freshly baked onion roll and smothered with onions and peppers. Burgers, BLTs, and rotisserie chicken are also served, but why bother?

Other locations include the Valley's Universal CityWalk (☎ 818/622-JODY), and inside LAX Terminals 3, 4, and 6, where you can pick up some last-minute vacuum-packed sausages for home. Having elevated sausage-worship to an art form, Jody's now boasts a helpful and humorous cookbook, plus its own Web site.

Kay 'n Dave's Cantina. 262 26th St. (south of San Vicente Blvd.), Santa Monica. ☎ **310/260-1355.** Reservations accepted only for parties of 8 or more. Main courses $5–$10. MC, V. Mon–Thurs 11am–9:30pm; Fri 11am–10pm; Sat 8:30am–10pm; Sun 8:30am–9:30pm. Metered street parking. HEALTHY MEXICAN.

A beach community favorite for "really big portions of really good food at really low prices," Kay 'n Dave's cooks with no lard and has a vegetarian-friendly menu with plenty of meat items, too. Come early (and be prepared to wait) for breakfast, as local devotees line up for five kinds of fluffy pancakes, zesty omelets, or one of the best breakfast burritos in town. Grilled tuna Veracruz, spinach and chicken enchiladas in tomatillo salsa, seafood fajitas tostada, vegetable-filled corn tamales, and other Mexican specialties really are served in huge portions, making this mostly locals minichain a great choice to energize for (or reenergize after) an action-packed day of beach sightseeing. Bring the family—there are a kids' menu and crayons on every table.

✪ **Sidewalk Cafe.** 1401 Ocean Front Walk (between Horizon Ave. and Market St.), Venice. ☎ **310/399-5547.** Main courses $6–$13. MC, V. Sun–Thurs 8am–11pm; Fri–Sat 8am–midnight. Free parking with validation. AMERICAN/BREAKFAST.

Nowhere in L.A. is the people-watching better than along Ocean Front Walk. The constantly bustling Sidewalk Cafe is ensconced in one of Venice's few remaining early 20th-century buildings. The best seats, of course, are out front, around overcrowded open-air tables, all with a perfect view of the crowd, which provides nonstop entertainment. The menu is extensive, and the food is a whole lot better than it has to be at a location like this. Choose from the seriously overstuffed sandwiches or other over-sized American favorites: omelets, salads, and burgers.

3 L.A.'s Westside & Beverly Hills

For a map of restaurants in L.A.'s Westside and Beverly Hills, see p. 44.

In addition to the choices listed below, consider dining at the Daily Grill (11677 San Vicente Blvd.; ☎ 310/442-0044), which offers terrific American cuisine in a clubby setting. Other locations include Los Angeles (100 N. La Cienega Blvd.; ☎ 310/659-3100), and Studio City (12050 Ventura Blvd.; ☎ 818/769-6336).

EXPENSIVE

✪ **Four Oaks.** 2181 N. Beverly Glen Blvd., Los Angeles. ☎ **310/470-2265.** Reservations required. Main courses $22–$29. AE, DISC, MC, V. Tues–Sat 11:30am–2pm and 6–10pm; Sun 10:30am–2pm and 6–10pm. Valet parking $4. CALIFORNIA.

Just looking at the menu here makes us swoon. The country-cottage ambience and chef Peter Roelant's superlative blend of fresh ingredients with luxurious continental flourishes make a meal at the Four Oaks one of our favorite luxuries. Dinner is served beneath trees festooned with twinkling lights. Appetizers like lavender-smoked salmon with crisp potatoes and horseradish crème fraîche complement mouth-watering dishes like roasted chicken with sage, Oregon forest mushrooms, artichoke hearts, and port-balsamic sauce. If you're looking for someplace special, head to this canyon hideaway—you won't be disappointed.

✪ **Jozu.** 8360 Melrose Ave. (at Kings Rd.), West Hollywood. ☎ **323/655-5600.** www.jozu.com. Reservations recommended. Main courses $16–$25. AE, MC, V. Thurs–Fri 12noon–2pm and 5:30–10:30pm; Sat–Wed 5:30–10:30pm. Valet parking $3.50. PACIFIC RIM/CALIFORNIA.

Jozu means "excellent" in Japanese, and the word perfectly describes everything about this tranquil restaurant. All meals begin with a complimentary sake from Jozu's premium sake list. Chef Hisashi Yoshiara's menu presents Asian flavors interpreted with an international inventiveness. Outstanding dishes include delicately roasted sea bass on a bed of crunchy cabbage, accented with tangy *ponzu* sauce; albacore tuna wrapped in a crispy potato nest and bathed in soy butter; and rack of lamb perfectly charbroiled and

ⓕ Family-Friendly Restaurants

Pinot Bistro *(p. 101)* This upscale offshoot of chic Patina doesn't often come to mind when you're searching for family eats, and many kids are certainly too antsy to behave during an entire bistro meal. But the Pinot dynasty welcomes little ones with a special child-friendly menu., and kids under 10 eat free of charge. It's a great way to enjoy L.A.'s finest and stay close to your budget, too.

On the other end of the scale is **Pink's Hot Dogs** *(see p. 95)* in Hollywood, an institution in its own right that has been serving politically incorrect franks for what seems like forever. Everyone loves Pink's chili dogs, but you may never get the orange grease stains out of your kids' clothes.

Miceli's *(see p. 102)* in Universal City is a cavernous Italian restaurant that the whole family is sure to love. The gimmick? The waistaff sings show tunes or opera favorites while serving dinner (and sometimes instead of). Kids will love the boisterous atmosphere, which might even drown them out.

Jerry's Famous Deli *(see p. 102)* in Studio City is frequented mostly by industry types who populate this Valley community; their kids often sport baseball caps or production T-shirts from Mom or Dad's latest project. Jerry's has the most extensive deli menu in town and a casual, coffee-shop atmosphere. Families flock here for lunch, early dinner, and (crowded) weekend breakfast.

presented over a warm bell-pepper and arugula *ragout.* Appetizers range from shrimp sui-mai in rich lobster sauce to spicy halibut sashimi. The dessert of choice is Asian pear tart, lightly caramelized fruit laid in a buttery crust. The restaurant's interior is warmly comfortable and subtly lit; plenty of beautiful Hollywood types dine here, but it's quiet enough for real dinner conversation.

Lawry's The Prime Rib. 100 N. La Cienega Blvd. (north of Wilshire Blvd.), Beverly Hills. ☎ **310/652-2827.** Reservations recommended. Main courses $20–$30. AE, CB, DC, DISC, JCB, MC, V. Mon–Thurs 5–10pm; Fri 5–11pm; Sat 4:30–11pm; Sun 4–10pm. Valet parking $3.50. STEAKS/SEAFOOD.

Most Americans know Lawry's only as a brand of seasoned salt (which was invented here). Going to this family-run institution is an Old-World event. The main menu offerings are four cuts of prime rib that vary in thickness from two fingers to an entire hand. Every standing rib roast is dry-aged for 2 to 3 weeks, sprinkled with Lawry's famous seasoning, and then roasted on a bed of rock salt. A carver wheels the cooked beef tableside, then slices it properly, rare to well done. All dinners come with creamy whipped horse-radish, Yorkshire pudding, and the Original Spinning Bowl Salad (drenched in Lawry's signature sherry French dressing). Lawry's moved across the street from its original location a few years ago but retained its throwback-to-the-1930s clubroom atmosphere, complete with Persian-carpeted oak floors, high-backed chairs, and European oil paintings.

✪ **Lucques.** 8474 Melrose Ave. (east of La Cienega), West Hollywood. ☎ 323/655-6277. Reservations recommended. Main courses $16–$25. Tues–Sat 6pm–1:30am; Sun 6pm–midnight. Metered street parking or valet. FRANCO-MEDITERRANEAN.

Once Los Angeles became accustomed to this restaurant's unusual name—"Lucques" is a variety of French olive, pronounced "Luke"—local foodies fell hard for this quietly and comfortably sophisticated new home of former Campanile chef Suzanne Goin. The old brick building, once silent star Harold Lloyd's car-riage house, is decorated in mute, clubby colors with subdued lighting that extends to the handsome enclosed patio behind. Goin cooks with bold flavors, fresh-from-the-farm produce, and an instinctive feel for the food of the Mediterranean. The short and oft-changed menu makes the most of unusual ingredients like salt cod and oxtails. Standout dishes include Tuscan bean soup with tangy greens and pistou, grilled chicken served along-side spinach sautéed with pancetta and shallots, rustic *mascarpone* polenta topped with wild mushroom ragout and wilted greens, and perfect vanilla *pôt de crème* for dessert. Lucques's bar menu, featuring steak *frites* bearnaise, omelets, and tantalizing hors d'oeuvres (olives, warm almonds, sea salt, chewy bread), is a godsend for late-night diners.

✪ **Matsuhisa.** 129 N. La Cienega Blvd. (north of Wilshire Blvd.), Beverly Hills. ☎ 310/659-9639. Reservations recommended. Main courses $14–$26; sushi $4–$13 per order; full omakase dinner from $65. AE, DC, MC, V. Mon–Fri 11:45am–2:15pm; daily 5:45–10:15pm. Valet parking $3.50. JAPANESE/ PERUVIAN.

Japanese chef/owner Nobuyuki Matsuhisa arrived in Los Angeles via Peru and opened what may be the most creative restaurant in the entire city. A true master of fish cookery, Matsuhisa creates fantastic, unusual dishes by combining Japanese flavors with South American spices and salsas. Broiled sea bass with black truffles, sautéed squid with garlic and soy, and Dungeness crab tossed with chilies and cream are good examples of the masterfully prepared delicacies that are available in addition to thickly sliced nigiri and creative sushi rolls. Matsuhisa is perennially popular with celebrities and hard-core foodies, so reserve early for those hard-to-get tables. The small crowded main dining room suffers from poor lighting and precious lack of privacy; many big names are ushered through to private dining rooms. If you dare, ask for omakase, and the chef will personally compose a selection of eccentric dishes.

✪ **Mimosa.** 8009 Beverly Blvd. (west of Fairfax), Los Angeles. ☎ **323/ 655-8895.** Reservations recommended. Main courses $13–$24. AE, MC, V. Mon–Fri 11:30am–3pm; daily 5:30pm–midnight. Metered street parking. FRENCH PROVENÇAL.

It takes seasoned maitre d' Silvio de Mori to fend off the throngs clamoring to get into chef Jean-Pierre Bosc's country French bistro—"Provençal" is the magic culinary buzzword these days, and this stylish spot leads the pack. Decked out in traditional bistro garb (butter-yellow walls, artistic photos, French posters), Mimosa also attracts plenty of French expatriates and Euro-style denizens with a truly authentic menu. You won't get the classic French of caviar and truffles, but rather regional peasant specialties like rich veal daube, tripe sausage (*andouillette*), perfect steak fries, and a slow-cooked pork roast with horseradish lentils. The appetizer list usually includes a splendid terrine, and bowls of house-cured *cornichons* and spicy Dijon mustard accompany bread to every table. Despite the occasional tinge of trendy attitude—usually precipitated by the presence of habitues like Tom Cruise, Nicole Kidman, and Brad Pitt—Mimosa should be appreciated for its casual, comforting bistro fare.

Spago Beverly Hills. 176 N. Canon Dr. (north of Wilshire). ☎ **310/ 385-0880.** www.wolfgangpuck.com. Reservations required. Main courses $18–$34 tasting menu $85. AE, CB, DC, DISC, JCB, MC, V. Sun and Tues–Thurs 6–10pm; Fri–Sat 5:30–11pm. CALIFORNIA.

Wolfgang Puck is more than a great chef, he's also a masterful businessman and publicist who has made Spago one of the best-known restaurants in the United States. Despite all the hoopla— and almost 20 years of service—Spago remains one of L.A.'s top-rated restaurants. Talented Puck henchman Lee Hefter presides over the kitchen, delivering the culinary sophistication demanded by an upscale Beverly Hills crowd. This high-style indoor/outdoor space glows with the aura of big bucks, celebrity, and the perfectly honed California cuisine that can honestly take credit for setting the standard. Spago is also one of the last places in L.A. where men will feel most comfortable in jacket and tie (suggested, but not required). All eyes may be on the romantically twinkle-lit outdoor patio (the most coveted tables), but the food takes center stage. You simply can't choose wrong—highlights include the appetizer of *foie gras* "three ways"; savory duck either honey-lacquered and topped with foie gras, or Cantonese-style with a citrus tang; and rich Austrian dishes from "Wolfie's" childhood, like spicy beef goulash or perfect veal schnitzel.

Though the famous original location has been upstaged by the flashy new BH flagship, **Spago Hollywood,** 1114 Horn Ave. (at Sunset Boulevard; ☎ **310/652-4025**), is still a treat. Overlooking the Sunset Strip and boasting a more casual atmosphere and menu, this iconic space (remember all those star-studded Swifty Lazar Oscar parties?) is where you can still relish the imaginative "gourmet" pizzas that skyrocketed Puck to fame. Rumors continue to circulate that the WeHo original will one day close its doors; until then, there seem to be plenty of Spago-hungry diners to go around.

MODERATE

✪ **Bombay Cafe.** 12021 W. Pico Blvd. (at Bundy). ☎ **310/473-3388.** Reservations recommended for dinner. Main courses $9–$17. AE, MC, V. Tues–Thurs 11:30am–10pm; Fri–Sat 11:30am–11pm; Sun 5–10pm. Metered street parking. INDIAN.

This friendly sleeper may well be L.A.'s best Indian spot, serving excellent curries and kurmas typical of South Indian street food. Once seated, immediately order *sev puri* for the table; these crispy little chips topped with chopped potatoes, onions, cilantro, and chutneys are the perfect accompaniment to what's sure to be an extended menu-reading session. Also recommended are the burrito-like "frankies," juicy little bread rolls stuffed with lamb, chicken, or cauliflower. The best dishes come from the tandoor and include spicy yogurt-marinated swordfish, lamb, and chicken. While some dishes are authentically spicy, plenty of others have a mellow flavor for less incendiary palates. This restaurant is phenomenally popular and gets its share of celebrities: Meg Ryan and Dennis Quaid hired the Bombay Cafe to cater an affair at their Montana ranch.

✪ **Chaya Brasserie.** 8741 Alden Dr. (east of Robertson Blvd.). ☎ **310/ 859-8833.** Reservations recommended on weekends. Main courses $15–$27; lunch $10–$16. AE, CB, DC, MC, V. Mon–Fri 11am–2:30pm; Mon–Thurs 6–10:30pm; Fri–Sat 6–11pm; Sun 6–10pm. Valet parking $3.50. FRANCO-JAPANESE.

Now open for 17 years, Chaya has become well ensconced as one of Los Angeles's finest restaurants. This continental bistro with Asian overtones is popular with film agents during lunch and a particularly beautiful assembly of stars at night (spotted recently: George Clooney, Marky Mark, the Baldwin brothers). The place is loved for its exceptionally good food and refreshingly unpretentious atmosphere. Despite a high noise level, the stage-lit dining room feels sensuous and swoony. On warm afternoons and evenings, the best tables are on the outside terrace, overlooking the busy street. Chaya is best known for superb grilled fish and meats, like seared soy-marinated Hawaiian tuna and Long Island duckling. Chef Shigefumi Tachibe's lobster ravioli with pesto-cream sauce is both stylish and delicious, as is tangy grilled chicken Dijon, a house specialty. Chaya is also a hot late-night rendezvous, with a short but choice supper menu served until 12:15am Tuesday through Saturday.

Kate Mantilini. 9101 Wilshire Blvd. (at Doheny Dr.), Beverly Hills. ☎ **310/ 278-3699.** Reservations accepted only for parties of 6 or more. Main courses $7–$16. AE, MC, V. Mon–Thurs 7:30am–1am; Fri 7:30am–2am; Sat 11am–2am; Sun 10am–midnight. Validated valet parking. AMERICAN/BREAKFAST.

It's rare to find a restaurant that feels comfortably familiar yet cutting-edge trendy at the same time—and also happens to be one of L.A.'s few late-night eateries. Kate Mantilini fits the bill perfectly. One of the first to bring meat loaf back into fashion, Kate's offers a huge menu of upscale truck-stop favorites like "white" chili (made with chicken, white beans, and Jack cheese), grilled steaks and fish, a few token pastas, and just about anything you might crave. At 2am, nothing quite beats a steaming bowl of lentil-vegetable soup and some garlic-cheese toast, unless your taste runs to fresh oysters and a dry martini—Kate has it all. The huge mural of the Hagler-Hearns boxing match that dominates the stark, open interior provides the only clue to the namesake's identity: Mantilini was an early female boxing promoter, around 1947.

✪ **La Serenata Gourmet.** 10924 W. Pico Blvd., West L.A. ☎ **310/ 441-9667.** Main courses $8–$13. AE, MC, V. Daily 11am–3:30pm and 5–10pm (Fri–Sat until 10:30pm). Metered street parking. MEXICAN.

Westsiders rejoiced when this branch of Boyle Heights's award-winning La Serenata de Girabaldi began serving its authentic, but innovative, Mexican cuisine just a block away from the Westside Pavilion shopping center. This place is casual, fun, and intensely delicious. Specialties like shrimp enchiladas, fish tacos, and pork *gorditas* are all accented with hand-patted corn tortillas, fresh chips dusted with *añejo* cheese, and flavorful fresh salsas. Always packed to capacity, the restaurant finally expanded in 1998, but try to avoid the prime lunch and dinner hours nevertheless.

Adventurous diners head to the original La Serenata de Gira-baldi, 1842 1st St. (between Boyle and State sts; ☎ **213/ 265-2887**), reopened in 2000 after an extensive remodel. The menu is more formal, the ambiance is more authentic, and secured valet parking is provided for those worried about the sketchy neighborhood.

Maui Beach Cafe. 1019 Westwood Blvd. (at Le Conte), Westwood. ☎ **310/ 209-0494.** www.mauibeachcafe.com. Reservations suggested for dinner. Main courses $6–$12 lunch, $8–$22 dinner. AE, DC, MC, V. Mon–Thurs 11:30am–3pm and 5–10pm; Fri 11:30am–3pm and 5–11pm; Sat 11:30am–11pm; Sun 11:30am–10pm. Metered street or lot parking. PACIFIC RIM/HAWAIIAN.

Enormously popular with both students from nearby UCLA and foodies from throughout the Westside, this casual and noisy island party zone features looming interior palm trees and wavy walls that glow tropical-wave blue. The menu is refreshingly different, offering a true sampling of Hawaiian Regional Cuisine, an amalgam of influences from Japan, China, Thailand, Korea, and Portugal—all composed using fresh Hawaiian fish, lush fruits, and tropical produce. Island-born chef Mako Segawa-Gonzales trained on Maui with HRC guru Roy Yamaguchi, and he tosses a few Latin elements into the mix, in honor of his new L.A. home. You can feast on Asian "tapas" like baby back ribs glazed with guava-hoisin; slurp up pastas such as thick Shanghai noodles tossed with crispy vegetables and roasted garlic; or dig your chopsticks into "Da Maui Bowls," nicely composed one-bowl meals atop rice (white or brown) or noodles (udon or soba).

✪ **Pastis.** 8114 Beverly Blvd. (west of Crescent Heights), Los Angeles.
☎ **323/655-8822.** Reservations recommended. Main courses $15–$20. AE,
MC, V. Mon–Fri 11am–2pm; daily 5:30–10pm. Metered street parking or valet
parking. FRENCH PROVENÇAL.

Of the new wave of country French bistros in town, Pastis usually
takes a back seat to the ultrahip, celebrity-frequented Mimosa,
which happens to be just a block away. But locals and regulars often
prefer this rustic yet civilized spot, named for the licorice-flavored
liqueur imbibed throughout the south of France. Intimate and
friendly, with sidewalk tables and a warmly ochre-toned dining
room, Pastis manages to be both elegant and the kind of place you
can scrape your chair, raise your voice, or drink a little too much
wine. Distinctive menu selections include curly endive salad
with bacon and poached-egg garnish, wine-braised rabbit, and
Marseilles-style seafood bouillabaisse. For chocolate lovers only:
Dessert is chocolat pôt au crème, a beautiful thick custard served in
rustic glazed pots.

INEXPENSIVE

✪ **The Apple Pan.** 10801 Pico Blvd. (east of Westwood Blvd.). ☎ **310/
475-3585.** Most menu items under $5. No credit cards. Tues–Thurs and Sun
11am–midnight; Fri–Sat 11am–1am. SANDWICHES/AMERICAN.

There are no tables, just a U-shaped counter, at this classic American burger shack and L.A. landmark. Open since 1947, the
Apple Pan is a diner that looks—and acts—the part. It's famous
for juicy burgers, bullet-speed service, and an authentic frills-free
atmosphere. The hickory burger is best, though the tuna
sandwich also has its huge share of fans. Ham, egg-salad, and
Swiss-cheese sandwiches round out the menu. Definitely order
fries and, if you're in the mood, the home-baked apple pie, too.

Nate & Al's. 414 N. Beverly Dr. (at Brighton Way), Beverly Hills. ☎ **310/
274-0101.** Main courses $8–$13. AE, DISC, MC, V. Daily 7:30am–9pm. Free
parking with validation. BREAKFAST/DELI.

If you want to know where old money, rich-and-famous types go
for comfort food, look no further. Despite its location in the center of Beverly Hills's "Golden Triangle," Nate & Al's has remained
unchanged since it opened in 1945, from the Naugahyde booths
to the motherly waitresses, who treat you the same whether you're
a house-account celebrity regular or just a visitor stopping in for
an overstuffed pastrami on rye. Their too-salty chicken soup
keeps Nate & Al's from being the best L.A. deli (actually, I'd be

hard pressed to choose any one deli as the city's best), but staples like chopped liver, dense potato pancakes, blintzes, borscht, and well-dilled pickles more than make up for it.

Skewers'. 8939 Santa Monica Blvd. (between Robertson and San Vicente blvd.), West Hollywood. ☎ **310/271-0555.** Main courses $7–$9; salads and pitas $4–$7. AE, MC, V. Daily 11am–midnight. MIDDLE EASTERN.

Santa Monica Boulevard is the heart of West Hollywood's commercial strip, and Skewers' sidewalk tables are a great place to see all kinds of neighborhood activity (and audacity). Inside is a New York–like narrow space with changing artwork adorning bare brick walls. From the zesty marinated carrot sticks you get the moment you're seated, to sweet, sticky squares of baklava for dessert, this Mediterranean grill is sure to please. You'll get baskets of warm pita bread for scooping up traditional salads like *baba ghanoush* (grilled eggplant with tahini and lemon) and *tabbouleh* (cracked wheat, parsley, and tomatoes). Try marinated chicken and lamb off the grill, or dolmades (rice- and meat-stuffed grape leaves) seared with a tangy tomato glaze.

4 Hollywood

For a map of Hollywood restaurants, see p. 56.

EXPENSIVE

✪ **Campanile.** 624 S. La Brea Ave. (north of Wilshire Blvd.). ☎ **323/938-1447.** www.campanilerestaurant.com. Reservations required. Main courses $18–$32. AE, MC, V. Mon–Thurs 11:30am–2:30pm and 6–10pm; Fri 7:30–10am, 11:30am–2:30pm, and 5:30–11pm; Sat 9:30am–1:30pm and 5:30–11pm; Sun 9:30am–1:30pm. Valet parking $3.50. BREAKFAST/CALIFORNIA-MEDITERRANEAN.

Built as Charlie Chaplin's private offices in 1928, this lovely building has a multilevel layout with flower-bedecked interior balconies, a bubbling fountain, and a skylight through which diners can see the *campanile* (bell tower). The kitchen, headed by Spago alumnus chef/owner Mark Peel, gets a giant leg up from baker (and wife) Nancy Silverton, who runs the now-legendary La Brea Bakery next door. Meals here might begin with fried zucchini flowers drizzled with melted mozzarella or lamb carpaccio surrounded by artichoke leaves—a dish that arrives looking like one of van Gogh's sunflowers. Chef Peel is particularly known for his grills and roasts; try the grilled prime rib smeared with black-olive tapenade or papardelle with braised rabbit, roasted tomato, and collard greens. And don't skip dessert—the restaurant's many enthusiastic sweets fans have turned Nancy's dessert book into a best-seller. Breakfast is a surprising crowd-pleaser and a terrific way to appreciate this beautiful space on a budget.

✪ **Patina.** 5955 Melrose Ave. (west of Cahuenga Blvd.). ☎ **323/467-1108.** www.patina-pinot.com. Reservations required. Main courses $18–$30. AE, DC, DISC, JCB, MC, V. Sun–Thurs 6–9:30pm (Tues also noon–2pm); Fri 6–10:30pm; Sat 5:30–10:30pm. CALIFORNIA-FRENCH.

Joachim Splichal, arguably L.A.'s very best chef, is also a genius at choosing and training top chefs to cook in his kitchens while he jets around the world. Patina routinely wins the highest praise from demanding gourmands, who are happy to empty their bank accounts for unbeatable meals that almost never miss their intended mark. The dining room is straightforwardly attractive, low key, well lit, and professional, without the slightest hint of stuffiness. The menu is equally disarming: "Mallard Duck with Portobello Mushrooms" gives little hint of the brilliant colors and flavors that appear on the plate. The seasonal menu features partridge, pheasant, venison, and other game in winter and spotlights exotic local vegetables in warmer months. Seafood is always available; if Maine lobster cannelloni or asparagus-wrapped John Dory is on the menu, order it. Patina is justifiably famous for its mashed potatoes and potato-truffle chips; be sure to include one (or both) with your meal.

MODERATE

Authentic Cafe. 7605 Beverly Blvd. (at Curson Ave.). ☎ **323/939-4626.** Reservations accepted only for parties of 8 or more. Main courses $9–$19. AE, MC, V. Mon–Thurs 11:30am–10pm; Fri 11:30am–11pm; Sat 9:30am–11pm; Sun 9:30am–10pm. SOUTHWESTERN/ECLECTIC.

True to its name, this restaurant serves authentic Southwestern food in a casual atmosphere. It's a winning combination that quickly made this place an L.A. favorite, although popularity has dropped off recently due to the decline of Southwestern cuisine and the rush for the next big thing. But Authentic Cafe still has a loyal following of locals who appreciate generous portions and lively flavor combinations. You'll sometimes find an Asian flair to chef Roger Hayot's dishes. Look for brie, papaya, and chili quesadillas; other worthwhile dishes are the chicken casserole with a corn-bread crust, fresh corn and red peppers in chili-cream sauce, and meat loaf with caramelized onions.

Ca' Brea. 346 S. La Brea Ave. (north of Wilshire Blvd.). ☎ **323/938-2863.** Reservations recommended. Main courses $9–$21; lunch $7–$20. AE, CB, DC, MC, V. Mon–Sat 11:30am–2:30pm; Mon–Thurs 5:30–10:30pm; Fri–Sat 5:30pm–midnight. Valet parking $3.50. NORTHERN ITALIAN.

When Ca' Brea opened in 1991, its talented chef/owner Antonio Tommasi was catapulted into a public spotlight shared by only a handful of L.A. chefs—Wolfgang Puck, Michel Richard, and Joachim Splichal. Since then, Tommasi has opened two other celebrated restaurants, Locanda Veneta in Hollywood and Ca' Del Sole in the Valley, but, for many, Ca' Brea remains tops. The restaurant's refreshingly bright two-story dining room is a happy place, hung with colorful, oversize contemporary paintings and backed by an open prep-kitchen where you can watch as your seafood cakes are sautéed and your Napa cabbage braised. Booths are the most coveted seats; but with only 20 tables in all, be thankful you're sitting anywhere. Detractors might complain that Ca' Brea isn't what it used to be since Tommasi began splitting his time between three restaurants, but Tommasi stops in daily and keeps a very close watch over his handpicked staff. Consistently excellent dishes include the roasted pork sausage, the butter squash–stuffed ravioli, and a different risotto each day—always rich, creamy, and delightfully indulgent.

Georgia. 7250 Melrose Ave. (at Alta Vista Ave.). ☎ **323/933-8420.** Reservations recommended. Main courses $15–$22. AE, MC, V. Mon–Sat 6:30–11pm; Sun 5:30–10pm. Valet parking $3. SOUTHERN.

Soul food and power ties come together at this calorie-unconscious ode to Southern cooking in the heart of Melrose's funky shopping district. Owned by a group of investors that includes Denzel Washington and Eddie Murphy, the restaurant is popular with Hollywood's African-American crowd and others who can afford L.A.'s highest-priced pork chops, fried chicken, and grits. It's great for people-watching. The antebellum-style dining room is built to resemble a fine Southern house, complete with mahogany floors, Spanish moss, and wrought-iron gates; a bourbon bar continues the theme. The smoked baby back ribs are particularly good and, like many other dishes, are smothered in onion gravy or rémoulade, and sided with corn pudding, grits, string beans, or an excellent creamy garlic coleslaw. Other recommendations include turtle soup, grilled gulf shrimp, and a Creole-style catfish that's more delicately fried than it would traditionally be.

۞ Lola's. 945 N. Fairfax Ave. (south of Santa Monica Blvd.), Los Angeles. ☎ **323/736-5652.** Reservations recommended. Main courses $10–$18. AE, MC, V. Daily 5:30pm–2am. Valet parking $3.50. NEW AMERICAN.

As the song goes, "Whatever Lola wants, Lola gets . . ."—and Lola must have wanted to open a stylish restaurant and martini bar that would instantly become the in-crowd's darling. This centrally located place has a lot going for it: Not only is the circa-1935 Hollywood building a perfect foil for Lola's semi-Gothic decor, but the menu also is reasonably priced (and better than it reads), and then there's the famed martini bar. All of the several dozen colorful concoctions are available tableside, served up in enormous chilled conical glasses. Menu selections are unfussy and flavorful, featuring mesquite-grilled meats, simple pasta dishes, and internationally flavored appetizers. Be sure to try "Domenick's Mashed Potatoes," a creamy dollop of mash atop a nest of crispy shoestring potatoes. The star dessert is Lola's "Chocolate Kiss Cake," a dense and rich treat.

۞ Musso & Frank Grill. 6667 Hollywood Blvd. (at Cherokee Ave.). ☎ **323/467-7788.** Reservations recommended. Main courses $13–$32. AE, CB, DC, MC, V. Tues–Sat 11am–11pm. Self parking $2.25 with validation. AMERICAN/CONTINENTAL.

A survey of Hollywood restaurants that leaves out Musso & Frank is like a study of Las Vegas singers that fails to mention Wayne Newton. As L.A.'s oldest eatery (since 1919), Musso & Frank is the paragon of Old Hollywood grill rooms. This is where Faulkner and Hemingway drank during their screenwriting days and where Orson Welles used to hold court. The restaurant is still known for its bone-dry martinis and perfectly seasoned Bloody Marys. The setting is what you'd expect: oak-beamed ceilings, red-leather booths and banquettes, mahogany room dividers, and chandeliers with tiny shades. The extensive menu is a veritable survey of American/continental cookery. Hearty dinners include veal scaloppine Marsala, roast spring lamb with mint jelly, and broiled lobster. Grilled meats are a specialty, as is the Thursday-only chicken potpie. Regulars also flock in for Musso's trademark "flannel cakes," crêpe-thin pancakes flipped to order.

Sofi. 8030³/₄ W. 3rd St. (between Fairfax Ave. and Crescent Heights Blvd.). ☎ **323/651-0346.** Reservations recommended. Main courses $7–$14. AE, DC, MC, V. Mon–Sat noon–3pm; daily 5:30–11pm. Metered street parking or valet parking $3. GREEK.

Look for the simple black awning over the narrow passageway that leads from the street to this hidden Aegean treasure. Be sure to ask for a table on the romantic patio amid twinkling lights, and immediately order a plate of their thick, satisfying *tsatziki* (yogurt-cucumber-garlic spread) accompanied by a basket of warm pitas for dipping. Other specialties (recipes courtesy of Sofi's old-world grandmother) include herbed rack of lamb with rice, fried calamari salad, *saganaki* (kasseri cheese flamed with ouzo), and other hearty taverna favorites. Sofi's odd, off-street setting, near the Farmers Market in a popular part of town, has made it an insiders' secret.

✪ **Tahiti.** 7910 W. 3rd St. (at Fairfax), Los Angeles. ☎ **323/651-1213.** Reservations recommended. Main courses $11–$17. AE, MC, V. Mon–Fri 11:30am–2:30pm; Mon–Thurs 6–10pm; Fri–Sat 6–11pm; Sun 5–9pm. Valet parking $3.75. WORLD CUISINE.

Tahiti has a rapidly growing fan base of showbiz types and artists who inhabit the eclectic surrounding neighborhood. Chef/owner Tony DiLembo's distinctive "world cuisine" is a provocative mix of zesty influences that produces diverse specialties like rare ahi tuna drizzled with lime-ginger butter, sprinkled with toasted sesame seeds, and served with wasabi horseradish and papaya garnish; Argentinean-style T-bone with chimichurri dipping sauce; sherry-sautéed chicken and spinach potstickers accented with mint; and perennial standout rosemary chicken strips with fettuccine in sun-dried tomato/cream sauce. The relaxing decor is sophisticated South Seas with a modern twist, incorporating thatch, batik, rattan, and palm fronds. In the adjacent Tiki Lounge, tropical concoctions contribute to the island ambiance. If the weather is nice, try to get a table on the patio. And don't forget to save room for Tahiti's tropical-tinged desserts.

INEXPENSIVE

✪ **El Cholo.** 1121 S. Western Ave. (south of Olympic Blvd.). ☎ **323/734-2773.** Reservations recommended. Main courses $8–$14. AE, DC, MC, V. Mon–Thurs 11am–10pm; Fri–Sat 11am–11pm; Sun 11am–9pm. Free self-parking or valet parking $3. MEXICAN.

There's authentic Mexican and then there's traditional Mexican—El Cholo is comfort food of the latter variety, south-of-the-border cuisine regularly craved by Angelenos. They've been serving it up in this pink adobe hacienda since 1927, even though the once-outlying mid-Wilshire neighborhood around them has turned into Koreatown. El Cholo's expertly blended margaritas, invitingly messy nachos, and classic combination dinners don't break new culinary ground, but the kitchen has perfected these standards over 70 years. We wish they bottled their rich enchilada sauce! Other specialties include seasonally available green-corn tamales and creative sizzling vegetarian fajitas that go way beyond just eliminating the meat. The atmosphere is festive, as people from all parts of town dine happily in the many rambling rooms that compose the restaurant. There's valet parking as well as a free self-park lot directly across the street.

Westsiders head to El Cholo's Santa Monica branch at 1025 Wilshire Blvd. (☎ **310/899-1106**).

Hollywood Hills Coffee Shop. 6145 Franklin Ave. (between Gower and Vine sts.). ☎ **323/467-7678.** Most items less than $10. AE, DISC, MC, V. Daily 7am–10pm. Free parking. DINER.

Having for years served as the run-of-the-mill coffee shop for the attached freeway-side Best Western, this place took on a life of its own when chef Susan Fine commandeered the kitchen and spiked the menu with quirky Mexican and Asian touches. Hotel guests spill in from the lobby to rub noses with the actors, screenwriters, and other artistic types who converge from nearby canyons while awaiting that sitcom casting call or feature-film deal—a community immortalized in the 1996 film *Swingers,* which was filmed in the restaurant. Prices have gone up (to pay for the industrial-strength cappuccino maker visible behind the counter?), and the dinner menu features surprisingly sophisticated entrees. But breakfast and lunch are still bargains, and the comfy Americana atmosphere is a nice break from the bright lights of nearby Hollywood Boulevard.

Pink's Hot Dogs. 709 N. La Brea Ave. (at Melrose Ave.). ☎ **323/931-4223.** Hot dogs $2.10. Sun–Thurs 9:30am–2am; Fri–Sat 9:30am–3am. HOT DOGS.

Pink's isn't your usual guidebook recommendation, but then again, this crusty corner stand isn't your usual doggery either. The heartburn-inducing chili dogs are craved by even the most upstanding, health-conscious Angelenos. Bruce Willis reportedly proposed to Demi Moore at the 59-year-old shack that grew around the late Paul Pink's 10¢ wiener cart. Pray the bulldozers stay away from this little nugget of a place.

Swingers. 8020 Beverly Blvd. (west of Fairfax Ave.). ☎ **323/653-5858.**
Most items less than $8. AE, DISC, MC, V. Sun–Thurs 6am–2am; Fri–Sat
9am–4am. Metered street parking. DINER/AMERICAN.

Resurrected from a motel coffee shop so dismal we can't even
remember it, Swingers was transformed by a couple of L.A. hipster nightclub owners into a 1990s version of comfy Americana.
The interior seems like a slice of the 1950s until you notice
the plaid upholstery and Warholesque graphics, which contrast
nicely with the retro red-white-and-blue "Swingers" logo adorning *everything*. Guests at the attached Beverly Laurel Motor Hotel
chow down alongside body-pierced industry hounds from nearby
record companies, while a soundtrack that runs the gamut from
punk rock to "Schoolhouse Rock" plays in the background. It's
not all attitude here, though—you'll enjoy a menu of high-
quality diner favorites spiked with trendy crowd-pleasers:
Steel-cut Irish oatmeal, challah French toast, grilled Jamaican
jerk chicken, and a nice selection of tofu-enhanced vegetarian
dishes are just a few of the eclectic offerings. Sometimes we just
"swing" by for a malt or milk shake to go—they're among the best
in town.

✪ **Toi on Sunset.** 7505 ¹/₂ Sunset Blvd. (at Gardner). ☎ **323/
874-8062.** Reservations accepted only for parties of 6 or more. Main courses
$6–$11. AE, DISC, MC, V. Daily 11am–4am. THAI.

Because they're open *really* late, Toi has become an instant fave of
Hollywood hipsters like Sean Penn and Woody Harrelson, who
make post-clubbing excursions to this rock-and-roll eatery a few
blocks from the Sunset Strip. After all the hype, I was surprised to
find possibly L.A.'s best bargain Thai food, authentically prepared
and served in portions so generous the word *enormous* seems inad-
equate. Menu highlights include hot-and-sour chicken, coconut
soup, and the house specialty: chicken curry somen, a spicy dish
with green curry and mint sauce spooned over thin Japanese rice
noodles. Vegetarians will be pleased with the vast selection of
meat-free items like *pad kee mao,* rice noodles served spicy with
tofu, mint, onions, peppers, and chili. The interior is a noisy
amalgam of cultish movie posters, rock-and-roll memorabilia, and
haphazardly placed industrial-issue dinette sets; and the plates,
flatware, and drinking glasses are cheap coffee-shop issue. In other
words, it's all about the food and the scene—neither will
disappoint.

Westsiders can opt for ✪ **Toi on Wilshire,** 1120 Wilshire Blvd., Santa Monica (☎ **310/394-7804**), open daily from 11am to 3am.

5 Downtown

For a map of downtown restaurants, see p. 60.

EXPENSIVE

✪ **Water Grill.** 544 S. Grand Ave. (between 5th and 6th sts.). ☎ **213/891-0900.** Reservations recommended. Main courses $19–$31. AE, DC, DISC, MC, V. Mon–Tues 11:30am–9pm; Wed–Fri 11:30am–10pm; Sat 5–10pm; Sun 4:30–9pm. Valet parking $4. SEAFOOD.

This restaurant is popular with the suit-and-tie crowd at lunch and with concertgoers en route to the Music Center at night. The dining room is a stylish and sophisticated fusion of wood, leather, and brass, but it gets a lighthearted lift from cavorting papier-mâché fish that play against an aquamarine ceiling painted with bubbles. Water Grill, considered by many to be L.A.'s best seafood house, is best known for its shellfish; among the appetizers are a dozen different oysters. Main courses are imaginative dishes influenced by the cuisines of Hawaii, the Pacific Northwest, New Orleans, and New England. Try the appetizer seafood platter, a mouthwatering assortment served with well-made *aïoli;* bluefin tuna tartare; Santa Barbara spot prawns paired with fingerling potato salad; Maine lobster stuffed with Dungeness crab; perfectly pan-roasted Alaskan halibut; and simple desserts like *mascarpone* with figs and cherries.

MODERATE

Cha Cha Cha. 656 N. Virgil Ave. (at Melrose Ave.), Silver Lake. ☎ **323/664-7723.** Reservations recommended. Main courses $8–$15. AE, DC, DISC, MC, V. Sun–Thurs 8am–10:30pm; Fri–Sat 8am–11:30pm. Valet parking $3.50. BREAKFAST/CARIBBEAN.

Cha Cha Cha serves the West Coast's best Caribbean food in a fun and funky space on the seedy fringe of downtown. The restaurant is a festival of flavors and colors that are both upbeat and offbeat. It's impossible to feel down when you're part of this eclectic hodgepodge of pulsating Caribbean music, wild decor, and kaleidoscopic clutter; still, the intimate dining rooms cater to lively romantics, not obnoxious frat boys. Claustrophobes should choose seats in the airy covered courtyard. The very spicy black-pepper jumbo shrimp gets top marks, as does the paella, a generous mixture of chicken, sausage, and seafood blended with saffron rice. Other Jamaican-, Haitian-, Cuban-, and Puerto Rican–inspired recommendations include jerk pork and mambo gumbo, a zesty soup of okra, shredded chicken, and spices. Hardcore Caribbeanites might visit for breakfast, when the fare ranges from plantain, yucca, onion, and herb omelets to scrambled eggs with fresh tomatillos served on hot grilled tortillas.

Ciudad. 445 S. Figueroa St. ☎ **213/486-5171.** Reservations recommended. Main courses $12–$23, cuchifrito $5–$8. AE, MC, V. Mon–Fri 11:30am–10pm; Sat–Sun 5–10pm. Free parking days; valet parking (after 5pm) $3.50. LATIN.

The latest venture of TV's *Too Hot Tamales*—Susan Feniger and Mary Sue Milliken—is this intriguingly conceived restaurant in the heart of downtown's high-rises. The name, Ciudad, means "city" in Spanish and is a nod to the partners' long-ago venture City Restaurant. Here, amidst juicy sherbet pastel walls and 1950s geometric abstract designs, exuberant crowds gather to revel in a menu that brings together cuisines from the world's great Latin urban centers: Havana, Rio de Janeiro, Barcelona, and so on. Standout dishes include Honduran ceviche presented in a martini glass and accented with tropical coconut and pineapple, Argentine rib eye stuffed with jalapeño chiles and whole garlic cloves, and citrus-roasted Cuban-style chicken served with Puerto Rican rice and fried plantains. Between 3 and 7pm on weekdays, Ciudad presents *cuchifrito,* traditional Latin snacks served at the bar; it's easy to make a meal of several, choosing from sweet-savory pork-stuffed green tamales, *papas rellenos* (mashed potato fritters stuffed with oxtail stew), plantain gnocchi in tomatillo sauce, and more. As with the pair's Border Grill, desserts are worth saving room for, and large enough to share.

R23. 923 E. 3rd St. (between Alameda St. and Santa Fe Ave.). ☎ **213/687-7178.** Reservations recommended. Main courses $12–$20; sushi $4–$8. AE, MC, V. Mon–Fri noon–2pm and 6–10pm; Sat 6–10pm. Free parking. JAPANESE/SUSHI.

This gallery-like space in downtown's out-of-the-way warehouse/artist loft district has been the secret of sushi connoisseurs since 1991. At the back of R23's single, large dining room, the 12-seat sushi bar shines like a beacon; what appear at first to be ceramic wall ornaments are really stylish sushi platters hanging in wait for large orders. More functional art reveals itself in the corrugated cardboard chairs—they're funky, yet far more comfortable than wood! Genial sushi wizards stand in wait, cases of the finest fish before them. Salmon, yellowtail, shrimp, tuna, and scallops are among the always-fresh selections; an excellent and unusual offering is seared *toro,* where the rich belly tuna absorbs a faint and delectable smoky flavor from the grill. Though R23's sublimely perfect sushi is the star, the short but inventive menu also includes pungent red miso soup, creamy baked scallops, finely sliced beef "sashimi," and several other choices.

Traxx. In Union Station, 800 N. Alameda St. (at Cesar E. Chavez Ave.). ☎ 213/625-1999. Reservations suggested for dinner. Main courses $10–$15 lunch, $10–$25 dinner. AE, MC, V. Mon–Fri 11am–10pm; Sat 6–10pm. Free valet parking with validation. CALIFORNIA.

There's always been a restaurant—of some sort—inside the Union Station passenger concourse, but Traxx is the first to do justice to its grand, historic setting. Boasting just the right mix of retro-evocative art deco character with sleek contemporary touches, the interior blends seamlessly with the station's architecture, a unique fusion of Spanish Colonial Revival and Streamline Moderne. Elegant enough for a low-lit romantic dinner, yet welcoming to the casual commuter in search of a stylish lunch or sit-down snack, Traxx features a menu designed by executive chef Tara Thomas to have the same cosmopolitan flavor as the station itself. Samples range from "small plates" of ahi tuna Napoleon with crispy wonton or "Really Good" (and they are) crab cakes with a chipotle kick, to main dishes like grilled salmon with a Mediterranean flair or the much-talked-about Gorgonzola-crusted beef tenderloin presented atop crispy and mashed potatoes surrounded by a pool of demi-glace/herb reduction.

Yang Chow Restaurant. 819 N. Broadway (at Alpine St.), Chinatown. ☎ 213/625-0811. Reservations recommended on weekends. Main courses $8–$14. AE, MC, V. Daily 11:30am–2:30pm; Sun–Thurs 5–9:30pm; Fri–Sat 5–10:30pm. Free parking. MANDARIN/SZECHUAN.

Open for more than 30 years, family-operated Yang Chow is one of downtown's more popular Chinese restaurants. It's not the dining room's bland and functional decor that accrues accolades, however; what makes Yang Chow so popular is an interesting menu of seafood specialties complementing well-done Chinese standards. After covering the Mandarin and Szechuan basics— sweet-and-sour pork, shrimp with broccoli, moo shu chicken— the kitchen leaps into high gear, concocting dishes like spicy Dungeness crab, a tangy and hot sautéed squid, and sautéed shellfish with a pungent hoisin-based dipping sauce. The key to having a terrific meal is to first order the house specialty—plump steamed pork dumplings presented on a bed of fresh spinach—then respectfully ask for recommendations from your server.

INEXPENSIVE

✪ **The Original Pantry Cafe.** 877 S. Figueroa St. (at 9th St.). ☎ **213/ 972-9279.** Main courses $6–$11. No credit cards. Daily 24 hrs. Free parking with validation. AMERICAN/BREAKFAST.

An L.A. institution if there ever was one, this place has been serving huge portions of comfort food around the clock for more than 60 years. In fact, there isn't even a key to the front door. Owned by L.A. Mayor Richard Riordan, the Pantry is especially popular with politicos, who come here for weekday lunches, and with conferencegoers en route to the nearby L.A. Convention Center. The well-worn restaurant is also a welcoming beacon to clubbers after hours, when downtown becomes a virtual ghost town. A bowl of celery stalks, carrot sticks, and whole radishes greets you at your Formica table, and creamy coleslaw and sourdough bread come free with every meal. Famous for quantity rather than quality, the Pantry serves huge T-bone steaks, densely packed meat loaf, macaroni and cheese, and other American favorites. A typical breakfast (served all day) might consist of a huge stack of hotcakes, a big slab of sweet cured ham, home fries, and coffee.

Philippe the Original. 1001 N. Alameda St. (at Ord St.). ☎ **213/628-3781.** www.philippes.com. Most menu items under $7. No credit cards. Daily 6am–10pm. Free parking. BREAKFAST/SANDWICHES.

Good old-fashioned value is what this legendary landmark cafeteria is all about. Popular with both south-central project dwellers and Beverly Hills elite, Philippe's decidedly unspectacular dining room is one of the few places in L.A. where everyone can get along. Philippe's claims to have invented the French-dipped sandwich at this location in 1908; it remains the most popular menu item. Patrons push trays along the counter and watch while their choice of beef, pork, ham, turkey, or lamb is sliced and layered onto crusty French bread that's been dipped in meat juices. Other menu items include homemade beef stew, chili, and pickled pigs' feet. A hearty breakfast, served daily until 10:30am, is worthwhile if only for Philippe's uncommonly good cinnamon-dipped French toast. Beer and wine are available.

6 The San Fernando Valley

EXPENSIVE

Pinot Bistro. 12969 Ventura Blvd. (west of Coldwater Canyon Ave.), Studio City. ☎ 818/990-0500. www.patina-pinot.com. Reservations required. Main courses $7–$13 lunch, $16–$22 dinner. AE, DC, DISC, MC, V. Mon–Fri 11:30am–2:30pm; Mon–Thurs 6–10pm; Fri 6–10:30pm; Sat 5:30–10:30pm; Sun 5:30–9:30pm. Valet parking $4.50. CALIFORNIA-FRENCH.

When the Valley crowd doesn't want to make the drive to Patina, they pack into Pinot Bistro, one of Joachim Splichal's other hugely successful restaurants. The Valley's only great bistro is designed with dark woods, etched glass, and cream-colored walls that scream "trendy French" almost as loudly as the rich, straight-forward cooking. The menu, a symphony of California and continental elements, includes a beautiful warm potato tart with smoked whitefish, and baby lobster tails with creamy polenta—both studies in culinary perfection. The most popular dish here is chef Octavio Becerra's French-ified Tuscan bean soup, infused with oven-dried tomatoes and roasted garlic and served over crusty ciabatta bread. The generously portioned main dishes continue the gourmet theme: baby lobster risotto, braised oxtail with parsley gnocchi, and puff pastry stuffed with bay scallops, Manila clams, and roast duck. The service is good, attentive, and unobtrusive. Many regulars prefer Pinot Bistro at lunch, when a less expensive menu is served to a more easygoing crowd.

MODERATE

Casa Vega. 13371 Ventura Blvd. (at Fulton Ave.), Sherman Oaks. ☎ **818/788-4868.** Reservations recommended. Main courses $5–$11. AE, CB, DC, MC, V. Mon–Fri 11am–2am; Sat–Sun 4pm–2am. Metered street parking or $2.50 valet. MEXICAN.

I believe that everyone loves a friendly dive, and Casa Vega is one of my local favorites. A faux-weathered adobe exterior conceals red Naugahyde booths lurking among fake potted plants and 1960s amateur oil paintings of dark-eyed Mexican children and cape-waving bullfighters. (The decor achieves critical mass at Christmas, when everything drips with tinsel.) Locals love this place for its good, cheap margaritas (order on the rocks), bottomless baskets of hot and salty chips, and traditional combination dinners, which all come with Casa Vega's patented tostada-style dinner salad. Street parking is so plentiful here you should use the valet only as a last resort.

✪ **Jerry's Famous Deli.** 12655 Ventura Blvd. (just east of Coldwater Canyon Ave.), Studio City. ☎ **818/980-4245.** Main courses $9–$14 dinner, $2–$11 breakfast, $4–$12 sandwiches and salads. AE, MC, V. Daily 24 hr. Free parking. BREAKFAST/DELI.

Here's a simple yet sizable deli where all the Valley's hipsters go to relieve their late-night munchies. This place probably has one of the largest menus in America—a tome that spans cultures and continents, from Central America to China to New York. From salads to sandwiches to steak-and-seafood platters, everything— including breakfast—is served all day. Jerry's is consistently good at lox and eggs, pastrami sandwiches, potato pancakes, and all the deli staples. It's also an integral part of L.A.'s cultural landscape and a favorite of the show-business types who populate the adjacent foothill neighborhoods. It even has a full bar.

Miceli's. 3655 Cahuenga Blvd. (east of Lankershim), Los Angeles. ☎ **818/508-1221.** Main courses $7–$12; pizza $9–$15. AE, DC, MC, V. Mon–Thurs 5pm–midnight; Fri 5pm–1am; Sat 4pm–1am; Sun 4–11pm. Parking $2.50. ITALIAN.

Mostaccioli marinara, lasagna, thin-crust pizza, and eggplant parmigiana are indicative of the Sicilian-style fare at this cavernous, stained-glass windowed Italian restaurant adjacent to Universal City. The waitstaff sings show tunes or opera favorites in between serving dinner (and sometimes instead of); make sure you have enough Chianti to get into the spirit of it all. This is a great place for kids, but way too rollicking for romance.

If you're near Hollywood Boulevard, visit the original (since 1949) Miceli's at 1646 N. Las Palmas (☎ **323/466-3438**).

✪ **Paul's Cafe.** 13456 Ventura Blvd. (between Dixie Canyon and Woodman Ave.), Sherman Oaks. ☎ **818/789-3575.** Main courses $12–$17 dinner, $8–$11 lunch. AE, MC, V. Mon–Thurs 11:30am–2:30pm and 5:30–10pm; Fri 11:30am–2:30pm and 5:30–11pm; Sat 5–11pm; Sun 5–9:30pm. Metered street parking or valet parking $4. CALIFORNIA-FRENCH.

One of the Valley's hardest reservations (hint: call early, dine early, or both) is at this midsize neighborhood bistro, where a quietly elegant setting belies the friendly prices that have made Paul's a big success. Expect the seasonal menu to include plenty of seafood (roasted sea bass laid atop spinach with a mushroom vinaigrette, sautéed sea scallops with saffron risotto and lobster sauce), hearty meats (filet mignon with port sauce accompanied by a creamy sweet potato–gorgonzola gratin, garlic-rubbed rack of lamb sweetened with mint), and appetizers that ought to be main courses (pepper crusted seared ahi drizzled with scallion vinaigrette, crab cakes with lobster *aioli*). Soup or a small salad is only $1 with any dinner, and locals love the mere $2 corkage fee. Paul's manages to be intimate enough for lovers yet also welcoming for families—its success is no surprise.

INEXPENSIVE

Du-par's Restaurant & Bakery. 12036 Ventura Blvd. (1 block east of Laurel Canyon Blvd.), Studio City. ☎ **818/766-4437.** www.Dupars.com. All items under $10. AE, DC, DISC, MC, V. Sun–Thurs 6am–1am; Fri–Sat 6am–4am. Free parking. AMERICAN/DINER.

It's been called a "culinary wax museum," the last of a dying breed, the kind of coffee shop Donna Reed took the family to for blue-plate specials. This isn't a trendy new theme place, it's the real deal—and that motherly waitress who calls everyone under 60 "hon" has probably been slinging hash here for 20 or 30 years. Du-par's is popular among old-timers who made it part of their daily routine decades ago, show-business denizens who eschew the industry watering holes, a new generation that appreciates a tasty, cheap meal . . . well, everyone, really. It's common knowledge that Du-par's makes the best buttermilk pancakes in town, though some prefer the eggy, perfect French toast (extra-crispy around the edges, please). Mouth-watering pies (blueberry cream cheese, coconut cream, and more) line the front display case and can be had for a song.

West Hollywood denizens can visit the branch of Du-par's in the Ramada Hotel, 8571 Santa Monica Blvd., west of La Cienega (☎ **310/659-7009**); it's open until 3am on weekends *and* has a full bar. There's another Du-par's in Los Angeles at the Farmers Market, 6333 W. 3rd St. (☎ **323/933-8446**), but it doesn't stay open as late.

7 Pasadena & Environs

EXPENSIVE

✪ **The Raymond.** 1250 S. Fair Oaks Ave. (at Columbia St.), Pasadena. ☎ **626/441-3136.** Reservations required. Main courses $12–$19 lunch, $29–$33 dinner, $43–$47 4-course dinner, prix fixe 3-course dinner $29 (including wine). AE, CB, DC, DISC, MC, V. Tues–Thurs 11:30am–2:30pm and 6–9:30pm; Fri 11:30am–2:30pm and 5:45–10pm; Sat 11am–2:30pm and 5:45–10pm; Sun 10am–2:30pm and 4:30–8pm; afternoon tea Tues–Sun noon–4pm. Free parking. NEW AMERICAN/CONTINENTAL.

With its easy-to-miss setting in a sleepy part of Pasadena, the Raymond is a jewel even few locals know about. This Craftsman cottage was once the caretaker's house for a grand Victorian hotel called The Raymond. Though the city has grown to surround it, the place maintains an enchanting air of seclusion and serenity. Chef/owner Suzanne Bourg brings a romantic sensibility and impeccable culinary instincts to dishes that are mostly haute American—with an occasional European flair. The menu changes weekly. One night a grilled rack of lamb is sauced with orange, Grand Marnier, and peppercorns; another night it comes with a creamy white wine and chèvre sauce punctuated with dried cherries. Bourg's soups are always heavenly (the restaurant gladly gives out the recipes), and desserts are inspired. Tables are scattered throughout the house and in the lush English garden, and there's plenty of free, nonvalet parking. (You wouldn't find *that* on the Westside!)

MODERATE

Cafe Santorini. 64 W. Union St. (main entrance at the shopping plaza at the corner of Fair Oaks and Colorado), Pasadena. ☎ **626/564-4200.** www. cafesantorini.com. Reservations recommended on weekends. Main courses $9–$22. AE, DISC, MC, V. Daily 11am–11pm (until midnight Fri–Sat). Valet parking $3.50; self-parking in area structures $4. GREEK/MEDITERRANEAN.

Located at ground zero of Pasadena's crowded Old Town shopping mecca, this second-story gem has a secluded Mediterranean ambience, due in part to its historic brick building with splendid patio tables overlooking, but insulated from, the busy plaza below. In the evening, lighting is subdued and romantic, but the ambience is casual; many diners are coming from or going to an adjacent movie-theater complex. The food is outstanding and affordable, featuring expertly grilled meats and kebobs, pizzas, fresh and tangy hummus, plenty of warm pitas, and other staples of Greek cuisine. The menu includes regional flavors like lamb, feta cheese, spinach, or 'Armenian sausage; the vegetarian baked butternut squash is filled with fluffy rice and smoky roast vegetables.

Yujean Kang's Gourmet Chinese Cuisine. 67 N. Raymond Ave. (between Walnut St. and Colorado Blvd.), Pasadena. ☎ **626/585-0855.** Reservations recommended. Main courses $8–$19. AE, MC, V. Daily 11:30am–2:30pm and 5–10pm. Street parking. CONTEMPORARY CHINESE.

Many Chinese restaurants put the word *gourmet* in their name, but few really mean it—or deserve it. Not so at Yujean Kang's, where Chinese cuisine is taken to an entirely new level. A master of "fusion" cuisine, the eponymous chef/owner snatches bits of techniques and flavors from both China and the West, co-mingling them in an entirely fresh way. Can you resist such provocative dishes as "Ants on Tree" (beef sautéed with glass noodles in chili and black sesame seeds), or lobster with caviar and fava beans, or Chilean sea bass in passion-fruit sauce? Kang is also a wine aficionado and has assembled a magnificent cellar of California, French, and particularly German wines. Try pairing a German Spätlese with tea-smoked duck salad. The red-wrapped dining room is less subtle than the food, but just as elegant.

There's a second Yujean Kang's in West Hollywood, at 8826 Melrose Ave. (☎ **310/288-0806**). Even though Kang consulted with a *feng shui* master on the location and layout of the new space, some Angelenos grumble about the less adventurous menu and higher prices. Others are just grateful they don't have to trek to Pasadena anymore.

INEXPENSIVE

✪ Old Town Bakery & Restaurant. 166 W. Colorado Blvd. (at Pasadena Ave.), Pasadena. ☎ **626/792-7943.** Main courses $5–$11. DISC, MC, V. Sun–Thurs 7:30am–10pm; Fri–Sat 7:30am–midnight. Metered street parking. CALIFORNIA/BAKERY.

Set back from the street in a quaint fountain courtyard, this cheery bakery is an especially popular place to read the morning paper over a tasty breakfast such as pumpkin pancakes or zesty omelets. The display counters are packed with cakes, muffins, scones, and other confections, all baked expressly for this shop. The rest of the menu is a mishmash of pastas, salads, and the like, borrowing heavily from Latin and Mediterranean cuisines. This is a great place to spy on local Pasadenans in their natural habitat.

5

What to See & Do in Los Angeles

*T*hese are exciting times for the cultural scene in L.A. New museums are opening up regularly. By far, the most notable is the $1 billion Getty Center, which dominates the Brentwood hillside. Other recent museum additions include such diverse entities as the Petersen Automotive Museum and the Museum of Tolerance.

But it's not just the museums that are experiencing a renaissance. The city and its planners know what side their bread is buttered on. The Walk of Fame, the Hollywood sign, Santa Monica Pier, and other traditional tourist draws are being spruced up; newer ones, like Universal CityWalk, have been added to L.A.'s repertoire; and L.A.'s theme parks are continually adding new attractions.

To find out what's going on while you're in town, pick up a copy of the free tabloid *L.A. Weekly,* the monthly magazine *Los Angeles,* or the Sunday *Los Angeles Times* "Calendar" section; each has detailed listings covering what's going on around town, often accompanied by entertaining and helpful commentary on which activities might be worth your while.

1 The Top Attractions

SANTA MONICA & THE BEACHES

✪ **Venice Ocean Front Walk.** On the beach, between Venice Blvd. and Rose Ave.

This has long been one of L.A.'s most colorful areas. Founded at the turn of the century, the town of Venice was a theme development inspired by its Italian namesake. Authentic Venetian gondolas plied miles of inland waterways lined with rococo palaces. In the 1950s, Venice became the celebrated stomping grounds of Jack Kerouac, Allen Ginsberg, William S. Burroughs, and other beats. In the 1960s, this was the epicenter of L.A.'s hippie scene.

Today, Venice is still one of the world's most engaging bohemias. It's not an exaggeration to say that no visit to L.A. would be complete without a stroll along the famous beach path, an almost-surreal assemblage of every L.A. stereotype—and then some. Among stalls and stands selling cheap sunglasses, Mexican blankets, and "herbal ecstasy" pills swirls a carnival of humanity that includes bikini-clad in-line skaters, tattooed bikers, muscle-bound pretty boys, panhandling vets, beautiful wanna-bes, and plenty of tourists and gawkers. On any given day, you're bound to come across all kinds of performers: mimes, break-dancers, buskers, chain-saw jugglers, talking parrots, or an occasional apocalyptic evangelist.

L.A.'S WESTSIDE & BEVERLY HILLS

✪ **J. Paul Getty Museum at the Getty Center.** 1200 Getty Center Dr., Los Angeles. ☎ **310/440-7300.** www.getty.edu. Free admission. Tues–Wed 11am–7pm, Thurs–Fri 11am–9pm, Sat–Sun 10am–6pm. Closed major holidays. Advance reservations required. Parking $5.

Since opening in December 1997, the Richard Meier–designed Getty Center has quickly assumed its place in the L.A. landscape (literally and figuratively) as a cultural cornerstone and international mecca. Headquarters for the Getty Trust's

---

The "Hollywood" CityPass

Beginning in 2000, the folks at **CityPass** (☎ **707/256-0490;** www.citypass.net) added Los Angeles to their nationwide list of destinations with money-saving combination attraction passes. Despite the name, the participating eight attractions are scattered throughout the L.A. area, even as far as Simi Valley's **Reagan Presidential Library & Museum.** The main draw, and the primary reason to purchase CityPass, is **Universal Studios Hollywood;** the rest are the **Hollywood Entertainment Museum, American Cinemateque at the Egyptian Theatre, Museum of Television and Radio, Museum of Tolerance, Petersen Automotive Museum,** and **Autry Museum of Western Heritage.** Purchase the pass at any of the eight attractions, or visit the CityPass Web site to buy advance passes online, find links to the attraction Web sites, and peruse hotel packages that include CityPass. The pass costs $49.95 for adults ($38 for kids 3 to 11) and will expire 9 days from the first use.

Los Angeles Attractions at a Glance

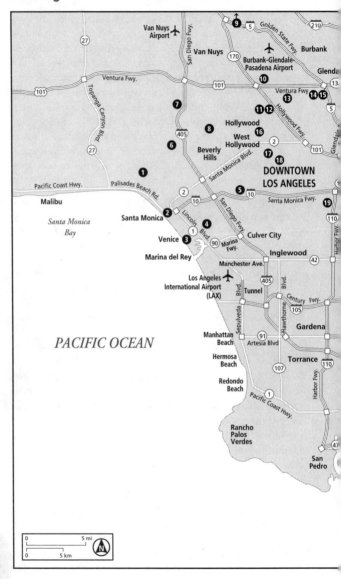

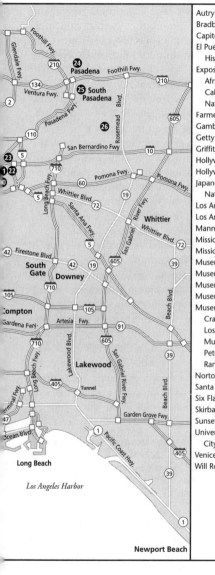

..search, education, and conservation concerns, the complex is most frequently visited for the museum galleries displaying collector J. Paul Getty's enormous collection of important art. Always known for antiquities, expanded galleries now allow the display of impressionist paintings, French decorative arts, fine illuminated manuscripts, and contemporary photography and graphic arts that were previously overlooked. A sophisticated system of programmable window louvers allows many outstanding works to be displayed in natural light for the first time in the modern era. One of these is van Gogh's *Irises,* one of the museum's finest holdings. Trivia buffs will enjoy knowing that the museum spent $53.9 million to acquire this painting; it's displayed in a complex that cost roughly $1 billion to construct.

Visitors to the center park at the base of the hill and ascend via a cable-driven electric tram. On clear days, the sensation is of being in the clouds, gazing across Los Angeles and the Pacific Ocean (and into a few chic Brentwood backyards). In addition to a casual cafe and several espresso/snack carts, the complex even has a bona fide restaurant on-site, complete with a panoramic view.

Parking reservations are in high demand on weekends, during the summer, and other vacation seasons when you're likely to be visiting. To be on the safe side, make your Getty Center reservations as early as possible. Even visitors without cars—those who arrive by taxi, tour bus, bicycle, and so on—aren't guaranteed admittance during high-volume periods. *Insider tip:* Avoid the crowds by visiting in the late afternoon or evening; the center is open until 9pm Thursdays and Fridays, the nighttime view is breathtaking, and you can finish with a late dinner on the Westside.

Rancho La Brea Tar Pits/George C. Page Museum. 5801 Wilshire Blvd. (east of Fairfax Ave.), Los Angeles. ☎ **323/934-PAGE.** www.tarpits.org. Admission $6 adults, $3.50 seniors 62 and older and students with ID, $2 children ages 5–12, free for kids age 4 and under; free for everyone the 1st Tues of every month. Daily 10am–5pm (museum).

An odorous, murky swamp of congealed oil continuously oozes to the earth's surface in the middle of Los Angeles. No, it's not a low-budget horror-movie set—it's the La Brea Tar Pits, an awesome, primal pool right on Museum Row, where hot tar has been bubbling from the earth for over 40,000 years. The glistening pools, which look like murky water, have enticed thirsty animals throughout history. Thousands of mammals, birds, amphibians,

and insects—many of which are now extinct—mis
crawled into the sticky sludge and stayed forever. In 1906
tists began a systematic removal and classification of entombed
specimens, including ground sloths, giant vultures, mastodons,
camels, bears, lizards, even prehistoric relatives of today's beloved
super-rats. The best finds are on display in the adjacent George
C. Page Museum of La Brea Discoveries, where an excellent
15-minute film documenting the recoveries is also shown.
Archaeological work is ongoing; you can watch as scientists clean,
identify, and catalog new finds in the Paleontology Laboratory.

HOLLYWOOD

Farmers Market. 6333 W. 3rd St. (corner of Fairfax Ave.). ☎ **323/933-9211.** Mon–Sat 9am–6:30pm, Sun 10am–5pm.

The original market was little more than a field clustered with
stands set up by farmers during the Depression so they could sell
directly to city dwellers. Eventually, permanent buildings grew
up, including the trademark shingled 10-story clock tower. Today
the place has evolved into a sprawling food marketplace with a
carnival atmosphere, a kind of "turf" version of San Francisco's
surfy Fisherman's Wharf. About 100 restaurants, shops, and gro-
cers cater to a mix of workers from the adjacent CBS Television
City complex, locals, and tourists, who are brought here by
the busload. Retailers sell greeting cards, kitchen implements,
candles, and souvenirs; but everyone comes here for the food
stands, which offer oysters, Cajun gumbo, fresh-squeezed orange
juice, roast-beef sandwiches, fresh-pressed peanut butter, and all
kinds of international fast foods. You can still buy produce here—
it's no longer a farm-fresh bargain, but the selection's better than
at the grocery stores. Don't miss **Kokomo,** a "gourmet" outdoor
coffee shop that has become a power breakfast spot for showbiz
types. Red turkey hash and sweet-potato fries are the dishes that
keep them coming back.

✪ **Griffith Observatory.** 2800 E. Observatory Rd. (in Griffith Park, at the
end of Vermont Ave.). ☎ **323/664-1191,** or 323/663-8171 for the Sky
Report, a recorded message on current planet positions and celestial events.
www.griffithobservatory.org. Free admission; planetarium show tickets $4
adults, $3 seniors, $2 children. June–Aug daily 12:30–10pm; Sept–May Tues–Fri
2–10pm, Sat–Sun 12:30–10pm.

Made world-famous in the film *Rebel Without a Cause,* Griffith
Observatory's bronze domes have been Hollywood Hills landmarks since 1935. Most visitors never actually go inside; they

come to this spot on the south slope of Mount Hollywood for unparalleled city views. On warm nights, with the lights twinkling below, this is one of the most romantic places in L.A.

The main dome houses a **planetarium,** where narrated projection shows reveal the stars and planets that are hidden from the naked eye by the city's lights and smog. Other shows take you on excursions into space to search for extraterrestrial life, or examine the causes of earthquakes, moonquakes, and starquakes. Presentations last about an hour. Show times vary, so call for information.

The adjacent **Hall of Science** holds exhibits on galaxies, meteorites, and other cosmic objects, including a telescope trained on the sun, a Foucault pendulum, and earth and moon globes 6 feet in diameter. On clear nights you can gaze at the heavens through the powerful 12-inch telescope.

Hollywood Sign. At the top of Beachwood Dr., Hollywood.

These 50-foot-high white sheet-metal letters have come to symbolize both the movie industry and the city itself. The sign was erected in 1923 as an advertisement for a fledgling real-estate development. The full text originally read HOLLYWOODLAND. Actress Peg Entwistle leapt to her death from the "H" in 1932. An earthquake-monitoring seismograph is now buried near its base. The installation of motion detectors around the sign just made this graffiti tagger's coup a target even more worth boasting about. A thorny hiking trail leads toward the sign from Durand Drive near Beachwood Drive, but the best view is from down below, at the corner of Sunset Boulevard and Bronson Avenue.

Hollywood Walk of Fame. Hollywood Blvd., between Gower St. and La Brea Ave.; and Vine St., between Yucca St. and Sunset Blvd. ☎ **323/469-8311.**

More than 2,500 celebrities are honored along the world's most famous sidewalk. Each bronze medallion, set into the center of a granite star, pays homage to a famous television, film, radio, theater, or recording personality. Although about a third of them are just about as obscure as Andromeda—their fame simply hasn't withstood the test of time—millions of visitors are thrilled by the sight of famous names like **James Dean** (1719 Vine St.), **John Lennon** (1750 Vine St.), **Marlon Brando** (1765 Vine St.), **Rudolph Valentino** (6164 Hollywood Blvd.), **Marilyn Monroe** (6744 Hollywood Blvd.), **Elvis Presley** (6777 Hollywood Blvd.), **Greta Garbo** (6901 Hollywood Blvd.), **Louis Armstrong** (7000 Hollywood Blvd.), and **Barbra Streisand** (6925 Hollywood Blvd).

The sight of bikers, metalheads, druggies, hookers, and hordes of disoriented tourists all treading on memorials to Hollywood's greats makes for quite a bizarre tribute indeed. But the Hollywood Chamber of Commerce has been doing a terrific job sprucing up the pedestrian experience with filmstrip crosswalks, swaying palms, and more. And at least one weekend a month, a privately organized group of fans calling themselves Star Polishers busy themselves scrubbing tarnished medallions.

The legendary sidewalk is continually adding new names. The public is invited to attend dedication ceremonies; the honoree is usually in attendance. Contact the **Hollywood Chamber of Commerce,** 6255 Sunset Blvd., Suite 911, Hollywood, CA 90028 (☎ **323/469-8311**), for information on who's being honored this week.

Mann's Chinese Theatre. 6925 Hollywood Blvd. (3 blocks west of Highland Ave.). ☎ **323/464-8111** or 323/461-3331. Movie tickets $8.50. Call for show times.

This is one of the world's great movie palaces and one of Hollywood's finest landmarks. The Chinese Theatre was opened in 1927 by entertainment impresario Sid Grauman, a brilliant promoter who's credited with originating the idea of the paparazzi-packed movie "premiere." Outrageously conceived, with both authentic and simulated Chinese embellishments, gaudy Grauman's theater was designed to impress. Original Chinese heavenly doves top the facade, and two of the theater's exterior columns once propped up a Ming Dynasty temple.

Visitors flock to the theater by the millions for its world-famous entry court, where stars like Elizabeth Taylor, Paul Newman, Ginger Rogers, Humphrey Bogart, Frank Sinatra, Marilyn Monroe, and about 160 others set their signatures and hand- and footprints in concrete. It's not always hands and feet, though: Betty Grable made an impression with her shapely leg; Gene Autry with the hoofprints of his horse, Champion; and Jimmy Durante and Bob Hope with their trademark noses.

DOWNTOWN
El Pueblo de Los Angeles Historic Monument. Enter on Alameda St. across from Union Station. ☎ **213/628-1274.** www.cityofla.org/elp.

This historic district was built in the 1930s, on the site where the city was founded, as an alternative to the wholesale razing of a particularly unsightly slum. The result is a contrived nostalgic fantasy of the city's beginnings, a kitschy theme park portraying Latino culture in a Disneyesque fashion. Nevertheless, El Pueblo has proven wildly successful, as L.A.'s Latinos have adopted it as an important cultural monument.

El Pueblo is not entirely without authenticity. Some of L.A.'s oldest buildings are located here, and the area really does exude the ambience of Old Mexico. At its core is a Mexican-style marketplace on old Olvera Street. The carnival of sights and sounds is heightened by mariachis, colorful piñatas, and more-than-occasional folkloric dancing. Olvera Street, the district's primary pedestrian thoroughfare, and adjacent Main Street are home to about two dozen 19th-century buildings; one houses an authentic Mexican restaurant, **La Golondrina.** Stop in at the **visitor center,** 622 N. Main St. (☎ **213/628-1274;** open Monday to Saturday from 10am to 3pm). Don't miss the **Avila Adobe,** at E-10 Olvera St. (open Mon to Sat from 10am to 5pm); built in 1818, it's the oldest building in the city.

THE SAN FERNANDO VALLEY

✪ **Universal Studios Hollywood.** Hollywood Fwy. (Universal Center Dr. or Lankershim Blvd. exits), Universal City. ☎ **818/662-3801.** www.universalstudios. com. Admission $41 adults, $36 seniors 60 and over, $31 children ages 3–11, free for kids under age 3. Parking $7. Summer daily 8am–10pm; the rest of the year daily 9am–7pm.

Believing that filmmaking itself was a bona fide attraction, Universal Studios began offering tours to the public in 1964. The concept worked. Today Universal is more than just one of the largest movie studios in the world—it's one of the biggest amusement parks.

The main attraction continues to be the **Studio Tour,** a 1-hour guided tram ride around the company's 420 acres. En route you pass stars' dressing rooms and production offices before visiting famous back-lot sets that include an eerily familiar Old West town, a clean New York City street, and the famous town square from the *Back to the Future* films. Along the way the tram encounters several staged "disasters," which we won't divulge here lest we ruin the surprise.

Other attractions are more typical of high-tech theme-park fare, but all have a film-oriented slant. On **Back to the Future— The Ride,** you're seated in a mock time-traveling DeLorean and thrust into a fantastic multimedia roller-coasting extravaganza— it's far and away Universal's best ride. The **Waterworld** live-action

stunt show is thrilling to watch (and probably m
than the film that inspired it), while the special-eff
Jurassic Park—The Ride, is short in duration but long on
dinosaur illusions and computer magic lifted from the Universal
blockbuster. The latest thrill is **Terminator 2 3-D,** a virtual
adventure utilizing triple-screen technology to impact all the
senses. **Totally Nickelodeon** is an interactive live show from the
kids' TV network, providing adventure and gallons of green
slime.

Universal Studios is a really fun place. But just as in any theme
park, lines can be long; the wait for a 5-minute ride can sometimes last more than an hour. In summer, the stifling Valley heat
can dog you all day. To avoid the crowds, skip weekends, school
vacations, and Japanese holidays.

PASADENA & ENVIRONS

✪ **Huntington Library, Art Collections, and Botanical Gardens.** 1151
Oxford Rd., San Marino. ☎ **626/405-2141.** www.huntington.org. Admis-
sion $8.50 adults, $8 seniors 65 and over, $6 students and children age 12 and
over, free to children under age 12; free to all the 1st Thurs of each month.
Sept–May Tues–Fri noon–4:30pm; Sat–Sun 10:30am–4:30pm; June–Aug
Tues–Sun 10:30am–4:30pm. Closed major holidays.

The Huntington Library is the jewel in Pasadena's crown. The
207-acre hilltop estate was once home to industrialist and railroad
magnate Henry E. Huntington (1850 to 1927), who bought
books on the same massive scale on which he acquired businesses.
The continually expanding collection includes dozens of Shake-
speare's original works, Benjamin Franklin's handwritten autobi-
ography, a Gutenberg Bible from the 1450s, and the earliest
known manuscript of Chaucer's *Canterbury Tales.* Although some
rare works are available only to visiting scholars, the library has
a regularly changing (and always excellent) exhibit showcasing
different items in the collection.

If you prefer canvas to parchment, Huntington also put
together a terrific 18th-century British and French art collection.
The most celebrated paintings are Gainsborough's *The Blue Boy*
and *Pinkie,* a companion piece by Sir Thomas Lawrence depicting the youthful aunt of Elizabeth Barrett Browning. These and
other works are displayed in the stately Italianate mansion on the
crest of this hillside estate, so you can also get a glimpse of its
splendid furnishings.

But it's the **botanical gardens** that draw most locals to the Huntington. The Japanese Garden comes complete with a traditional open-air Japanese house, koi-filled stream, and serene Zen garden. The cactus garden is exotic, the jungle garden is intriguing, the lily ponds are soothing—and there are many benches scattered about so you can sit and enjoy the surroundings.

Because the Huntington surprises many with its size and wealth of activities to choose from, first-timers might want to start by attending one of the regularly scheduled 12-minute introductory slide shows; you can also take the more in-depth 1-hour garden tour, given each day at 1pm. We also recommend that you tailor your visit to include the popular English high tea served Tuesday through Sunday from 1:30 to 3:30pm. The charming tearoom overlooks the Rose Garden (home to 1,000 varieties displayed in chronological order of their breeding), and since the finger sandwiches and desserts are served buffet style, it's a genteel bargain (even for hearty appetites) at $11 per person. Phone ☎ **626/683-8131** for reservations.

2 TV Tapings

Being part of the audience for the taping of a television show might be the quintessential L.A. experience. This is a great way to see Hollywood at work, to find out how your favorite sitcom or talk show is made, and to catch a glimpse of your favorite TV personalities. Timing is important here—remember that most series productions go on hiatus between March and July. And tickets to the top shows, like *Friends* and *Everybody Loves Raymond,* are in greater demand than others, so getting your hands on them usually takes advance planning—and possibly some time waiting in line.

Request tickets as far in advance as possible. Several episodes may be shot on a single day, so you may be required to remain in the theater for up to 4 hours (in addition to the recommended 1-hour early check-in). If you phone at the last moment, you may luck into tickets for your top choice. More likely, however, you'll be given a list of shows that are currently filming, and you won't recognize many of the titles; studios are always taping pilots, few of which end up on the air. But you never know who may be starring in them—look at all the famous faces that have launched new sitcoms in the past couple of years. Tickets are always free, usually limited to two per person, and are distributed on a first-come, first-served basis. Many shows don't admit children under the age of 10; in some cases no one under the age of 18 is admitted.

Tickets are sometimes given away to the public outside popular tourist sites like Mann's Chinese Theatre in Hollywood and Universal Studios in the Valley; L.A.'s visitor information centers in downtown and Hollywood often have tickets as well (see "Orientation," in chapter 2). But if you're determined to see a particular show, contact the following suppliers:

Audiences Unlimited (☎ 818/506-0043 or 818/506-0067) is a good place to start. It distributes tickets for most of the top sitcoms, including *Friends, Saved by the Bell, Caroline in the City, Suddenly Susan, 3rd Rock from the Sun, Everybody Loves Raymond,* and many more. This service is organized and informative, and fully sanctioned by production companies and networks. ABC, for example, no longer handles ticket distribution directly, but refers all inquiries to Audiences Unlimited. **Television Tickets** (☎ 323/467-4697) distributes tickets for talk and game shows, including the popular *Jeopardy!* show.

You also may want to contact the networks directly for information on a specific show, including some whose tickets are not available at the above agencies. At **ABC,** all ticket inquiries are referred to Audiences Unlimited (see above), but you may want to check out ABC's Web site at **www.abc.com** for a colorful look at its lineup and links to specific shows' sites. For tickets to *Politically Incorrect with Bill Maher,* call the show's ticket line at ☎ 323/852-2655 to make a reservation (taken on a first-come, first-served basis), or order online at **www.abc.com/pi**.

For **CBS,** 7800 Beverly Blvd., Los Angeles, CA 90036 (☎ 323/852-2458), call to see what's being filmed while you're in town. Tickets for CBS tapings are distributed on a first-come, first-served basis; you can write in advance to reserve them or pick them up directly at the studio up to an hour before taping. Tickets for many CBS sitcoms, including *Everybody Loves Raymond,* are also available from Audiences Unlimited (see above). Tickets for *The Price Is Right* must be requested by mail; allow 4 to 6 weeks. For a virtual visit to CBS's shows, log on to **www.cbs.com**.

For **NBC,** 3000 W. Alameda Ave., Burbank, CA 91523 (☎ 818/840-4444 or 818/840-3537), call to see what's on while you're in L.A. Tickets for NBC tapings, including *The Tonight Show with Jay Leno,* can be obtained in two ways: either pick them up at the NBC ticket counter on the day of the show you want to see (they're distributed on a first-come, first-served basis at the ticket counter off California Avenue), or, at least 3 weeks before your visit, send a self-addressed, stamped envelope with your ticket request to the address above. All the NBC shows are represented online at **www.nbc.com**.

3 More City Sights & Attractions

ARCHITECTURAL HIGHLIGHTS

Los Angeles is a veritable Disneyland of architecture. The city is home to an amalgam of distinctive styles, from art deco to Spanish revival to coffee-shop kitsch to suburban ranch to postmodern—and much more.

The movie industry, more than anything else, has defined Los Angeles. The process of moviemaking isn't—and never has been—confined to studio offices and back lots; it spills out into the city's streets and other public spaces. The city itself is an extension of the movie set, and Angelenos have always seen it that way. Therefore, all of Los Angeles has an air of Hollywood sureality, even in its architecture. The whole city seems a bit larger than life. Cutting-edge, over-the-top styles that would be out of place in other cities, from Tail o' the Pup to the mansions lining the streets of Beverly Hills, are perfectly at home in L.A. The world's top architects, from Frank Lloyd Wright to Frank Gehry, have flocked to L.A., reveling in the artistic freedom here. Between 1945 and 1966, *Arts & Architecture* magazine focused the design world's attention on L.A. with its series of "Case Study Houses," modern prototypes for postwar living, many of which were designed by prominent émigrés like Pierre Koenig, Richard Neutra, and Eero Saarinen. Los Angeles has taken some hard criticism for not being a "serious" architectural center, but in terms of innovation and personal style, the city couldn't get higher marks.

Although much of it is gone, you'll still find some prime examples of the kitschy roadside art that defined L.A. in earlier days. The famous Brown Derby is no more, but you can still find an oversized hot dog (the aforementioned **Tail o' the Pup;** see below) and a neon-lit **1950s gas station/spaceship** (at the corner of Little Santa Monica Boulevard and Crescent Drive in Beverly Hills), in addition to some new structures carrying on the tradition, such as the **Chiat/Day offices** in Venice (see below).

Pacific Design Center. 8687 Melrose Ave., West Hollywood. ☎ **310/ 657-0800.**

The bold architecture and overwhelming scale of the Pacific Design Center, designed by Argentinean architect Cesar Pelli, aroused plenty of controversy when it was erected in 1975. Sheathed in gently curving cobalt-blue glass, the seven-story building houses over 750,000 square feet of wholesale interior-design showrooms and is known to locals as "the blue whale." When the property for the design center was acquired in the 1970s, almost all of the small businesses that lined this stretch of Melrose Avenue were demolished. Only tenacious Hugo's Plating, which still stands in front of the center, successfully resisted the wrecking ball. In 1988, a second box-like structure, dressed in equally dramatic kelly green, was added to the design center and surrounded by a protected outdoor plaza.

Schindler House. 835 N. Kings Rd. (north of Melrose Ave.), West Hollywood. ☎ **323/651-1510.** E-mail: MAKcenter@earthlink.net. Admission $5 adults, free to children age 12 and under. Free to all on Sept 10 (Schindler's birthday), May 24 (International Museum Day), Dec 1, and every Fri after 4pm. Wed–Sun 11am–6pm.

A protégé of Frank Lloyd Wright and contemporary of Richard Neutra, Austrian architect Rudolph Schindler designed this innovative modern house for himself in 1921–22. It's now home to the Los Angeles arm of Austria's Museum of Applied Arts (MAK). The house is noted for its complicated interlocking spaces; the interpenetration of indoors and out; simple, unadorned materials; and technological innovations. Docent-guided tours are conducted at no additional charge on weekends only.

The MAK Center offers guides to L.A.-area buildings by Schindler and other Austrian architects, and presents visiting related exhibitions and creative arts programming. Call for schedules.

✪ **Tail o' the Pup.** San Vicente Blvd. (between Beverly Blvd. and Melrose Ave.), West Hollywood. ☎ **310/652-4517.**

At first glance, you might not think twice about this hot dog–shaped bit of kitsch just across from the Beverly Center. But locals adored this closet-sized wiener dispensary so much that when it was threatened by the developer's bulldozer, they spoke out en masse to save it. One of the last remaining examples of 1950s representational architecture, the "little dog that could" also serves up a great Baseball Special.

Capitol Records Building. 1750 Vine St., Hollywood. ☎ **323/462-6252.**

Opened in 1956, this 12-story tower, just north of the legendary intersection of Hollywood and Vine, is one of the city's most recognizable buildings. This circular tower is often, but incorrectly, said to have been made to resemble a stack of 45s under a turntable stylus (it kinda does, though). Nat "King" Cole, songwriter Johnny Mercer, and other 1950s Capitol artists populate a giant exterior mural.

The Bradbury Building. 304 S. Broadway (at 3rd St.), Downtown. ☎ **213/626-1893.** Daily 9am–5pm.

This National Historic Landmark, built in 1893, is Los Angeles's oldest commercial building and one of the city's most revered architectural achievements. Capped by a magical five-story skylight, Bradbury's courtyard combines glazed brick, Mexican tile, rich Belgian marble, handsome oak paneling, and lacelike wrought-iron railings. The glass-topped atrium is often used as a movie and TV set; you've seen it in *Chinatown* and *Blade Runner.*

Central Library. 630 W. 5th St. (between Flower St. and Grand Ave.), Downtown. ☎ **213/228-7000.** www.lapl.org.

This is one of L.A.'s early architectural achievements. The city rallied to save the library when arson nearly destroyed it in 1986; the triumphant restoration has returned much of its original splendor. Working in the early 1920s, architect Bertram G. Goodhue employed the Egyptian motifs and materials popularized by the recent discovery of King Tut's tomb, and combined them with a more modern use of concrete block to great effect. *Warning:* Parking in this area can involve a heroic effort. Try visiting on the weekend and using the Flower Street parking entrance; the library will validate your ticket, and you can escape for only $2.

Union Station. Alameda St. (at Cesar E. Chavez Ave.), Downtown.

Union Station, completed in 1939, is one of the finest examples of California mission–style architecture. It was built with the opulence and attention to detail that characterize 1930s W.P.A. projects. The cathedral-size, richly paneled ticket lobby and waiting area of this fantastic cream-colored structure stand sadly empty most of the time, but the MTA does use Union Station for Blue Line commuter trains. When you're strolling through these grand historic halls, it's easy to imagine the glamorous movie stars who once boarded *The City of Los Angeles* and *The Super Chief* to journey back east during the glory days of rail travel; I also like to picture the many joyous reunions between returning soldiers and loved ones following the victorious end to World War II, in the station's heyday.

✪ **The Gamble House.** 4 Westmoreland Place, Pasadena. ☎ **626/ 793-3334.** www.gamblehouse.usc.edu. Admission $8 adults, $6 students and seniors 65+, free for children under 12. Thurs–Sun noon–3pm. Closed holidays.

The huge two-story Gamble House, built in 1908 as a California vacation home for the wealthy family of Procter and Gamble fame, is a sublime example of Arts-and-Crafts architecture. The interior, designed by the famous Pasadena-based Greene and Greene architectural team, abounds with handcraftsmanship, including intricately carved teak cornices, custom-designed furnishings, elaborate carpets, and a fantastic Tiffany glass door. No detail was overlooked. Every oak wedge, downspout, air vent, and switch plate contributes to the unified design. Admission is by 1-hour guided tour only, which departs every 15 minutes. No reservations are necessary.

If you can't fit the tour into your schedule but have a love of Craftsman design, visit the well-stocked bookstore and museum shop located in the former garage (you can also see the exterior and grounds of the house this way). The bookstore is open Tuesday through Sunday 10am to 5pm.

Additional elegant Greene & Greene creations (still privately owned) abound 2 blocks away along **Arroyo Terrace,** including address nos. **368, 370, 400, 408, 424,** and **440.** The Gamble House bookstore can give you a walking-tour map and also conducts guided neighborhood tours by appointment.

ORGANIZED TOURS OF ARCHITECTURAL INTEREST

The **L.A. Conservancy** (☎ 213/623-2489) conducts a dozen fascinating, information-packed walking tours of historic **Downtown L.A.,** seed of today's sprawling metropolis. The most popular is "Broadway Theaters," a loving look at movie palaces. Other intriguing tours include "Marble Masterpieces," "Art Deco," "Mecca for Merchants," "Terra-Cotta," and tours of the landmark Biltmore Hotel and City Hall. They cost $5 and are usually held on Saturday mornings. Call Monday to Friday between 9am and 5pm for exact schedule and information.

In **Pasadena,** various tours spotlighting architecture or neighborhoods are lots of fun, given this area's history of wealthy estates and ardent preservation. Call **Pasadena Heritage** (☎ **626/793-0617**) for a schedule of guided tours, or pick up "Ten Tours of Pasadena" (self-guided walking or driving maps), available at the **Pasadena Convention and Visitors Bureau,** 171 S. Los Robles Ave. (☎ **626/795-9311**).

For a unique and entertaining tour of Southern California's "vernacular architecture"—what we laypeople might call "kitsch"—sign up for a **Googie Tour** of L.A. and environs. Named for the defunct midcentury coffee-shop chain whose style was best captured in the cartoon chic of *The Jetsons,* the grass-roots safari takes you to an "Aztec/Egyptian/atomic bowling center," a Polynesian-themed cocktail lounge, and various other exuberant expressions of the Atomic Age. Reservations are required, and prices start at $40 per person for a 5-hour tour. For a current schedule, call ☎ **323/980-3480.**

MISSIONS

In the late 18th century, Franciscan missionaries established 21 missions up the California coast, from San Diego to Sonoma. Each uniquely beautiful mission was built 1 day's trek from the next, along a path known as El Camino Real (the Royal Road), remnants of which still exist today. The missions' construction marked the beginning of European settlement of California and the displacement of the Native American population. The two L.A.-area missions are located in the valleys that took their names: the San Fernando Valley and the San Gabriel Valley (near Pasadena). A third mission, San Juan Capistrano, is located in Orange County.

Mission San Fernando. 15151 San Fernando Mission Blvd., Mission Hills. ☎ **818/361-0186.** Admission $4 adults, $3 seniors and children under age 13. Daily 9am–5pm. From I-5, exit at San Fernando Mission Blvd. east and drive 5 blocks to the mission.

Established in 1797, Mission San Fernando once controlled more than 1^1/2 million acres, employed 1,500 Native Americans, and boasted more than 22,000 head of cattle and extensive orchards. The fragile adobe mission complex was destroyed several times, but it was always faithfully rebuilt with low buildings surrounding grassy courtyards. The aging church was replaced in the 1940s, and again in the 1970s after a particularly destructive earthquake. The Convento, a 250-foot-long colonnaded structure dating from 1810, is the compound's oldest remaining building. Some of the mission's rooms, including the old library and the private salon of the first bishop of California, have been restored to their late–18th-century appearance. A half-dozen padres and many hundreds of Shoshone Indians are buried in the adjacent cemetery.

Mission San Gabriel Arcangel. 428 S. Mission Dr., San Gabriel (15 min. south of Pasadena). ☎ **626/457-3035.** www.sangabrielmission.org. Admission $4 adults, $1 children ages 6–12, free for kids age 5 and under. Daily 9am–5pm. Closed holidays.

Founded in 1771, Mission San Gabriel Arcangel still retains its original facade, notable for its high oblong windows and large capped buttresses that are said to have been influenced by the cathedral in Cordova, Spain. The mission's self-contained compound encompasses an aqueduct, a cemetery, a tannery, and a working winery. Within the church stands a copper font with the dubious distinction of being the first one used to baptize a Native Californian. The most notable contents of the mission's museum are Native American paintings depicting the Stations of the Cross, done on sailcloth, with colors made from crushed desert flower petals.

MORE MUSEUMS & GALLERIES

Also see "The Top Attractions," above.

SANTA MONICA & THE BEACHES

Museum of Flying. At Santa Monica Airport, 2772 Donald Douglas Loop N., Santa Monica. ☎ **310/392-8822.** www.mof.org/mof. Admission $7 adults, $5 seniors, $3 children under age 16. Wed–Sun 10am–5pm.

Once headquarters of the McDonnell Douglas corporation, the Santa Monica Airport is the birthplace of the DC-3 and other pioneers of commercial aviation. The museum celebrates this bit of local history with 24 authentic aircraft displays and some interactive exhibits. In addition to antique Spitfires and Sopwith Camels, there's a new kid-oriented learning area, where hands-on exhibits detail airplane parts, pilot procedures, and the properties of air and aircraft design. The museum shop is full of scale models of World War II birds; the coffee-table book *The Best of the Past* beautifully illustrates 50 years of aviation history.

L.A.'s WESTSIDE & BEVERLY HILLS

Museum of Television and Radio. 465 N. Beverly Dr. (at Santa Monica Blvd.), Beverly Hills. ☎ **310/786-1000.** www.mtr.org/camsm. Suggested contribution $6 adults, $4 students and seniors, $3 kids age 12 and under. Wed and Fri–Sun noon–5pm, Thurs noon–9pm. Closed New Year's Day, July 4, Thanksgiving Day, and Christmas Day. Parking free for 2 hours with validation.

Want to see the Beatles on *The Ed Sullivan Show* (1964), or Edward R. Murrow's examination of Joseph McCarthy (1954), or Arnold Palmer's victory in the 1958 Masters Tournament, or listen to radio excerpts like FDR's first "Fireside Chat" (1933) and Orson Welles's famous *War of the Worlds* UFO hoax (1938)? All these, plus a gazillion episodes of *The Twilight Zone, I Love Lucy,* and other beloved series, can be viewed within the starkly white walls of architect Richard Meier's neutral, contemporary museum building. Like the ritzy Beverly Hills shopping district that surrounds it, the museum is more flash than substance. Once you gawk at the celebrity and industry-honcho names adorning every hall, room, and miscellaneous area, it becomes quickly apparent that "library" would be a more fitting name for this collection, since the main attractions are requested via sophisticated computer catalogs and viewed in private consoles. Although no one sets out to spend a vacation watching TV, it can be tempting once you start browsing the archives. This West Coast branch of the 20-year-old New York facility succeeds in treating our favorite pastime as a legitimate art form, with the respect history will prove it deserves.

Museum of Tolerance. 9786 W. Pico Blvd. (at Roxbury Dr.). ☎ **310/553-8403.** www.wiesenthal.com. Admission $8.50 adults, $6.50 seniors, $5.50 students, $3.50 children ages 3–12, free for children age 2 and under. Advance purchase recommended. Mon–Thurs 10am–4pm, Fri 10am–3pm (to 1pm Nov–Mar), Sun 11am–5pm (closing hours represent last entry time). Closed many Jewish and secular holidays; call for schedule.

The Museum of Tolerance is designed to expose prejudices and to teach racial and cultural tolerance. It's located in the Simon Wiesenthal Center, an institute founded by the legendary Nazi-hunter. While the Holocaust figures prominently here, this is not just a Jewish museum—it's an academy that broadly campaigns for a live-and-let-live world. Tolerance is an abstract idea that's hard to display, so most of this $50 million museum's exhibits are high-tech and conceptual in nature. Fast-paced interactive displays are designed to touch the heart as well as the mind, and engage both serious investigators and the MTV crowd. One of two major museums in America that deal with the Holocaust, the Museum of Tolerance is considered by many to be inferior to its Washington, D.C., counterpart. Visitors might be frustrated by the museum's policy of insisting that you follow a prescribed $2^{1}/_{2}$-hour route through the exhibits.

Skirball Cultural Center. 2701 No. Sepulveda Blvd. (at Mulholland Dr.). ☎ **310/440-4500.** www.skirball.org. Admission $8 adults, $6 students and seniors 65 and over, free for kids under 12. Tues–Sat noon–5pm, Sun 11am–5pm. Free parking. From I-405, exit at Skirball Center Dr./Mulholland Dr.

This strikingly modern museum/cultural center is quick to remind us that Jewish history is about more than the Holocaust. Nestled in the Sepulveda Pass uphill from the Getty Center, the Skirball explores American Jewish life, American democratic values, and the pursuit of the American Dream—a theme shared by many immigrant groups. The Skirball's core exhibits chronicle the journey of the Jewish people through the ages, with particular emphasis on American Jewry. Related events are held here throughout the year; one recent highlight was a rollicking festival of klezmer music (a traditional Jewish folk style).

HOLLYWOOD

✪ **Autry Museum of Western Heritage.** 4700 Western Heritage Way (in Griffith Park). ☎ **323/667-2000.** www.autry-museum.org. Admission $7.50 adults, $5 seniors 60 and over and students ages 13–18, $3 children ages 2–12, free for kids under age 2. Tues–Sun 10am–5pm (Thurs until 8pm). Free to all 2nd Tues each month.

If you're under the age of 45, you might not be familiar with Gene Autry, a Texas-born actor who starred in 82 westerns and became known as the "Singing Cowboy." Located north of Downtown in Griffith Park, his eponymous museum is one of California's best, a collection of art and artifacts of the European conquest of the West, remarkably comprehensive and intelligently displayed. Evocative exhibits illustrate the everyday lives of early pioneers, not only with antique firearms, tools, saddles, and the like, but with many hands-on displays that successfully stir the imagination and the heart. You'll find footage from Buffalo Bill's Wild West Show, movie clips from the silent days, contemporary films, the works of Wild West artists, and plenty of memorabilia from Autry's own film and TV projects. The "Hall of Merchandising" displays Roy Rogers bedspreads, Hopalong Cassidy radios, and other items from the collective consciousness—and material collections—of baby boomers.

Craft & Folk Art Museum. 5814 Wilshire Blvd. (at Curson Ave.). ☎ **323/ 937-4230.** Admission $3.50 adults, $2.50 seniors and students, free for children under age 12, free to all Thurs 5–9pm. Tues–Wed and Fri noon–5pm, Thurs noon–9pm, Sat 10am–4pm.

This gallery, housed in a prominent Museum Row building, has grown into one of the city's largest. "Craft and folk art" is a large rubric that encompasses everything from clothing, tools, religious artifacts, and other everyday objects to wood carvings, papier-mâché, weaving, and metalwork. The museum displays folk objects from around the world, but its strongest collection is masks from India, America, Mexico, Japan, and China. The museum is also well known for its annual International Festival of Masks, a colorful celebration held each October in Hancock Park, across the street.

✪ **Los Angeles County Museum of Art.** 5905 Wilshire Blvd. ☎ **323/ 857-6000.** www.lacma.org. Admission $7 adults, $5 students and seniors age 62 and over, $1 children ages 6–17, free for kids age 5 and under; regular exhibitions free for everyone the 2nd Tues of each month. Mon–Tues and Thurs noon–8pm, Fri noon–9pm, Sat–Sun 11am–8pm.

This is one of the finest art museums around. The huge complex was designed by three very different architects over a span of 30 years. The architectural fusion can be migraine inducing, but this city landmark is well worth delving into.

The newest wing is the **Japanese Pavilion,** which has exterior walls made of Kalwall, a translucent material that, like shoji screens, permits the entry of soft natural light. Inside is a collection of Japanese Edo paintings that's rivaled only by the holdings of the emperor of Japan. The **Anderson Building,** the museum's contemporary wing, is home to 20th-century painting and sculpture. Here you'll find works by Matisse, Magritte, and a good number of Dada artists. The **Ahmanson Building** houses the rest of the museum's permanent collections. Here you'll find everything from 2,000-year-old pre-Columbian Mexican ceramics to 19th-century portraiture to a unique glass collection spanning the centuries. Other displays include one of the nation's largest holdings of costumes and textiles, and an important Indian and Southeast Asian art collection. The **Hammer Building** is primarily used for major special-loan exhibitions. Free guided tours covering the museum's highlights depart on a regular basis from here.

The museum recently took over the former May Company department store 1 block away, converting the historic art deco building into gallery space. For information on film programs at the museum's **Leo S. Bing Theater,** see "Movies: Play It Again, Sam," p. 198, in chapter 7.

Museum of Miniatures. 5900 Wilshire Blvd. ☎ **323/937-MINI.** www.museumofminiatures.com. Admission $7.50 adults, $6.50 seniors, $5 students, $3 children. Tues–Sat 10am–5pm, Sun 11am–5pm.

With almost 200 exhibits, the Museum of Miniatures is the world's largest repository of diminutive mansions, pint-size automobiles, and intricately decorated minirooms. Completely unbeknownst to most, miniature making is a thriving and popular art; almost everything in this museum has been created within the past 15 years. And we're not talking mere dollhouses here (though they have those, too): The Museum of Miniatures has perfect one-twelfth–scale minis of an antebellum mansion, a Benedictine abbey, and an entire Victorian village. It even has an intricately detailed miniature re-creation of the *Titanic,* crafted from 75,000 toothpicks. Miniature 18K-gold train cars full of rubies, sapphires, and emeralds are pulled by an engine encrusted with almost 200 diamonds. The wonderful museum gift shop has tiny tea sets, clocks, and Louis XV "chair" brooches; bring your life-size wallet.

✪ **Petersen Automotive Museum.** 6060 Wilshire Blvd. (at Fairfax Ave.). ☎ **323/930-CARS.** www.petersen.org. Admission $7 adults, $5 seniors and students, $3 children ages 5–12, free for kids age 4 and under. Tues–Sun 10am–6pm. Parking $4.

When the Petersen opened in 1994, many locals were surprised that it had taken this long for the City of Freeways to salute its most important shaper. Indeed, this museum says more about the city than probably any other in L.A. Named for Robert Petersen, the publisher responsible for *Hot Rod* and *Motor Trend* magazines, the four-story museum displays more than 200 cars and motorcycles, from the historic to the futuristic. Cars on the first floor are exhibited chronologically, in period settings. Other floors are devoted to frequently changing shows of race cars, early motorcycles, and famous movie vehicles. Past shows have included a comprehensive exhibit of "woodies" and surf culture, and displays of the Flintstones' fiberglass-and-cotton movie car and of a three-wheeled scooter that folds into a Samsonite briefcase (created in a competition by a Mazda engineer).

DOWNTOWN

California African American Museum. 600 State Dr., Exposition Park.
☎ **213/744-7432.** www.caam.ca.gov. Free admission; donation requested.
Tues–Sun 10am–5pm. Closed Thanksgiving, Christmas, New Year's Day.
Parking $5.

This small museum is both a celebration of individual African Americans and a living showplace of contemporary culture. The best exhibits are temporary, and touch on themes as varied as the human experience. Recent shows have included a sculpture exhibit examining interpretations of home, a survey of African puppetry, and a look at black music in Los Angeles in the 1960s. Multimedia biographical retrospectives are also commonplace: An exhibit honoring jazz genius Duke Ellington included his instruments and handwritten music. In the gift shop you'll find sub-Saharan wooden masks and woven baskets, as well as hand-embroidered Ethiopian pillows. There are also posters, children's books, and calendars. The museum offers a full calendar of lectures, concerts, and special events; call for the latest.

California Science Center. 700 State Dr., Exposition Park. ☎ **213/SCI-ENCE**, or 213/744-7400; IMAX theater ☎ **213/744-2014.** www.casciencectr.org. Free admission to the museum; IMAX theater $7 adults, $4.75 ages 18–21, $4 seniors and children. Multishow discounts available. Parking $5. Daily 10am–5pm. Closed Thanksgiving, Christmas, and New Year's Day.

A $130 million remodel—reinvention, actually—has turned the former Museum of Science and Industry into Exposition Park's newest attraction. Using high-tech sleight-of-hand, the center stimulates kids of all ages with questions, answers, and lessons about the world. One of the museum's educational highlights is Tess, a 50-foot animatronic woman whose muscles, bones, organs, and blood vessels are revealed, demonstrating how the body reacts to a variety of external conditions and activities. (Appropriate for children of all ages, Tess doesn't possess reproductive organs.)

There are nominal fees to enjoy the science center's more thrilling attractions. You can pedal a bicycle across a high-wire suspended 43 feet above the ground (demonstrating the principle of gravity and counterweights) or get strapped into the Space Docking Simulator for a virtual-reality taste of zero-gravity. There's plenty more, and plans for expansion are already in the works. The newly expanded IMAX theater now boasts a screen seven stories high and 90 feet wide, with state-of-the-art surround sound and 3-D technology. Films are screened throughout the day until 9pm and are nearly always breathtaking, even the ones in 2-D.

Japanese American National Museum. 369 E. 1st St. (at Central Ave.). ☎ **213/625-0414.** www.janm.org. Admission $6 adults, $5 seniors, $3 students and kids 6–17, free for kids age 5 and under; free to all the 3rd Thurs of each month, and every Thurs after 5pm. Tues–Wed and Fri–Sun 10am–5pm, Thurs 10am–8pm.

Located in an architecturally acclaimed modern building in Little Tokyo, this museum is a private nonprofit institute created to document and celebrate the history of the Japanese in America. Its fantastic permanent exhibition chronicles Japanese life in the United States, while temporary exhibits highlight distinctive aspects of Japanese-American culture, from the internment-camp experience to the lives of Japanese-Americans in Hawaii. Don't miss the museum store, which carries everything from hand-fired sake sets to mini Zen gardening kits.

Los Angeles Children's Museum. 310 N. Main St. (at Los Angeles St.). ☎ **213/687-8800.** Admission $5, free for kids under age 2. Late June to early Sept Mon–Fri 11:30am–5pm, Sat–Sun 10am–5pm. Rest of the year Sat–Sun 10am–5pm.

This thoroughly enchanting museum is a place where children learn by doing. Everyday experiences are demystified by interesting interactive exhibits displayed in a playlike atmosphere. In the Art Studio, kids are encouraged to make finger puppets from a variety of media and shiny rockets out of Mylar. Turn the corner and you're in the unrealistically clean and safe City Street, where kids can sit on a police officer's motorcycle or pretend to drive a bus or a fire truck. Kids (and adults) can see their shadows freeze in the Shadow Box and play with giant foam-filled, Velcro-edged building blocks in Sticky City. Because this is Hollywood, the museum wouldn't be complete without its own recording and TV studios, where kids can become "stars."

Museum of Contemporary Art/Geffen Contemporary at MOCA. 250 S. Grand Ave. and 152 N. Central Ave. ☎ **213/626-6222** or 213/621-2766. www.moca-la.org. Admission $6 adults, $4 seniors and students, free for children age 11 and under. Tues–Wed and Fri–Sun 11am–5pm, Thurs 11am–8pm.

MOCA is Los Angeles's only institution exclusively devoted to art from 1940 to the present. Displaying works in a variety of media, it's particularly strong in works by Cy Twombly, Jasper Johns, and ıvıark Rothko, and shows are often superb. For many experts, MOCA's collections are too spotty to be considered world-class, and the conservative museum board blushes when offered controversial shows (it passed on a Whitney exhibit that included photographs by Robert Mapplethorpe). Nevertheless, we've seen some excellent exhibitions here.

MOCA is one museum housed in two buildings that are close to one another but not within walking distance. The Grand Avenue main building is a contemporary red sandstone structure by renowned Japanese architect Arata Isozaki. The museum restaurant, **Patinette** (☎ **213/626-1178**), located here, is the casual-dining creation of celebrity chef Joachim Splichal (see Patina, in chapter 4).

The museum's second space, on Central Avenue in Little Tokyo, was the "temporary" Contemporary while the Grand structure was being built, and it now houses a superior permanent collection in a fittingly neutral, warehouse-type space recently renamed for entertainment mogul and passionate art collector David Geffen. An added feature here is a detailed timeline corresponding to the progression of works. Unless there's a visiting exhibit of great interest at the main museum, we recommend that you start at the Geffen building—where it's also easier to park.

Natural History Museum of Los Angeles County. 900 Exposition Blvd., Exposition Park. ☎ **213/763-3466.** www.nhm.org. Admission $8 adults; $5.50 children ages 13–17, seniors, and students with ID; $2 children ages 5–12; free for kids age 4 and under; free for everyone the 1st Tues of each month. Mon–Fri 9:30am–5pm, Sat–Sun 10am–5pm.

The "Fighting Dinosaurs" are not a high-school football team but the trademark symbol of this massive museum: *Tyrannosaurus rex* and *Triceratops* skeletons poised in a stance so realistic that every kid feels inspired to imitate their Jurassic Park bellows. Opened in 1913 in a beautiful domed Spanish renaissance building, this museum is a 35-hall warehouse of Earth's history, chronicling the planet and its inhabitants from 600 million years ago to the present day. There's a mind-numbing number of exhibits of prehistoric fossils, bird and marine life, rocks and minerals, and North American mammals. The best permanent displays include the world's rarest shark, a walk-through vault of priceless gems, and an Insect Zoo.

The Dinosaur Shop sells ant farms and exploding volcano and model kits. The Ethnic Arts Shop has one-of-a-kind folk art and jewelry from around the world. The bookstore has an extensive selection of scientific titles and hobbyists' field guides.

Pasadena & Environs

✪ **Norton Simon Museum of Art.** 411 W. Colorado Blvd., Pasadena. ☎ **626/449-6840.** www.nortonsimon.org. Admission $6 adults, $3 seniors, free for students and kids 12 and under. Wed–Sun noon–6pm. Free parking.

Named for a food-packing king and financier who reorganized the failing Pasadena Museum of Modern Art, this has become one of California's most important museums. Comprehensive collections of masterpieces by Degas, Picasso, Rembrandt, and Goya are augmented by sculptures by Henry Moore and Auguste Rodin, including *The Burghers of Calais,* which greets you at the gates. The "Blue Four" collection of works by Kandinsky, Jawlensky, Klee, and Feininger is particularly impressive, as is a superb collection of Southeast Asian sculpture. *Still Life with Lemons, Oranges, and a Rose* (1633), an oil by Francisco de Zurbarán, is one of the museum's most important holdings. One of the most popular pieces is *The Flower Vendor/Girl with Lilies* by Mexican artist Diego Riveras. Architect Frank Gehry recently helped remodel the galleries.

Pacific Asia Museum. 46 N. Los Robles Ave., Pasadena. ☎ **626/449-2742.** www.pacasiamuseum.org. Admission $5 adults, $3 students and seniors, free for children under 12; free for everyone the 3rd Sat of each month. Wed–Fri noon–5pm (Thurs until 8pm), Sat–Sun 11am–5pm.

The most striking aspect of this museum is the building itself. Designed in the 1920s in Chinese Imperial Palace style, it's rivaled in flamboyance only by Mann's Chinese Theatre in Hollywood (see "The Top Attractions," above). Rotating exhibits of Asian art span the centuries, from 100 B.C. to the current day. This manageably sized museum is usually worth a peek.

PARKS

In addition to the two excellent examples of urban parkland discussed below, check out **Pan Pacific Park,** a hilly little retreat near the Farmer's Market and CBS Studios, named for the art deco auditorium that, unfortunately, no longer stands at its edge.

Griffith Park. Entrances along Los Feliz Blvd., at Riverside Dr., Vermont Ave., and Western Ave. (Hollywood). ☎ **323/913-4688.** www.cityofla.org/rap/grifmet/gp. Park admission free.

Mining tycoon Griffith J. Griffith donated these 4,000 acres to the city in 1896. Today, Griffith Park is the largest city park in

America. There's a lot to do here, including hiking, horseback riding, golfing, swimming, biking, and picnicking (see "Golf, Hiking & Other Fun in the Surf & Sun," later in this chapter). For a general overview of the park, drive the mountainous loop road that winds from the top of Western Avenue, past Griffith Observatory, and down to Vermont Avenue. For a more extensive foray, turn north at the loop road's midsection, onto Mt. Hollywood Drive. To reach the golf courses, the **Autry Museum** (see p. 125 for a full listing), or **Los Angeles Zoo** (see p. 134 for a full listing), take Los Feliz Boulevard to Riverside Drive, which runs along the park's western edge.

Near the zoo, in a particularly dusty corner of the park, you'll find the **Travel Town Transportation Museum,** 5200 Zoo Dr. (☎ 323/662-5874), a little-known outdoor museum with a small collection of vintage locomotives and old airplanes. Kids love it. The museum is open Monday to Friday from 10am to 4pm, Saturday to Sunday from 10am to 5pm; admission is free.

Will Rogers State Park. 1501 Will Rogers State Park Rd., Pacific Palisades (between Santa Monica and Malibu). ☎ **310/454-8212.** Park entrance $6 per vehicle. Daily 8am–sunset. House opens daily at 10am; guided tours can be arranged for groups of 10 or more. From Santa Monica, take the Pacific Coast Hwy. (Calif. 1) north, turn right onto Sunset Blvd., and continue to the park entrance.

Will Rogers State Park was once Will Rogers's private ranch and grounds. Willed to the state of California in 1944, the 168-acre estate is now both a park and a historic site, supervised by the Department of Parks and Recreation. Visitors may explore the grounds, the former stables, and the 31-room house filled with the original furnishings, including a porch swing in the living room and many Native American rugs and baskets. Charles Lindbergh and his wife, Anne Morrow Lindbergh, hid out here in the 1930s during part of the craze that followed the kidnap and murder of their first son. There are picnic tables, but no food is sold.

Will Rogers (1879 to 1935) was born in Oklahoma and became a cowboy in the Texas Panhandle before drifting into a Wild West show as a folksy, speechifying roper. The "crackerbarrel philosopher" performed lariat tricks while carrying on a humorous deadpan monologue on current events. The showman moved to Los Angeles in 1919, where he become a movie actor as well as the author of numerous books detailing his down-home "cowboy philosophy."

THEME PARKS

You'll find L.A.'s most famous theme park, **Universal Studios Hollywood,** under "The Top Attractions," above.

Six Flags California (Magic Mountain & Hurricane Harbor). Magic Mountain Pkwy. (off Golden State Fwy. [I-5] north), Valencia. ☎ **661/ 255-4100** or 818/367-5965. www.sixflags.com. Magic Mountain $39 adults, $19.50 seniors 55+ and children age 2 to 48 in. high, free for kids under age 2; Hurricane Harbor $19 adults, $12 seniors, $12 children; adult combo ticket $50. Magic Mountain open daily April–Sept; weekends and holidays only rest of year. Hurricane Harbor open daily Memorial Day–Labor Day; weekends May and Sept; closed Oct–Apr. Both parks open 10am, closing hours vary between 6pm and midnight. Take the San Diego Fwy. (I-405) or the Hollywood Fwy. (U.S. 101/170) north; both will eventually merge with I-5; from I-5, take the Magic Mountain Pkwy. exit.

What started as a countrified little amusement park with a couple of relatively tame roller coasters in 1971 has since been transformed by Six Flags into a thrill-a-minute daredevil's paradise. Located about 20 to 30 minutes north of Universal Studios, **Magic Mountain** is the lesser known of the two Six Flags parks, but it is enormously popular with teenagers and young adults— height-based ride restrictions make the place a big bore for little kids who haven't yet sprouted over 48 inches tall. Bring an iron constitution; rides with names like Ninja, Viper, Colossus, and Psyclone will have your cheeks flapping with the G-force, and queasy expressions are common at the exit. But where else can you experience zero-gravity weightlessness, careen down vertical tracks into relentless hairpin turns, or "race" another train on a side-by-side wooden roller coaster? Some rides are themed to action-film characters (like Superman—The Escape and Batman—The Ride); others are loosely tied to their themed surroundings, like a Far East pagoda or gold-rush mining town. Arcade games and summer-only entertainment (stunt shows, zany carnivals, and parades) round out the park's attractions.

Hurricane Harbor is Six Flags's over-the-top water park. While it's advertised as a companion to Magic Mountain, you really can't see both in 1 day—combo tickets allow you to return within a year's time. Bring your own swimsuit; the park has changing rooms with showers and lockers. Like Magic Mountain, areas have themes like a tropical lagoon or an African river (complete with ancient temple ruins). The primary activities are swimming, water slides, rafting, volleyball, and lounging; many areas are designed especially for the "little buccaneer."

THE ZOO

Los Angeles Zoo. Zoo Dr., Griffith Park. ☎ **323/644-6400.** www.lazoo. org. Admission $8.25 adults, $3.25 kids ages 2–12, $5.25 seniors 65 and over, free to children under age 2. Daily 10am–5pm. Closed Christmas Day. Free parking.

The L.A. Zoo, which shares its parking lot with the Autry Museum, has been welcoming visitors and busloads of schoolkids since 1966. In 1982, the zoo inaugurated a display of cuddly koalas, still one of its biggest attractions. While mature shade trees now help cool the once-barren grounds, and new habitats are light-years ahead of the cruel concrete roundhouses originally used to exhibit animals, there are still some depressing remnants of the humble old zoo—like a polar bear whose enclosure looks much more like a suburban swimming pool than the Arctic. Stick with the newer, more humane exhibits, like the interactive and educational Adventure Island (though promoted as the Children's Zoo, it's actually just as cool for grown-ups too), and the brand-new Chimpanzees of the Mahale Mountains habitat, where visitors can see plenty of primate activity. The year 2000 saw the opening of Red Ape Rain Forest, a natural orangutan habitat. The facility is renowned in zoological circles for the successful breeding and releasing of California condors, and occasionally it has some of these majestic and endangered birds on exhibit.

4 Studio, Sightseeing & Other Organized Tours

STUDIO TOURS

NBC Studios. 3000 W. Alameda Ave., Burbank. ☎ **818/840-3537.** Tours $6 adults, $5.50 seniors, $3.75 children ages 6–12. Mon–Fri 9am–3pm.

According to a security guard, John Wayne and Redd Foxx once got into a fight here after Wayne refused to ride in the same limousine as Foxx, who called the movie star a "redneck." Well, your NBC tour will probably be a bit more docile than that. The guided 1-hour tour includes a behind-the-scenes look at *The Tonight Show with Jay Leno* set; wardrobe, makeup, and set-building departments; and several sound studios. The tour also includes some cool video demonstrations of high-tech special effects.

Paramount Pictures. 5555 Melrose Ave. ☎ **323/956-1777.** Tours $15 per person. Mon–Fri 9am–2pm. www.paramount.com.

Paramount's 2-hour walking tour around its Hollywood headquarters is both a historical ode to filmmaking and a real-life look at a working studio. Tours depart hourly; the itinerary varies, depending on what productions are in progress. Visits might include a walk through the soundstages of TV shows or feature films, though you can't enter while taping is taking place. Cameras, recording equipment, and children under 10 are not allowed.

✪ **Warner Brothers Studios.** Olive Ave. (at Hollywood Way), Burbank. ☎ **818/972-TOUR;** www.virtuallot.com/cmp/main/vip.htm or www. warnerbros.com. Reservations required 2–4 weeks in advance. Tours $30 per person. Mon–Fri 9am–4pm.

Warner Brothers offers the most comprehensive—and the least theme-park like—of the studio tours. The tour takes visitors on a 2-hour informational drive-and-walk jaunt around the studio's faux streets. After a brief introductory film, you'll pile into glorified golf carts and cruise past parking spaces marked "Clint Eastwood," "Michael Douglas," and "Sharon Stone," then walk through active film and television sets. Whether it's an orchestra scoring a film or a TV show being taped or edited, you'll get a glimpse of how it's done. Stops may include the wardrobe department or the mills where sets are made. Whenever possible, you can also visit working sets to watch actors filming actual productions. Reservations are required; children under 8 are not admitted.

SIGHTSEEING TOURS

L.A. Tours (☎ **800/881-7715** or 323/937-3361; www.la-tours. com) operates regularly scheduled tours of the city. Plush shuttle buses (27 passengers maximum) pick up riders from major hotels for morning or afternoon tours of Sunset Strip, the movie studios, Farmers Market, Hollywood, homes of the stars, and other attractions. Different itineraries are available, if you're interested in downtown and the Music Center, for example, or want to spend your time exploring the beaches and shopping in Santa Monica. Tours vary in length from a half day to a full day and cost $42 to $58 for adults. There are discounts for kids; book online for a $4-per-person discount. Advance reservations are required.

Next Stage Tour Company offers a unique Insomniacs' Tour of L.A. (☎ **213/939-2688**), a 3am tour of the predawn city that usually includes trips to the *Los Angeles Times;* the flower, produce, and fish markets; and the top of a skyscraper to watch the sun rise over the city. The fact-filled tour lasts about 6¹/₂ hours and includes breakfast. Tours depart twice monthly and cost $47 per person. Phone for information and reservations.

Grave Line Tours (☎ 323/469-4149) is a terrific journey through Hollywood's darker side. You're picked up in a renovated hearse and taken to the murder sites and final residences of the stars. You'll see the Hollywood Boulevard hotel where female impersonator/actor Divine died, the liquor store where John Belushi threw a temper tantrum shortly before his overdose, and more. Tours are $44 per person and last about 2^1/2 hours. They depart at 9:30am daily from the corner of Orchid Street and Hollywood Boulevard, by Mann's Chinese Theatre. Reservations are required.

The ✪ **L.A. Conservancy** (☎ 213/623-2489) conducts a dozen fascinating, information-packed walking tours of historic downtown L.A., seed of today's sprawling metropolis. The most popular is "Broadway Theaters," a loving look at movie palaces. Other intriguing ones include "Marble Masterpieces," "Art Deco," "Mecca for Merchants," "Terra-Cotta," and tours of the landmark Biltmore Hotel and City Hall. They're usually held on Saturday mornings and cost $5. Call Monday through Friday between 9am and 5pm for the exact schedule and information.

In Pasadena, various tours spotlighting architecture or neighborhoods are lots of fun, given this area's history of wealthy estates and ardent preservation. Call **Pasadena Heritage** (☎ 626/793-0617) for a schedule of guided tours, or pick up "Ten Tours of Pasadena," self-guided walking or driving maps available at the **Pasadena Convention and Visitors Bureau,** 171 S. Los Robles Ave. (☎ 626/795-9311).

GUIDED RUNS

Off 'N Running Tours (☎ 800/523-TOUR or 310/246-1418) combines sporting with sightseeing, taking out-of-town joggers on guided jaunts through the streets of Los Angeles. One-on-one tours are customized to take in the most beautiful areas around your hotel and can accommodate any skill level for 4 to 12 miles. It's a smart way to get the most out of your first morning's jog. Tours cost about $35 (for 6 miles).

5 Beaches

Los Angeles County's 72-mile coastline sports over 30 miles of beaches, most of which are operated by the **Department of Beaches & Harbors,** 13837 Fiji Way, Marina del Rey (☎ 310/305-9503). County-run beaches usually charge for parking

($4 to $8). Alcohol, bonfires, and pets are prohibited. For recorded **surf conditions** (and coastal weather forecast), call ☎ **310/ 457-9701.** The following are the county's best beaches, listed from north to south.

EL PESCADOR, LA PIEDRA & EL MATADOR BEACHES These relatively rugged and isolated beaches front a 2-mile stretch of the Pacific Coast Highway (Calif. 1) between Broad Beach and Decker Canyon roads, about a 10-minute drive from the Malibu Pier. Picturesque coves with unusual rock formations are perfect for sunbathing and picnicking, but swim with caution as there are no lifeguards or other facilities. These beaches can be difficult to find; they're marked only by small signs on the highway. Visitors are limited by the small number of parking spots atop the bluffs. Descend to the beach via stairs that cling to the cliffs.

✪ **ZUMA BEACH COUNTY PARK**   Jam-packed on warm weekends, L.A. County's largest beach park is located off the Pacific Coast Highway (Calif. 1), a mile past Kanan Dume Road. While it can't claim to be the most lovely beach in the Southland, Zuma has the most comprehensive facilities: plenty of rest rooms, lifeguards, playgrounds, volleyball courts, and snack bars. The southern stretch, toward Point Dume, is Westward Beach, separated from the noisy highway by sandstone cliffs. A trail leads over the point's headlands to Pirate's Cove, once a popular nude beach.

PARADISE COVE   This private beach in the 28000 block of the Pacific Coast Highway (Calif. 1) charges $15 to park and $5 per person if you walk in. Changing rooms and showers are included in the price. The beach is often full by noon on weekends.

✪ **MALIBU LAGOON STATE BEACH**   Not just a pretty white-sand beach but an estuary and wetlands area as well, Malibu Lagoon is the historic home of the Chumash Indians. The entrance is on the Pacific Coast Highway (Calif. 1) south of Cross Creek Road, and there's a small admission charge. Marine life and shorebirds teem where the creek empties into the sea, and the waves are always mild. The historic Adamson House is here, a showplace of Malibu tile now operating as a museum.

✪ **SURFRIDER BEACH**   Without a doubt, L.A.'s best waves roll ashore here. One of the city's most popular surfing spots, this beach is located between the Malibu Pier and the lagoon. In surf lingo, few "locals-only" wave wars are ever fought here—surfing

Los Angeles Beaches & Coastal Attractions

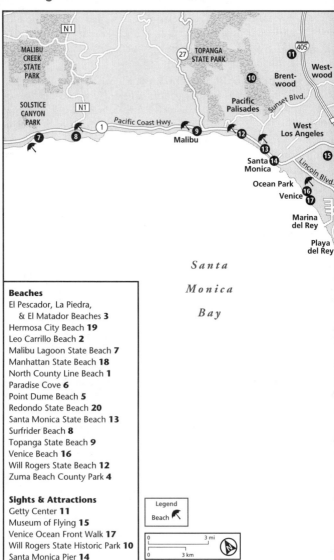

Beaches
El Pescador, La Piedra,
& El Matador Beaches **3**
Hermosa City Beach **19**
Leo Carrillo Beach **2**
Malibu Lagoon State Beach **7**
Manhattan State Beach **18**
North County Line Beach **1**
Paradise Cove **6**
Point Dume Beach **5**
Redondo State Beach **20**
Santa Monica State Beach **13**
Surfrider Beach **8**
Topanga State Beach **9**
Venice Beach **16**
Will Rogers State Beach **12**
Zuma Beach County Park **4**

Sights & Attractions
Getty Center **11**
Museum of Flying **15**
Venice Ocean Front Walk **17**
Will Rogers State Historic Park **10**
Santa Monica Pier **14**

Legend
Beach

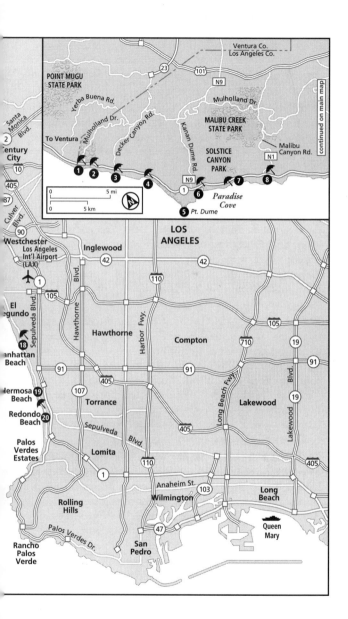

continued on main map

Ventura Co.
Los Angeles Co.

POINT MUGU
STATE PARK

Yerba Buena Rd.

Mulholland Dr.

Mulholland Dr.

MALIBU CREEK
STATE PARK

Decker Canyon Rd.

Kanan Dume Rd.

SOLSTICE
CANYON
PARK

Malibu
Canyon Rd.

Santa
Monica
Blvd.

entury
City

To Ventura

*Paradise
Cove*

Pt. Dume

0   5 mi
0   5 km

LOS
ANGELES

Westchester
Los Angeles
Int'l Airport
(LAX)

Inglewood

Culver
Blvd.

El
egundo

Sepulveda Blvd.

anhattan
Beach

Hawthorne

Blvd.

Hawthorne

Harbor Fwy.

Compton

Long Beach Fwy.

Lakewood Blvd.

lermosa
Beach

Redondo
Beach

Torrance

Sepulveda   Blvd.

Lakewood

Palos
Verdes
Estates

Lomita

Rolling
Hills

Anaheim St.

Wilmington

Long
Beach

Queen
Mary

Palos Verdes Dr.

Rancho
Palos
Verde

San
Pedro

139

is not as territorial here as it can be in other areas, where out-of-towners can be made to feel unwelcome. Surfrider is surrounded by all of Malibu's hustle and bustle; don't come here for peace and quiet.

TOPANGA STATE BEACH   Noise from the highway prevents solitude at this short, narrow strip of sand located where Topanga Canyon Boulevard emerges from the mountains. Why go? Ask the surfers who wait in line to catch Topanga's excellent breaks. There are rest rooms and lifeguard services here, but little else.

WILL ROGERS STATE BEACH   Three miles along the Pacific Coast Highway (Calif. 1), between Sunset Boulevard and the Santa Monica border, are named for the American humorist whose ranch-turned-state-historic-park (see "Parks," above) is nestled above the palisades that provide the striking backdrop for this popular beach. A pay parking lot extends the entire length of Will Rogers, and facilities include rest rooms, lifeguards, and a snack hut in season. While the surfing is only so-so, the waves are friendly for swimmers of all ages.

SANTA MONICA STATE BEACH   The beaches on either side of the Santa Monica Pier (see "Piers," above) are popular for their white sands and easy accessibility. There are big parking lots, eateries, and lots of well-maintained rest rooms. A paved beach path runs along here, allowing you to walk, bike, or skate to Venice and points south. Colorado Boulevard leads to the pier; turn north on the Pacific Coast Highway (Calif. 1) below the coastline's striking bluffs, or south along Ocean Avenue; you'll find parking in both directions.

✪ **VENICE BEACH**   Moving south from the city of Santa Monica, the paved pedestrian Promenade becomes Ocean Front Walk and gets progressively weirder until it reaches an apex at Washington Boulevard and the Venice fishing pier. Although there are people who swim and sunbathe, Venice Beach's character is defined by the sea of humanity on the Ocean Front Walk, plus the bevy of boardwalk vendors and old-fashioned pedestrian streets a block away (see "The Top Attractions," earlier in this chapter). Park on the side streets or in the plentiful lots west of Pacific Avenue.

MANHATTAN STATE BEACH   The Beach Boys used to hang out at this wide, friendly beach backed by beautiful ocean-view homes. Plenty of parking on 36 blocks of side streets (between Rosecrans Avenue and the Hermosa Beach border) draws weekend crowds from the L.A. area. Manhattan has some of the best surfing around, along with rest rooms, lifeguards, and volleyball courts. Manhattan Beach Boulevard leads west to the fishing pier and adjacent seafood restaurants.

✪ **HERMOSA CITY BEACH**   A very, very wide, white-sand beach with tons to recommend it, Hermosa extends to either side of the pier and includes "The Strand," a pedestrian lane that runs its entire length. Main access is at the foot of Pier Avenue, which itself is lined with interesting shops. There are plenty of street parking, rest rooms, lifeguards, volleyball courts, a fishing pier, playgrounds, and good surfing.

REDONDO STATE BEACH   Popular with surfers, bicyclists, and joggers, Redondo's white sand and ice-plant–carpeted dunes are just south of tiny King Harbor, along "The Esplanade" (South Esplanade Drive). Get there via the Pacific Coast Highway (Calif. 1) or Torrance Boulevard. Facilities include rest rooms, lifeguards, and volleyball courts.

6 Golf, Hiking & Other Fun in the Surf & Sun

BICYCLING   Los Angeles is great for biking. If you're into distance pedaling, you can do no better than the flat 22-mile paved **Ocean Front Walk** that runs along the sand from Pacific Palisades in the north to Torrance in the south. The path attracts all levels of riders and gets pretty busy on weekends. For information on this and other city bike routes, phone the **Metropolitan Transportation Authority** (☎ 213/244-6539).

The best place to mountain bike is along the trails of **Malibu Creek State Park** (☎ 800/533-7275 or 818/880-0350), in the Santa Monica Mountains between Malibu and the San Fernando Valley. Fifteen miles of trails rise to a maximum of 3,000 feet and are appropriate for intermediate to advanced bikers. Pick up a trail map at the park entrance, 4 miles south of U.S. 101 off Las Virgenes Road, just north of Mulholland Highway. Park admission is $5 per car.

Sea Mist Rental, 1619 Ocean Front Walk (at the pier), Santa Monica (☎ 310/395-7076), rents 10-speed cruisers for $5 per hour and $14 per day; 15-speed mountain bikes rent for $6 per hour and $20 per day.

FISHING   Del Rey Sport Fishing, 13759 Fiji Way (☎ **310/ 822-3625;** www.delreysportfishing.com), has four deep-sea boats departing daily on half- and full-day ocean fishing trips. Of course, it depends on what's running when you're out, but bass, barracuda, halibut, and yellowtail are the most common catches on these party boats. Excursions cost from $22 to $30; tackle rental is available. Phone for reservations.

No permit is required to cast from shore or drop a line from a pier. Local anglers will hate me for giving away their secret spot, but the **best saltwater fishing spot** in all of L.A. is at the foot of Torrance Boulevard in Redondo Beach.

GOLF   The greater Los Angeles area has more than 100 golf courses, which vary in quality from abysmal to superb. Most of the city's public courses are administered by the Department of Recreation and Parks, which follows a complicated registration/ reservation system for tee times. While visitors cannot reserve start times in advance, you're welcome to play any of the courses by showing up and getting on the call sheet. Expect to wait for the most popular tee times, but try to use your flexible vacationer status to your advantage by avoiding the early-morning rush.

Of the city's seven 18-hole and three 9-hole courses, you can't get more central than the **Rancho Park Golf Course,** 10460 W. Pico Blvd. (☎ **310/838-7373**), located smack-dab in the middle of L.A.'s Westside. The par-71 course has lots of tall trees, but not enough to blot out the towering Century City buildings next door. Rancho also has a 9-hole, par-3 course.

For a genuinely woodsy experience, try one of the three courses inside Griffith Park, northeast of Hollywood (see "Parks," above). The courses are extremely well maintained, challenging without being frustrating, and (despite some holes alongside I-5) a great way to leave the city behind. Bucolic pleasures abound, particularly on the nine-hole **Roosevelt,** on Vermont Avenue across from the Greek Theatre; early-morning wildlife often includes deer, rabbits, raccoons, and skunks (fore!). **Wilson** and **Harding** are each 18 holes and start from the main clubhouse off Riverside Drive, the park's main entrance.

Greens fees on all city courses are $17 Monday through Friday, and $22 on weekends and holidays; nine-hole courses cost $8.50 weekdays, $11.50 on weekends and holidays. For details on other city courses, or to contact the starter directly by phone, call the Department of Recreation and Parks at ☎ **213/485-5566.**

Industry Hills Golf Club, 1 Industry Hills Pkwy., City of Industry (☎ **818/810-4455**), has two 18-hole courses designed by William Bell. Together they encompass eight lakes, 160 bunkers, and many long fairways. The Eisenhower Course, which consistently ranks among *Golf Digest's* top 25 public courses, has extra-large undulating greens and the challenge of thick kikuyu rough. An adjacent driving range is lit for night use. Greens fees are $50 Monday through Thursday and $65 Friday through Sunday, including cart; call in advance for tee times.

HANG GLIDING   Up and down the California coast, it's not uncommon to see people poised on the crests of hills, hanging from enormous colorful kites. You can too. **Windsports International,** 16145 Victory Blvd., Van Nuys (☎ **818/988-0111;** www.windsports.com), offers flight instruction and rentals for both novices and experts. A 1-day lesson in a solo hang glider on a bunny hill costs $120. If it's more of a thrill you're looking for, choose the $125, 3,000-foot-high tandem flight, where you are flying with an instructor. Lessons take off from varying spots in the San Fernando Valley, depending on the winds. Phone for reservations.

HIKING   The **Santa Monica Mountains,** a small range that runs only 50 miles from Griffith Park to Point Mugu, on the coast north of Malibu, makes Los Angeles a great place for hiking. The mountains, which peak at 3,111 feet, are part of the Santa Monica Mountains National Recreation Area, a contiguous conglomeration of 350 public parks and 65,000 acres. Many animals live in this area, including deer, coyote, rabbit, skunk, rattlesnake, fox, hawk, and quail. The hills are also home to almost 1,000 drought-resistant plant species, including live oak and coastal sage.

Hiking is best after spring rains, when the hills are green, flowers are in bloom, and the air is clear. Summers can be very hot; hikers should always carry fresh water. Beware of poison oak, a hearty shrub that's common on the west coast. Usually found among oak trees, poison oak has leaves in groups of three, with waxy surfaces and prominent veins. If you come into contact with this itch-producing plant, bathe yourself in calamine lotion, or the ocean.

For trail maps and more information, contact the **National Parks Service** (☎ **818/597-1036**), or stop by its visitor center at 30401 Agoura Rd., Suite 100, in Agoura Hills. It's open Monday to Friday from 8am to 5pm, and Saturday and Sunday from 9am to 5pm. Some areas are administered by the **California Department of Parks** (☎ **818/880-0350**); the offices are located in Calabasas at 1925 Las Virgenes Rd.

Santa Ynez Canyon, in Pacific Palisades, is a long and difficult climb that rises steadily for about 3 miles. At the top, hikers are rewarded with fantastic views over the Pacific. Also at the top is Trippet Ranch, a public facility providing water, rest rooms, and picnic tables. From Santa Monica, take Pacific Coast Highway (Calif. 1) north. Turn right onto Sunset Boulevard, then left onto Palisades Drive. Then continue for 2¹/₂ miles, turn left onto Verenda de la Montura, and park at the cul-de-sac at the end of the street, where you'll find the trailhead.

Temescal Canyon, in Pacific Palisades, is far easier than the Santa Ynez trail and, predictably, far more popular, especially among locals. This is one of the quickest routes into the wilderness. Hikes here are anywhere from 1 to 5 miles. From Santa Monica, take Pacific Coast Highway (Calif. 1) north; turn right onto Temescal Canyon Road, and follow it to the end. Sign in with the gatekeeper, who can also answer your questions.

Will Rogers State Historic Park, Pacific Palisades, is also a terrific place for hiking. An intermediate-level hike from the park's entrance ends at Inspiration Point, a plateau from which you can see a good portion of L.A.'s Westside. See "Parks," above, for complete information.

HORSEBACK RIDING   The **Griffith Park Livery Stable,** 480 Riverside Dr. (in the Los Angeles Equestrian Center), Burbank (☎ **818/840-8401**), rents horses by the hour for western or English riding through Griffith Park's hills. There's a 200-pound weight limit, and children under 12 are not permitted to ride. Horse rental costs $15 per hour; maximum rental is 2 hours. You can also arrange for private 1-hour lessons ($35). The stables are open daily from 8am to 5pm, and cash is required for payment.

JET SKIING   **Nature Tours,** 1759 9th St., Suite 201, Santa Monica (☎ **310/453-8754**), offers Personal Watercraft (PWC) rentals and lessons, teaching all levels of riders how to get the most out of jet skis and the more popular, sit-down-style

WaveRunners. Riders of all levels learn in the harbor's calm water and then venture into open Santa Monica Bay. Rates range from $62 to $80 an hour for different size crafts—the larger ones even have a small ice-chest built in under the seat!

SEA KAYAKING Sea kayaking is all the rage in Southern California; if you've ever tried it, you know why. Unlike river kayaks, in which your legs are actually inside the boat's hull, paddlers sit on top of sea kayaks, which can be maneuvered more easily than canoes.

Southwind Kayak Center (☎ **800/768-8494** or 949/261-0200; www.southwindkayaks.com) rents sea kayaks for use in the bay or open ocean at rates of $10 to $15 per hour; instructional classes are available on weekends only. The center also conducts bird-watching kayak expeditions into Upper Newport Bay Ecological Reserve at rates of $40 to $65.

SKATING The 22-mile-long Ocean Front Walk that runs from Pacific Palisades to Torrance is one of the premiere skating spots in the country. In-line skating is especially popular, but conventionals are often seen here, too. Skating is allowed just about everywhere bicycling is, but be advised that cyclists have the right of way. **Spokes 'n' Stuff,** 4175 Admiralty Way, Marina del Rey (☎ **310/306-3332**), is just one of many places to rent wheels near the Venice portion of Ocean Front Walk. In the South Bay, in-line skate rentals are available 1 block from the Strand at **Hermosa Cyclery,** 20 13th St. (☎ **310/374-7816**). Skates cost around $5 per hour; knee pads and wrist guards come with every rental.

SURFING Surfing was invented by the Polynesians; Captain Cook made note of it in Oahu in 1778. George Freeth (1883 to 1918), who first surfed Redondo Beach in 1907, is widely credited with introducing the sport to California. But surfing didn't catch on until the 1950s, when California Institute of Technology graduate Bob Simmons invented a more maneuverable lightweight fiberglass board. The Beach Boys and other surf-music groups popularized Southern California in the minds of beach-babes and -dudes everywhere, and the rest, as they say, is history.

Boards are available for rent at shops near all top surfing beaches in the L.A. area. **Zuma Jay Surfboards,** 22775 Pacific Coast Hwy., Malibu (☎ **310/456-8044**), is about a quarter mile south of Malibu Pier. Rentals are $20 per day, plus $8 to $10 for wet suits in winter.

TENNIS   While soft-surface courts are more popular on the east coast, hard surfaces are most common in California. If your hotel doesn't have a court and can't suggest any courts nearby, try the well-maintained, well-lit **Griffith Park Tennis Courts,** on Commonwealth Road, just east of Vermont Avenue (☎ 323/485-5555). Or call the **City of Los Angeles Department of Recreation and Parks** (☎ 213/485-5555) to make a reservation at a municipal court near you.

WINDSURFING   Invented and patented by Hoyle Schweitzer of Torrance in 1968, windsurfing, or sail-boarding, is a fun sport that's much more difficult than it looks. The **Long Beach Windsurfing Center,** 3850 E. Ocean Ave., Long Beach (☎ 562/433-1014), offers lesson and rentals in Alamitos Bay. Twenty-five dollars will get you the use of a board for 4 hours; an $89 learner's package includes instruction from 8am to noon, use of board and wet suit, and a certificate for a free half-day rental once you've gotten the hang of it. Kayak and in-line skate rentals and instruction are also available.

7 Spectator Sports

BASEBALL   The **Los Angeles Dodgers** (☎ 213/224-1500) play at Dodger Stadium, 1000 Elysian Park, near Sunset Boulevard. L.A.'s baseball fans have put up with a lot lately; not since migrating from their former Brooklyn home have the Dodgers been the center of so much controversy. We hope that by the time you read this, L.A.'s beloved boys of summer will be back on track—check the *L.A. Times* sports section for the latest. The team's slick, interactive Web site (**www.dodgers.com**) offers everything from game schedules to souvenir merchandise online.

The Disney-owned **California Angels** (☎ 714/634-2000; www.angelsbaseball.com) play at Anaheim Stadium, at 2000 S. State College Blvd. (near Katella Avenue), in Anaheim. More often than not, games are populated by displaced fans there to see the visiting team rather than diehard Angels' supporters. If you go to cheer on your hometown Yankees, Red Sox, or Twins, you'll probably feel right at home.

BASKETBALL Los Angeles has two NBA franchises, the **L.A. Lakers** (☎310/419-3100; www.nba.com/lakers) and the **L.A. Clippers** (☎ 213/745-0400; www. nba.com/clippers). Both teams play in the new $300 million **STAPLES Center** in downtown L.A., 1111 S. Figueroa St. (☎ 877/673-6799; www.staplescenterla.com). Celebrity fans like Jack Nicholson and Dyan Cannon have the best tickets, but this 20,000-seater should have room for you too.

HORSE RACING The scenic **Hollywood Park Racetrack,** 1050 S. Prairie Ave., in Inglewood (☎ 310/419-1500; www.hollywoodpark.com), with its lakes and flowers, features thoroughbred racing from early April through July, as well as in November and December. The $1 million Hollywood Gold Cup is also run here. Well-placed monitors project views of the back stretch as well as stop-action replays of photo finishes. Races are usually held Wednesday through Sunday. Post times are 1pm in summer (7pm on Fri), and 12:30pm weekends and holidays. General admission is $6; admission to the clubhouse is $25.

One of the most beautiful tracks in the country, **Santa Anita Racetrack,** 285 W. Huntington Dr., Arcadia (☎ 626/574-RACE; www.santaanita.com), offers thoroughbred racing from October through mid-November and December through late April. The track was featured in the Marx Brothers' film *A Day at the Races* and in the 1954 version of *A Star Is Born.* On weekdays during the racing season, the public is invited to watch morning workouts from 7:30 to 9:30am. Post time is 12:30 or 1pm. Admission is $4.

ICE HOCKEY The NHL's **L.A. Kings** (☎ 310/673-6003; www.lakings.com) also call the new STAPLES Center home (see "Basketball," above).

8 A Side Trip to Disneyland

Opened in 1955, Disneyland—along with its Florida sibling, Walt Disney World—is the original mega–theme park, and it remains unsurpassed despite constant threats from pretenders to the crown. At no other park is fantasy elevated to such an art form. Nowhere else is as fresh and fantastic every time you walk through the gates, whether you're 6 or 60—and no matter how many times you've done it before. There's nothing like Disney Magic.

ESSENTIALS

GETTING THERE   Disneyland is located at 1313 Harbor Blvd. in Anaheim. It's about an hour's drive from downtown Los Angeles. Take I-5 south; at press time construction was drawing to a close on dedicated Disneyland exits from both directions of the interstate. By the time you read this, you'll be easily whisked off the freeway and directly to brand-new, multilevel Disney parking lots.

ADMISSION, HOURS & INFORMATION   At press time, admission to Disneyland, including unlimited rides and all festivities and entertainment, was $41 for adults and children age 10 and over, $39 for seniors age 60 and over, and $31 for children ages 3 to 9; children under age 3 enter free. These figures are given only as a guideline, since new prices will go into effect once California Adventure opens in February of 2001. Multi-day admission is available as well; 2- and 3-day passports offer substantial savings for adults and children. The days needn't be consecutive, but must be used within 7 days (for the 2-day) or 14 days (for the 3-day). You should expect to pay a parking charge between $7-$10 (which may be included in some admission packages).

Disneyland is open every day of the year but, because operating hours vary, we recommend that you call for information that applies to the specific day(s) of your visit (☎ **714/781-4565** or 213/626-8605, ext. 4565). The same information, including ride closures, can also be found online at www.disneyland.com. Generally speaking, the park is open from 9 or 10am to 6 or 7pm on weekdays, fall to spring; and from 8 or 9am to midnight or 1am on weekends, on holidays, and during winter, spring, or summer vacation periods.

TOURING THE PARK

The Disneyland complex is divided into several themed "lands," each of which has a number of rides and attractions that are, more or less, related to that land's theme.

MAIN STREET U.S.A.   At the park's entrance, Main Street U.S.A. is a cinematic version of turn-of-the-century small-town America. The whitewashed Rockwellian fantasy is lined with gift shops, candy stores, a soda fountain, and a silent theater that continuously runs early Mickey Mouse films. Here you'll find the practical things you might need, such as stroller rentals and storage lockers.

Because there are no rides, it's best to tour Main Street during the middle of the afternoon, when lines for rides are longest, and in the evening, when you can rest your feet in the theater that features "Great Moments with Mr. Lincoln," a patriotic (and audio-animatronic) look at America's 16th president. There's always something happening on Main Street; stop in at the information booth to the left of the main entrance for a schedule of the day's events.

You might start your day by circumnavigating the park by train. An authentic 19th-century steam engine pulls open-air cars around the park's perimeter. Board at the Main Street Depot and take a complete turn around the park, or disembark at any one of the lands.

ADVENTURELAND   Inspired by the most exotic regions of Asia, Africa, India, and the South Pacific, Adventureland is home to several popular rides. Here's where you can cavort inside **Tarzan's Treehouse,** a climb-around attraction based on Disney's recent animated success. Frequent visitors might recognize the former Swiss Family Treehouse, remodeled with jungle vines and moss. Its neighbor is the **Jungle Cruise,** where passengers board a large authentic-looking Mississippi River paddleboat and float along an Amazon-like river. En route, audio-animatronic wild animals and hostile natives threaten the boat, while a tour guide entertains with running patter.

A spear's throw away is the **Enchanted Tiki Room,** one of the most sedate attractions in Adventureland. Inside, you can sit down and watch a 20-minute musical comedy featuring electronically animated tropical birds, flowers, and "tiki gods."

The **Indiana Jones Adventure** is Adventureland's newest ride. Based on the Steven Spielberg films, this ride takes adventurers into the Temple of the Forbidden Eye, in joltingly realistic all-terrain vehicles. Riders follow Indy and experience the perils of bubbling lava pits, whizzing arrows, fire-breathing serpents, collapsing bridges, and the familiar cinematic tumbling boulder (an effect that's very realistic in the front seats!). Disney "Imagineers" reached new heights with the design of this ride's line, which—take my word for it—has so much detail throughout its twisting path that 30 minutes or more simply flies by.

California Adventure: Disney's Latest Addition

By the time you read this, Disney is scheduled to be putting the finishing touches on **California Adventure**, a brand new "sister" theme park adjacent to Disneyland (frequent visitors will actually notice it's built on space originally occupied by Disney's mammoth outdoor parking lot). At press time it appeared the new park would concentrate more on interactive and educational experiences than thrill rides; all tied together by the theme of celebrating California's unique climate, lifestyle, and diversity. Among the planned attractions are:

- a nostalgic boardwalk re-creation, complete with classic rides, fun zone, sandy beach, and street artists,

- Pacific Wharf, which celebrates California's best unique foods. The highlight promises to be Robert Mondavi's wine country experience, featuring real vineyards and wine-tasting counters. Other participants include a fully operational Mission tortilla factory, and a Boudin sourdough bread bakery that uses the original mother starter from 1850,

- a Hollywood-style studio district with hands-on animation exhibits, plus a one-of-a-kind TV studio where visitors are both the stars and the audience,

- an area celebrating California outdoor adventures, with chances for more daring guests to "soar" in hang gliders over the state's most picturesque locales, explore forests, deserts, subterranean caverns, or even take a white water "rafting" expedition,

- Muppet Vision 3-D, an action- and illusion-packed show featuring the familiar faces of Kermit, Miss Piggy, and others in a venue reminiscent of the original "Muppet Show" theater—complete with hecklers Statler and Waldorf in the balcony.

NEW ORLEANS SQUARE   A large grassy green dotted with gas lamps, New Orleans Square is home to the **Haunted Mansion.** It's the most high-tech ghost house we've ever seen. The spookiness has been toned down so kids won't get nightmares, and the events inside are as funny as they are scary.

Even more fanciful is **Pirates of the Caribbean,** one of Disneyland's most popular rides. Visitors float on boats through mock underground caves, entering an enchanting world of swashbuckling, rum-running, and buried treasure. Even in the middle of the afternoon you can dine by the cool moonlight and to the sound of crickets in the Blue Bayou restaurant, situated in the middle of the ride itself.

CRITTER COUNTRY An ode to the backwoods, Critter Country is a sort of Frontierland without those pesky settlers. Little kids like to sing along with the *audio-animatronic critters in the musical **Country Bear Jamboree***. Older kids and grown-ups head straight for **Splash Mountain,** one of the largest water-flume rides in the world. Loosely based on the Disney movie *Song of the South,* the ride is lined with about 100 characters who won't stop singing "Zip-A-Dee-Doo-Dah." Be prepared to get wet, especially if someone sizable is in the front seat of your log-shaped boat.

FRONTIERLAND Inspired by 19th-century America, Frontierland is full of dense "forests" and broad "rivers" inhabited by hearty-looking (but, luckily, not hearty-smelling) "pioneers." You can take a raft to **Tom Sawyer Island,** a do-it-yourself play area with balancing rocks, caves, and a rope bridge, and board the **Big Thunder Mountain Railroad,** a runaway roller coaster that races through a deserted 1870s gold mine. You'll also find a petting zoo and an Abe Lincoln–style log cabin here; both are great for exploring with the little ones.

On Saturdays, Sundays, and holidays, and during vacation periods, head to Frontierland's **Rivers of America** after dark to see the FANTASMIC! show. It mixes magic, music, live performers, and sensational special effects. Just as he did in *The Sorcerer's Apprentice,* Mickey Mouse appears and uses his magical powers to create giant water fountains, enormous flowers, and fantasy creatures. There's plenty of pyrotechnics, lasers, and fog, as well as a 45-foot-tall dragon that breathes fire and sets the water of the Rivers of America aflame. Cool!

MICKEY'S TOONTOWN This is a colorful, whimsical world inspired by the "Roger Rabbit" films—a wacky, gag-filled land populated by toons. There are several rides, including **Roger Rabbit's CarToonSpin,** but they take a back seat to Toontown itself—a trippy, smile-inducing world without a straight line or right angle in sight. This is a great place to talk with Mickey, Minnie, Goofy, Roger Rabbit, and the rest of your favorite toons.

You can even visit their "houses." Mickey's red-shingled home and movie barn are filled with props from some of his greatest cartoons.

FANTASYLAND   With a storybook theme, this is the catchall "land" for stuff that doesn't quite fit anywhere else. Most of the rides are geared to the under-6 set, including the **King Arthur Carousel,** the **Dumbo the Flying Elephant ride,** and the **Casey Jr. Circus Train.** Some, like **Mr. Toad's Wild Ride** and **Peter Pan's Flight,** appeal to grown-ups as well. You'll also find Alice in Wonderland, Snow White's Scary Adventures, Pinocchio's Daring Journey, and more.

The most lauded attraction is **It's a Small World,** a slow-moving indoor river ride through a saccharine nightmare of all the world's children singing the song everybody loves to hate. For a different kind of thrill, try the **Matterhorn Bobsleds,** a zippy roller coaster through chilled caverns and drifting fog banks. It's one of the park's most popular rides. An indoor live-action theater features a musical extravaganza called "Classic Disney Characters."

TOMORROWLAND   Conceived as an optimistic look at the future, Tomorrowland has always had a hard time keeping ahead of real advances. The 1955 "Rocket to the Moon" became "Mission to Mars" in 1975, only to be a dated laughingstock by the early 1980s. In 1998, Disney architects unveiled a redesigned land that employs an angular, metallic look popularized by futurists like Jules Verne.

The high-speed ride **Rocket Rods** joined Tomorrowland favorites **Space Mountain** (a pitch-black indoor roller coaster that assaults your equilibrium and ears) and **Star Tours** (the original Disney–George Lucas joint venture; it's a 40-passenger StarSpeeder that encounters a space-load of misadventures on the way to the Moon of Endor, achieved with wired seats and video effects—not for the queasy). A redesigned **Autopia** was introduced in 2000, with updated cars, an extended track, and interactive "road hazards" along the way.

Other attractions include "Honey, I Shrunk the Audience," which uses a variety of theatrical effects to impart the sensation that you've dwindled to thumbnail size. The interactive pavilion of near-future technology called "Innoventions" is a feature close to what old Walt originally envisioned for Tomorrowland, when he created exhibits like the "House of the Future" and "Bathroom of Tomorrow" that featured imaginative technology of the day.

The "lands" themselves are only half the adventure. Other joys include roaming Disney characters, penny arcades, restaurants and snack bars galore, summer fireworks, mariachi and ragtime bands, parades, shops, marching bands, and much more. Oh, yeah—there's also the storybook Sleeping Beauty Castle. Can you spot the evil witch peering from one of the top windows?

WHERE TO STAY AND DINE

The **Disneyland Hotel** (☎ 714/778-6600) is attached to Disneyland by a monorail system, and offers Disney package deals. It is an all-inclusive resort, with many dining options on the premises. **WestCoast Anaheim Hotel** (☎ 800/426-0670) is located just across the street from Disneyland and offers comfortable rooms with many amenities. **Candy Cane Inn** (☎ 800/345-7057) is a treat for the stylish bargain hunter, with cobblestone drives and old-time lamps.

There are many of dining options inside Disneyland, including the Creole-themed **Blue Bayou,** where you can eat under the stars inside the Pirates of the Caribbean ride—no matter what time of day it is.

6

Shopping

Whether you're looking for souvenirs with traditional Southern California images (someone is gonna love that "UCLA . . . on a clear day" T-shirt), fine goods available only here, cutting-edge Melrose Avenue fashions, Hollywood memorabilia, books on topics of local interest, or just some quirky thing that will always remind you of your trip to L.A., I guarantee you'll enjoy the diversity of the city's shopping scene as much as the residents do.

A note on hours: Street shops are generally open Monday through Saturday from 10 or 11am to 5 or 6pm. Many are open Sunday, particularly those near the beaches, movie theaters, or clusters of other stores. In addition, quite a few choose 1 night a week, often Wednesday or Thursday, to offer extended evening hours. Mall shops take their cue from the anchor department stores; as a rule, they open around 10am and do business until 8 or 9pm. Sundays shave an hour or two off each side, while holiday periods increase mall hours substantially.

Sales tax in Los Angeles is 8.25%; savvy out-of-state shoppers know to have larger items shipped directly home to save the tax.

1 L.A.'s Top Shopping Streets & Neighborhoods

Here's a rundown of L.A.'s most interesting shopping areas— from the fine and chic to the funky and cheap—along with some highlights of each neighborhood, to give you an idea of what you'll find there. If addresses and phone numbers are *not* given here, refer to the store's expanded listing by category in "Shopping A to Z."

SANTA MONICA & THE BEACHES
Main Street. Between Pacific St. and Rose Ave., Santa Monica and Venice.

An excellent streetscape for strolling, Main Street boasts a healthy combination of mall standards as well as upscale, left-of-center individual boutiques. You'll also find plenty of casually hip cafes and restaurants. The primary strip connecting Santa Monica and

Venice, Main Street has a relaxed, beach-community vibe that sets it apart from similar strips. The stores here straddle the fashion fence between upscale trendy and beach-bum edgy. Highlights include **C.P. Shades,** a San Francisco ladies' clothier whose loose and comfy cotton and linen line is carried by many department stores and boutiques. **Horizons West,** 2011 Main St. (south of Pico Boulevard; ☎ **310/392-1122**), sells brand-name surfboards, wet suits, leashes, magazines, waxes, lotions, and everything else you need to catch the perfect wave. Stop in and say hi to Randy, and pick up a free tide table. If you're looking for some truly sophisticated, finely crafted eyewear, friendly **Pepper's Eyeware,** 2904 Main St. (between Ashland and Pier streets; ☎ **310/392-0633**), is for you. Ask for frames by cutting-edge L.A. designers Bada and Koh Sakai. If you're lucky enough to have perfect vision, consider some stylish shades. Outdoors types will get lost in 5,600-square-foot **Patagonia,** 2936 Main St. (☎ **310/314-1776;** www.patagonia.com), where climbers, surfers, skiers, and hikers can gear up in the functional, colorful duds that put this environmentally friendly firm on the map.

Montana Avenue. Between 17th and 7th sts., Santa Monica.

This breezy stretch of slow-traffic Montana is one of our favorite regentrified parts of the city. Okay, so it's gotten a lot more pricey than in the late 1970s when tailors and Laundromats ruled the roost, but we're just happy the specialty shops still outnumber the chains. Look around and you'll see upscale moms with strollers and cell phones shopping for designer fashions, country home decor, and gourmet takeout.

Montana is still original enough for residents from across town to make a special trip to shop here, seeking out distinctive shops like **Shabby Chic,** 1013 Montana Ave. (☎ **310/394-1975**), a much-copied purveyor of slipcovered sofas and flea-market furnishings. Vintage-jewelry buffs keep coming back to **Brenda Cain,** 1211 Montana Ave. (☎ **310/395-1559**), for platinum rings, bracelets, earrings, and brooches from the 1920s, while clotheshorses shop for designer wear at minimalist **Savannah,** 706 Montana Ave. (☎ **310/458-2095**); ultrahip **Jill Roberts,** 920 Montana Ave. (☎ **310/260-1966**); and sleekly professional **Weathervane,** 1209 Montana Ave. (☎ **310/393-5344**). Upscale moms can find tiny fashions at **Real Threads,** 1527 Montana Ave. (☎ **310/393-3175**), and kid-sized bedroom furnishings at

Little Folk Art, 1120 Montana Ave. (☎ **310/576-0909**). For more grown-up style, head to **Ponte Vecchio,** 702 Montana Ave. (☎ **310/394-0989**), which sells Italian hand-painted dishes and urns, or to **Cinzia,** 1129 Montana Ave. (☎ **310/393-7751**), which features a smattering of both Tuscan and English home accessories. The stylish choice for lunch is **Wolfgang Puck Cafe,** 1323 Montana Ave. (☎ **310/393-0290**).

Third Street Promenade. 3rd St. from Broadway to Wilshire Blvd., Santa Monica.

Packed with chain stores and boutiques as well as dozens of restaurants and a large movie theater, Santa Monica's pedestrians-only section of 3rd Street is one of the most popular shopping areas in the city. The Promenade bustles on into the evening with a seemingly endless assortment of street performers and shoppers. Stores stay open late (often till 1 or 2am on the weekends) for the moviegoing crowds. There's plenty of metered parking in structures on the adjacent streets, so bring lots of quarters!

Highlights include **Hennessey & Ingalls,** a bookstore devoted to art and architecture; **Midnight Special Bookstore,** a medium-size general bookshop known for its good small-press selection and regular poetry readings; **Na Na,** 1245 Third Street Promenade (☎ **310/394-9690**), a punk clothing store featuring clunky shoes and baggy streetwear; and **Puzzle Zoo,** 1413 Third Street Promenade (☎ **310/393-9201**), where you'll find the double-sided World's Most Difficult Puzzle, the Puzzle in a Bottle, and many other brain-teasing challenges. Puzzle Zoo was voted "Best in L.A." by *Los Angeles* magazine. Music lovers can get CDs and vinyl at **Hear Music** and **Pyramid Music** and can check out the rock-and-roll collectibles at **Mayhem.**

L.A.'S WESTSIDE & BEVERLY HILLS

La Brea Avenue. North of Wilshire Blvd.

This is L.A.'s artsiest shopping strip. La Brea is anchored by the giant **American Rag, Cie.** alterna-complex, and it is also home to lots of great urban antiques stores dealing in deco, arts and crafts, 1950s modern, and the like. You'll also find vintage clothiers, furniture galleries, and other warehouse-size stores, as well as some of the city's hippest restaurants, such as Campanile (see chapter 4 for a compete listing).

Bargain hunters find flea-market furnishings at **Nick Metropolis,** 100 S. La Brea Ave. (☎ **323/934-3700**), while more upscale seekers of home decor head to **Mortise & Tenon,** 446 S. La Brea Ave. (☎ **323/937-7654**), where hand-crafted heavy wood pieces sit next to overstuffed velvet-upholstered sofas and even vintage steel desks. The best place for a snack is Nancy Silverton's **La Brea Bakery,** 624 S. La Brea Ave. (☎ **323/939-6813**), which foodies know from gourmet markets and the attached Campanile restaurant. Although the art of millinery often seems to have gone the way of white afternoon gloves for ladies, inventive ✪ **Drea Kadilak,** 463 S. La Brea Ave. (at 6th St.; ☎ **323/931-2051**), charms us with her tiny, reasonably priced hat shop. Drea designs in straw, cotton duck, wool felt, and a number of more unusual fabrics. She does her own blocking, cheerfully takes measurements for custom ladies' headwear, and gives away signature hatboxes with your purchase.

Stuffed to the rafters with hardware and fixtures of the past 100 years, **Liz's Antique Hardware,** 453 S. La Brea Ave. (☎ **323/939-4403;** www.lizshardware.com), thoughtfully keeps a canister of wet wipes at the register—believe me, you'll need one after sifting through bags and crates of doorknobs, latches, finials, and any other home hardware you can imagine needing. Perfect sets of Bakelite drawer pulls and antique ceramic bathroom fixtures are some of the more intriguing items. Be prepared to browse for hours, whether you're redecorating or not! **The Swell Store,** 126 N. La Brea Ave. (☎ **323/937-2096**), might be single-handedly responsible for bringing back Hush Puppies; it stocks every configuration and shade of these newly hip-again suede retro loafers. There's also a respectable collection of coordinatingly trendy clothing for men and women. Hipsters also head up the street to **Yellowstone** for vintage duds, and souvenir seekers know to visit **Moletown** for studio merchandise featuring logo graphics from the hottest new movies.

Rodeo Drive and Beverly Hills' Golden Triangle. Between Santa Monica Blvd., Wilshire Blvd., and Crescent Dr., Beverly Hills.

Everyone knows about Rodeo Drive, the city's most famous shopping street. Couture shops from high fashion's Old Guard are located along these 3 hallowed blocks, along with plenty of newer high-end labels. And there are two examples of the Beverly Hills version of minimalls, albeit more insular and attractive—the **Rodeo Collection,** 421 N. Rodeo Dr.; and **Two Rodeo,** at Wilshire Boulevard. The 16-square-block area surrounding Rodeo Drive is known as the "Golden Triangle." Shops off Rodeo are generally not as name-conscious as those on the strip (you might actually be able to buy something!), but they're nevertheless plenty upscale. Little Santa Monica Boulevard has a particularly colorful line of specialty stores, and Brighton Way is as young and hip as relatively staid Beverly Hills gets.

The big names to look for here are **Giorgio Beverly Hills,** 327 N. Rodeo Dr. (☎ **800/GIORGIO** or 310/274-0200); **Gucci,** 347 N. Rodeo Dr. (☎ **310/278-3451**); **Hermès,** 343 N. Rodeo Dr. (☎ **310/278-6440**); **Louis Vuitton,** 307 N. Rodeo Dr. (☎ **310/859-0457**); **Polo/Ralph Lauren,** 444 N. Rodeo Dr. (☎ **310/281-7200**); and **Tiffany & Co.,** 210 N. Rodeo Dr. (☎ **310/273-8880**). The newest arrival is **Tommy Hilfiger,** 468 N. Rodeo Dr. (☎ **310/888-0132**). **Niketown,** corner of Wilshire Boulevard and Rodeo Drive (☎ **310/275-9998**), is a behemoth shrine to the reigning athletic-gear king.

West Street. Between Fairfax and Robertson blvd.

You can shop till you drop on this trendy strip, anchored on the east end by the Farmers Market (see "The Top Attractions," in chapter 5). Many of Melrose Avenue's shops have relocated here, alongside some terrific up-and-comers, several cafes, and the much-lauded restaurant Locanda Veneta (see chapter 4 for a full listing). "Fun" is more the catchword here than "funky," and the shops (including the vintage clothing stores) tend a bit more to the refined than do those along Melrose. **The Cook's Library** is where the city's top chefs find both classic and deliciously offbeat cookbooks and other food-oriented tomes. Browsing is welcomed, even encouraged, with tea, tasty treats, and rocking chairs. **Traveler's Bookcase** is truly one of the best travel bookshops in the West, stocking a huge selection of guidebooks and travel literature, as well as maps and travel accessories. Nearby **Memory Lane** is filled with 1940s, 1950s, and 1960s collectibles.

There's lots more to see along this always-growing street, enough to take up several hours. Refuel at **Chado Tea Room,** 8422 W. 3rd St. (☎ **323/655-2056**), a temple for tea lovers. Chado is designed with a nod to Paris's renowned Mariage Frères tea purveyor; one wall is lined with nooks whose recognizable brown tins are filled with more than 250 different varieties of tea from around the world. Among the choices are 15 kinds of Darjeeling, Indian teas blended with rose petals, and ceremonial Chinese and Japanese blends. You can also get tea meals here, featuring delightful sandwiches and individual pots of any loose tea in the store.

HOLLYWOOD

Hollywood Boulevard. Between Gower St. and La Brea Ave.

One of Los Angeles's most famous streets is, for the most part, a sleazy strip. But along the Walk of Fame, between the T-shirt shops and greasy pizza parlors, you'll find some excellent poster shops, souvenir stores, and Hollywood-memorabilia dealers that are worth getting out of your car for—especially if there's a chance of getting your hands on that long-sought-after Ethel Merman autograph or 200 Motels poster.

Some long-standing purveyors of memorabilia include **Book City Collectibles,** which has more than 70,000 color prints of past and present stars available, along with a good selection of famous autographs. **Hollywood Book and Poster Company** has an excellent collection of movie posters (from about $15 each), particularly strong in horror and exploitation flicks. Photocopies of about 5,000 movie and television scripts are sold for $10 to $15 each, and the store also carries music posters and photos. The **Collector's Book Store** is a movie buff's dream, with enough printed memorabilia for an afternoon of browsing; vintage copies of *Photoplay* and other fan mags cost $2 to $5, and the selection of biographies is outstanding.

Larchmont Boulevard. Between Beverly Blvd. and 2nd St.

Neighbors congregate on this old-fashioned little street just east of busy Vine Avenue. As the surrounding Hancock Park homes become increasingly popular with artists and young Industry types, the shops and cafes lining Larchmont get more stylish. Sure, chains like Jamba Juice and the Coffee Bean are infiltrating this formerly mom-and-pop terrain, but plenty of unique shopping awaits amidst charming elements like diagonal parking, shady trees, and sidewalk bistro tables.

One of L.A.'s landmark independent bookstores is **Chevalier's Books,** 126 N. Larchmont Blvd. (☎ **323/465-1334**), a 60-year Larchmont tradition. Women in search of stylish comfort from only local clothing lines and designers head to **Southern Comfort,** 205 N. Larchmont Blvd. (☎ **323/469-5220**), where flowing dresses rule year-round. A fashionable antiques and home-decor store is **Hollyhock,** 214 N. Larchmont Blvd. (☎ **323/931-3400**), whose mix of genuine antiques and timeless new accessories makes for excellent browsing. If your walking shoes are letting you down, stop into **Village Footwear,** 240 N. Larchmont Blvd. (☎ **323/ 461-3619**), which specializes in comfort lines like Josef Siebel.

Melrose Avenue. Between Fairfax and La Brea aves.

It's showing some wear—some stretches have become downright ugly—but this is still one of the most exciting shopping streets in the country for cutting-edge fashions—and some eye-popping people-watching to boot. There are scores of shops selling the latest in clothes, gifts, jewelry, and accessories. Melrose is a playful stroll, dotted with plenty of hip restaurants and funky shops that are sure to shock. Where else could you find green patent-leather cowboy boots, a working 19th-century pocket watch, an inflatable girlfriend, and glow-in-the-dark condoms in the same shopping spree? From east to west, here are some highlights.

Condomania, 7306 Melrose Ave. (☎ **323/933-7865**), carries a vast selection of condoms, lubricants, and kits that creatively encourage safe sex. Curious? Check out its Web site at www. condomania.com. **Retail Slut,** 7308 Melrose Ave. (☎ **323/ 934-1339**), is a famous rock-and-roll shop carrying new clothing and accessories for men and women. The unique designs are for a select crowd (the name says it all), so don't expect to find anything for your next PTA meeting here. **Betsey Johnson Boutique** is a favorite among the young and pencil-thin; the New York–based designer has brought to L.A. her brand of fashion—trendy, cutesy, body-conscious womenswear in colorful prints and faddish fabrics. Across the street, **Off The Wall** is filled with neon-flashing, bells-and-whistles kitsch collectibles, from vintage Wurlitzer jukeboxes to life-size fiberglass cows. The L.A. branch of a Bay Area hipster hangout, **Wasteland** has an enormous steel-sculpted facade. There's a lot of leather and denim, and some classic vintage—but mostly funky 1970s garb, both vintage and contemporary. More racks of vintage treasures (and trash) are found at **Aardvark's Odd Ark,** which stocks everything, from suits and dresses to neckties, hats, handbags, and jewelry. This place also manages to anticipate some of the hottest new street fashions.

SILVER LAKE & LOS FELIZ

Located at the eastern end of Hollywood, and technically part of just plain Los Angeles, these two communities have been steadily rising on the hipness-meter. Silver Lake, named for the man-made

Silver Lake reservoir at its center, is a bohemian community of artists and ethnic families that's popular for nightclubbing and bar hopping. Los Feliz is northwest of Silver Lake, centered on Vermont and Hillhurst avenues between Sunset and Los Feliz boulevards; it's slightly tamer, and filled with 1920s and 1930s buildings. You'll find tons of unique businesses of all sorts, including artsy boutiques, music stores, and furniture dealers that have inspired some to compare the area with New York's SoHo.

Because so many alternative bands call Silver Lake home, it's not surprising to find cutting-edge music stores around every corner. A neighborhood mainstay with lots of used CDs, collectible discs, and new releases is **Rockaway Records,** 2395 Glendale Blvd. (south of Silver Lake Boulevard; ☎ **323/664-3232;** www.rockaway.com). **Destroy All Music,** 3818 Sunset Blvd. (south of Santa Monica Boulevard; ☎ **323/663-9300**), covers all punk bases, from hard-core to ska, indie, and lo-fi, while platter collectors head to the local branch of Melrose's **Vinyl Fetish,** 1750 N. Vermont Ave. (☎ **323/660-4500**), for new and used vinyl records (yes, it carries CDs, too). Vintage clothing is another big draw in these parts. The most reliable yet eclectic selections to browse through are at **Ozzie Dots,** 4637 Hollywood Blvd. (west of Hillhurst; ☎ **323/663-2867**); **Pull My Daisy,** 3908 Sunset Blvd. (at Griffith Park Boulevard; ☎ **323/663-0608**); and **Squaresville,** 1800 N. Vermont Ave. (south of Franklin; ☎ **323/669-8464**).

Hollywood set designers know to prowl the vintage furniture stores of Silver Lake: The best for midcentury gems are **Edna Hart,** 2945 Rowena Ave. (south of Hyperion; ☎ **323/661-4070**); and **Rubbish,** 1630 Silver Lake Blvd. (north of Sunset; ☎ **323/661-5575**). Plastic decorative items from the 1950s-on reign at the aptly named **Plastica,** 4685 Hollywood Blvd. (east of Vermont; ☎ **323/644-1212**). One not-to-be-missed neighborhood highlight is the wacky and eclectic **Soap Plant/Wacko/La Luz de Jesus Art Gallery,** 4633 Hollywood Blvd. (west of Hillhurst; ☎ **323/663-0122**), a three-in-one business with candles, art books, erotic toys, soap and bathing items, and a large selection of lava lamps. Local fixture **Y-Que,** 1770 N. Vermont Ave. (☎ **323/664-0021**), almost defies description, selling a variety of wacky stuff ranging from a knock-off *Austin Powers* penis pump to psychedelic lava lamps. Truly left-of-center bibliophiles head to the R-rated **Koma Bookstore,**

1764 N. Vermont Ave. (☎ **323/665-0956;** www.komabookstore. com), still called Amok by the faithful legions who come for hard-to-find volumes on Satanic rituals, radical political tracts, and lurid 1940s pulp erotica.

DOWNTOWN

Since the late, lamented grande dame department store Bullock's closed in 1993 (its deco masterpiece salons were rescued to house the Southwestern Law School's library), Downtown has become even less of a shopping destination than ever. But although many of the once-splendid streets are lined with cut-rate luggage and cheap electronics storefronts, shopping here can be a rewarding if gritty experience for the adventuresome.

Savvy Angelenos still go for bargains in the garment and fabric districts (see "Discount" under "Fashions," below); florists and bargain hunters arrive at the vast Flower Mart before dawn for the city's best selection of fresh blooms; and families of all ethnicities stroll the ✪ **Grand Central Market,** 317 S. Broadway (between 3rd and 4th streets; ☎ **213/624-2378**). Opened in 1917, this bustling market has watched the face of downtown L.A. change while changing little itself. Today, it serves Latino families, enterprising restaurateurs, and home cooks in search of unusual ingredients and bargain-priced fruits and vegetables. On weekends you'll be greeted by a lively mariachi band at the Hill Street entrance, near my favorite market feature—the fruit-juice counter, which dispenses 20 fresh varieties from wall spigots and blends up the tastiest, healthiest "shakes" in town. Farther into the market you'll find produce sellers and prepared-food counters, plus spice vendors who seem straight out of a Turkish alley, and a grain and bean seller who'll scoop out dozens of exotic rices and dried legumes.

THE SAN FERNANDO VALLEY

Studio City. Ventura Blvd. between Laurel Canyon Blvd. and Fulton Ave.

Long beloved by Valley residents, Studio City is conveniently located, freeway- and canyon-close to Hollywood and the Westside. Ventura Boulevard has a distinct personality in each of several Valley communities it passes through; Studio City is where you'll find small boutiques and antiques stores, quirky little businesses (many dating from the 1940s and 1950s), and less congested branches of popular chains like **The GAP, Pier 1**

Imports, and **Blockbuster.** Antiques hounds always check the **Cranberry House (Studio City Antique Mall),** and camera buffs stop into the full-service **Studio City Camera Exchange** for everything from film processing to camera repairs. Parking is a cinch on the street except during holiday season, when many stores team up to gaily decorate these friendly blocks and often observe extended evening hours. The 4 blocks between Laurel Canyon Boulevard and Whitsett Avenue are the most concentrated and are easily walkable in an afternoon. Start with the city's best pancakes at **Du-par's Restaurant & Bakery** (see chapter 4) and have fun!

PASADENA & ENVIRONS

Compared to L.A.'s behemoth shopping malls, the streets of pretty, compact Pasadena are a true pleasure to stroll. As a general rule, stores are open daily from about 10am, and while some close at the standard 5 or 6pm, many stay open till 8 or 9pm to accommodate the before- and after-dinner/movie crowds.

Old Pasadena. Centered around the intersection of Colorado Blvd. and Fair Oaks Ave.

In my opinion, Old Pasadena has some of the best shopping in L.A., but I hope the area retains more of the mom-and-pop businesses currently being pushed out by the likes of Banana Republic and Crate & Barrel. As you move eastward, the mix begins to include more eclectic shops and galleries commingling with dusty, pre-yuppie relics.

At the contemporary crafts gallery **Del Mano,** 33 E. Colorado Blvd. (☎ **626/793-6648**), it's a whole lot of fun to see the creations—some whimsical, some exquisite—of American artists working with glass, wood, ceramics, or jewelry. Across the street, **Penny Lane,** 12 W. Colorado Blvd. (☎ **626/564-0161**), carries new and used CDs, plus a great selection of music magazines and kitschy postcards. The stock is less picked-over here than at many record stores in Hollywood. Travelers always seem to find something they need at **Distant Lands Bookstore and Outfitters,** a duo of related stores. The bookstore has a terrific selection of maps, guides, and travel-related literature, while the recently opened outfitter two doors away offers everything from luggage and pith helmets to space-saving and convenient travel accessories. An Old Town mainstay is **Rebecca's Dream,** 16 S. Fair Oaks Ave. (☎ **626/796-1200**), where both men and women can find vintage clothing treasures. The store is small and meticulously organized (by color scheme); be sure to look up at the vintage hats adorning the walls.

OTHER PASADENA SHOPPING

In addition to Old Town Pasadena, there are numerous good hunting grounds in the surrounding area. Antique hounds might want to head to the **Green Street Antique Row,** 985–1005 E. Green St., east of Lake Avenue; or the **Pasadena Antique Center,** on South Fair Oaks Boulevard south of Del Mar. Each has a rich concentration of collectibles that can captivate for hours.

You never know what you'll find at the **Rose Bowl Flea Market,** at the Rose Bowl, 991 Rosemont Ave., Pasadena (☎ **626/577-3100;** www.rgcshows.com/rosebowl.asp). The horseshoe-shaped Rose Bowl, built in 1922, is one of the world's most famous football stadiums, home to UCLA's Bruins, the annual Rose Bowl Game, and an occasional Super Bowl. California's largest monthly swap meet, held here on the second Sunday of every month from 9am to 3pm, is a favorite of Los Angeles antiques hounds (who know to arrive as early as 6am for the best finds). Antique furnishings, clothing, jewelry, and other collectibles are assembled in the parking area to the left of the entrance, while the rest of the flea market surrounds the exterior of the Bowl. Expect everything from used surfboards and car stereos to one-of-a-kind lawn statuary and bargain athletic shoes. Admission is $5 after 9am (early-bird admission $10 to $15).

Anglophiles will delight in **Rose Tree Cottage,** 824 E. California Blvd., just west of Lake Avenue (☎ **818/793-3337;** www.rosetreecottage.com), and its charming array of all things British. This cluster of historic Tudor cottages surrounded by traditional English gardens holds three gift shops and a tearoom, where a superb $19.50 high tea is served thrice daily among the knickknacks (and supervised by the resident cat, Miss Moffett). In addition to imported teas, linens, and silver trinkets, Rose Tree Cottage sells homemade English delicacies like steak and kidney pies, hot cross buns, and shortbread. It's also the local representative of the British Tourist Authority and offers a comprehensive array of travel publications.

2 Shopping Malls

SANTA MONICA & THE BEACHES

Santa Monica Place. Colorado Ave. (at 2nd St.), Santa Monica. ☎ **310/394-5451.** www.smweb.com/smplace.htm.

About 140 shops occupy these three bright stories, anchored by **Robinson's/May** and **Macy's** department stores. The usual mall shops are augmented by more unusual finds like a branch of **Frederick's of Hollywood** and KCET Public Television's **Store of Knowledge,** which offers lots of thought-provoking and fun stuff for kids. The mall's food pavilion sells an array of fast foods, and it includes several health-oriented eateries.

L.A.'S WESTSIDE & BEVERLY HILLS

The Beverly Center. 8500 Beverly Blvd. (at La Cienega Blvd.). ☎ **310/854-0070.**

When the Beverly Center opened on L.A.'s Westside, there was more than a bit of concern about the impending "mallification" of Los Angeles. Loved for its convenience and disdained for its penitentiary-style architecture (and the "no validations" parking fee), Beverly Center contains about 170 standard mall shops (leaning toward the high end); it's anchored on each side by **Macy's** and **Bloomingdale's** department stores. You can see it blocks away, looking like a gigantic angular boulder with the **Hard Rock Cafe's** roof-mounted Cadillac on one corner.

Century City Marketplace. 10250 Santa Monica Blvd., Century City. ☎ **310/277-3898.**

This open-air mall, anchored by **Macy's** and **Bloomingdale's,** is located on what was once a Twentieth-Century Fox back lot, just west of Beverly Hills. Most of the dozens of smaller shops here are upscale chain-store fare. Among the offerings are the **Pottery Barn, Ann Taylor, Joan & David,** and **Brentano's,** as well as a giant **Crate & Barrel** and a multiplex with about a hundred (well, not quite) movie screens. If you have to "mall it" in the L.A. area, this is the most pleasant place to do it.

Pacific Design Center. 8687 Melrose Ave., West Hollywood. ☎ **310/657-0800.** www.pacificdesigncenter.com.

Something of an architectural and cultural landmark, the Pacific Design Center is the West Coast's largest facility for interior design goods and fine furnishings. It houses 200 showrooms filled with furniture, fabrics, flooring, wallcoverings, kitchen and bath fixtures, lighting, art, and accessories. Locals refer to the PDC as the "Blue Whale" in reference to its exterior, composed entirely of brilliant blue glass. Technically, businesses here sell to the trade only, and their wholesale prices reflect that; for a small fee, however, the center will provide a decorator-for-the-day to serve as official broker for your purchase.

THE SAN FERNANDO VALLEY

Universal CityWalk. Universal Center Dr., Universal City. ☎ **818/622-4455.**

Designed to resemble an almost-cartoonish depiction of an urban street, Universal CityWalk gets mention here because it's so utterly unique. Situated next door to Universal Studios—in fact, you're forced to walk through if you use Universal City's main parking structure—CityWalk is dominated by brightly colored, outrageously surreal oversize storefronts. The heavily touristed faux street is home to an inordinate number of restaurants, including **B.B. King's Blues Club,** the newest **Hard Rock Cafe,** and a branch of the **Hollywood Athletic Club** featuring a restaurant and pool hall. It's been called the commercial equivalent to the gated community, a place where the fear-driven middle class can shop and dine in sanitized safety. In terms of shopping, CityWalk is not worth a special visit; but kids will love the noisy carnival atmosphere and the **Warner Brothers** store. You can get an online preview at **www.mca.com/citywalk**.

3 Shopping A to Z

ANTIQUES

The Antique Guild. 3225–31 Helms Ave. (at Venice Blvd.), near Culver City. ☎ **310/838-3131.**

Billing itself as "the world's largest antique outlet," the Guild is a veritable warehouse of history, with more than 2 acres of antiques displayed in the former Helms Bakery headquarters. Its buyers regularly purchase entire contents of European castles, beer halls, estates, and mansions. Look for everything from old armoires to chandeliers to stained glass, crystal, china, clocks, washstands, tables, mirrors, and much more.

Arte de Mexico. 5356 Riverton Ave., North Hollywood. ☎ **818/769-5090.**

Seven warehouses full of carved furniture and wrought iron once sold only to moviemakers and restaurants are now available to the public. This is one of the most fascinating places in North Hollywood.

The Cranberry House (Studio City Antique Mall). 12318 Ventura Blvd. (2 blocks east of Whitsett), Studio City. ☎ **818/506-8945.**

Several storefront windows under a berry-colored awning hint at the treasures within this antiques and collectibles store featuring more than 100 different sellers. Be sure to haggle . . . even front-desk staff are often authorized by the individual dealers to strike a bargain.

Memory Lane. 8387 3rd St. (at Orlando), Los Angeles. ☎ **323/655-4571.**

This narrow shop filled with 1940s, 1950s, and 1960s collectibles features such treasures as Formica dinette sets, Bakelite radios, cocktail shakers and sets, unusual lamps, and a few well-chosen coats, dresses, and accessories.

Off The Wall. 7325 Melrose Ave., Los Angeles. ☎ **323/930-1185.**

This collection of oversized antiques includes kitschy statues, deco furnishings, carved wall reliefs, Wurlitzer jukeboxes, giant restaurant and gas-station signs, pinball machines, and lots and lots of neon.

✪ **Piccolo Pete's Art Deco.** 13814 Ventura Blvd. (west of Woodman Ave.), Sherman Oaks. ☎ **818/907-9060.** www.piccolopetes.com.

This lovely shop sells art nouveau, deco, and Moderne furnishings and art, including clocks, lighting fixtures, pottery, and dinnerware. A recent museum exhibition on art deco wasn't even as nice as the perfect specimens in Piccolo Pete's—but expect the prices to reflect that iperfection.

ART

Bergamot Station. 2525 Michigan Ave. (east of Cloverfield Blvd.), Santa Monica. ☎ **310/829-5854.**

Once a station for the Red Car trolley line, this industrial space is now home to the **Santa Monica Museum of Art,** plus two dozen art galleries, a cafe, a bookstore, and offices. Most of the galleries are closed Monday. The train yard is located at the terminus of Michigan Avenue, west of Cloverfield Boulevard.

Exhibits change often and vary widely, ranging from a Julius Shulman black-and-white photo retrospective of L.A.'s Case Study Houses, to a provocative exhibit of Vietnam War propaganda posters from the United States and Vietnam, to whimsical furniture constructed entirely of corrugated cardboard. A sampling of offerings includes the **Gallery of Functional Art** (☎ 310/829-6990), which features one-of-a-kind and limited-edition furniture, lighting, bathroom fixtures, and other functional art pieces, as well as smaller items like jewelry, flatware, ceramics, and glass. **The Rosamund Felson Gallery** (☎ 310/828-8488) is well known for showcasing L.A.-based contemporary artists; this is a good place to get a taste of current trends. **Track 16 Gallery** (☎ 310/264-4678) has exhibitions that range from pop art to avant-garde inventiveness—try to see what's going on here.

Every Picture Tells a Story. 7525 Beverly Blvd. (between Fairfax and La Brea aves.), Los Angeles. ☎ **323/932-6070.**

This gallery, devoted to the art of children's literature, is frequented by young-at-heart art aficionados as well as parents introducing their kids to the concept of an art gallery. Works by Maurice Sendak (*Where the Wild Things Are*), Tim Burton (*The Nightmare Before Christmas*), and original lithos of *Curious George* and *Charlotte's Web,* are featured. Call to see what's going on; the store usually combines exhibitions of illustrators with story readings and interactive workshops.

PaceWildenstein. 9540 Wilshire Blvd., Beverly Hills. ☎ **310/205-5522.** www.pacewildenstein.com/la.html.

This stark, modern space showcases blue-chip art by international stars such Claes Oldenburg and legends like Picasso and Noguchi. PaceWildenstein draws art-minded members of L.A.'s entertainment elite, such as Steve Martin and David Geffen.

BOOKS

Barnes & Noble Booksellers. 10850 W. Pico Blvd. (Westside Pavilion), Los Angeles. ☎ **310/475-4144.**

This national chain is represented throughout the city. B&N offers discounts on best-sellers and also comfy chairs to shoppers who like to read a bit before they buy. The Westwood branch is one of their larger stores and is conveniently attached to the vast Westside Pavilion shopping mall; there's plenty of free parking downstairs.

You'll also find branches in Santa Monica (1201 Third Street Promenade; ☎ 310/260-9110) and Pasadena (111 W. Colorado Blvd.; ☎ 626/585-0362).

✪ **Book Soup.** 8818 Sunset Blvd., West Hollywood. ☎ **310/659-3110.** www.booksoup.com.

This has long been one of L.A.'s most celebrated bookshops, selling both mainstream and small-press books and hosting regular book signings and author nights. Book Soup is a great browsing shop; it has a large selection of show-biz books and an extensive outdoor news and magazine stand on one side. The owners recently annexed an adjacent cafe space so they can better cater to hungry intellectuals. The **Book Soup Bistro** has an appealing bar, a charming outdoor patio, and a classical bistro menu.

Borders Books & Music. 1360 Westwood Blvd., Westwood. ☎ **310/ 475-3444.** Also at 330 S. La Cienega Blvd. (at 3rd St.), Los Angeles. ☎ **310/ 659-4045.**

Borders offers convenient one-stop shopping for books, CDs, greeting cards, and even cappuccino. The La Cienega branch is a block away from the Beverly Center; the Westwood branch is favored by students from nearby UCLA.

C.G. Jung Bookstore & Library. 10349 W. Pico Blvd. (east of Beverly Glen Blvd.), Los Angeles. ☎ **310/556-1196.**

This bookshop specializes in analytical psychology, folklore, fairy tales, alchemy, dream studies, myths, symbolism, and other related topics. Tapes and videocassettes are also sold.

The Cook's Library. 8373 W. 3rd St. ☎ **323/655-3141.** www. cookslibrary.com.

There's a specialty bookshop for everyone in L.A.; this is where the city's top chefs find both classic and deliciously offbeat cookbooks and other food-oriented tomes. Browsing is welcomed, even encouraged, with tea, tasty treats, and rocking chairs.

Dutton's Brentwood Books. 11975 San Vicente Blvd. (west of Montana Ave.), Los Angeles. ☎ **310/476-6263.** www.duttonsbrentwood.com.

This huge bookshop is well known not only for an extensive selection of new books, but also for its good children's section and an eclectic collection of used and rare books. There are more than 120,000 titles in stock at any one time. Dutton's hosts regular author readings and signings, and sells cards, stationery, prints, CDs, and select software.

Hennessey & Ingalls. 1254 Third Street Promenade, Santa Monica. ☎ **310/ 458-9074.** www.hennesseyingalls.com.

This bookstore is devoted to art and architecture, from magnificent coffee-table photography books to graphic arts titles and obscure biographies of artists and art movements.

Los Angeles Audubon Society Bookstore. 7377 Santa Monica Blvd., West Hollywood. ☎ **323/876-0202.** www.LAAudubon.org.

A terrific selection of books on nature, adventure travel, and ecology is augmented by bird-watching equipment and accessories. Phone for information on L.A. nature walks. Closed Monday.

Midnight Special Bookstore. 1318 Third Street Promenade, Santa Monica. ☎ **310/393-2923.** www.msbooks.com.

This medium-size general bookshop, located on the Third Street Promenade, is known for its good small-press selection and regular poetry readings.

Mysterious Bookshop. 8763 Beverly Blvd. (between Robertson and San Vicente blvd.), West Hollywood. ☎ **310/659-2959.** www.mysteriousbookshop.com.

More than 20,000 used, rare, and out-of-print titles make this the area's best mystery, espionage, detective, and thriller bookshop. Author appearances and other special events are hosted regularly.

Samuel French Book Store. 7623 Sunset Blvd. (between Fairfax and La Brea aves.), Hollywood. ☎ **323/876-0570.** www.samuelfrench.com.

This is L.A.'s biggest theater and movie bookstore. Plays, screenplays, and film books are all sold here, as well as scripts for Broadway and Hollywood blockbusters. Also in Studio City at 11963 Ventura Blvd. (☎ **818/762-0535**).

Traveler's Bookcase. 8375 W. 3rd St. ☎ **323/655-0575.** www.travelbooks.com.

This store, one of the best travel bookshops in the West, stocks a huge selection of guidebooks and travel literature, as well as maps and travel accessories. A quarterly newsletter chronicles the travel adventures of the genial owners, who know firsthand the most helpful items to carry. Look for regular readings by well-known travel writers.

CAMERA EQUIPMENT & REPAIR

Studio City Camera Exchange. 12174 Ventura Blvd. (1 block west of Laurel Canyon Blvd.), Studio City. ☎ **818/762-4749.** www.studiocitycamera.com.

There's comfort in the 1940s architecture of this corner photography store. Studio City Camera is there if you need film, developing, batteries, frames or albums, and used cameras (some quite collectible). You're also welcome to stop just to talk shop with fellow shutterbugs behind the counter.

CDS & MUSIC

Hear Music. 1429 Third Street Promenade, Santa Monica. ☎ **310/319-9527.**

At the first L.A. branch of Boston's Hear Music chain, albums are grouped by genre, theme, and mood. Headphones are everywhere, so you can test a brand-new disc before you buy.

Pyramid Music. 1340 Third Street Promenade, Santa Monica. ☎ **310/393-5877.**

Seemingly endless bins of used compact discs and cassette tapes line the walls of this long, narrow shop on the Promenade. LPs, posters, cards, buttons, and accessories are also available.

L.A.'s Westside & Beverly Hills

✪ **Rhino Records.** 1720 Westwood Blvd., Westwood. ☎ **310/474-8685.** www.rhinowestwood.com.

This is L.A.'s premier alternative shop, specializing in new artists and independent-label releases. In addition to new releases, there's also a terrific used selection; music-industry types come here to trade in the records they don't want for the records they do, so you'll be able to find never-played promotional copies of brand-new releases at half the retail price. You'll also find the definitive collection of records on the Rhino label.

Tower Records. 8811 W. Sunset Blvd., Hollywood. ☎ **310/657-7300.** www.towerrecords.com.

Tower insists that it has L.A.'s largest selection of compact discs—more than 125,000 titles—despite the Virgin Megastore's contrary claim. Even if Virgin has more, Tower's collection tends to be more interesting and browser friendly. And the enormous shop's blues, jazz, and classical selections are definitely better than the competition's. Open 365 days a year.

Virgin Megastore. 8000 Sunset Blvd., Hollywood. ☎ **323/650-8666.**

Some 100 CD "listening posts" and an in-store "radio station" make this megastore a music lover's paradise. Virgin claims to stock 150,000 titles, including an extensive collection of hard-to-find artists.

FASHIONS
For Men & Women

American Rag, Cie. 150 S. La Brea Ave., Los Angeles. ☎ **323/935-3157.**

First to draw shoppers back to industrial La Brea back in the early 1980s, American Rag has grown from a small vintage clothing store to include trendy new fashions on its own label, as well as adjacent boutiques selling shoes and children's clothes; there's even a kitchen and housewares shop with a small cafe in back. Once a best-kept secret of hip teenagers, the American Rag dynasty today draws more tourists than trendsetters.

Maxfield. 8825 Melrose Ave., West Hollywood. ☎ **310/274-8800.**

Here you'll find some of L.A.'s best-quality avant-garde designs, including men's and women's fashions by Yamamoto, Comme des Garçons, Dolce & Gabbana, Jil Sander, and the like. Furniture and home accessories are also sold. The store's provocative window displays have ranged from sharp political statements to a Jerry Garcia tribute.

For Women

Betsey Johnson Boutique. 7311 Melrose Ave., Los Angeles. ☎ **323/931-4490.** www.betseyjohnson.com.

The New York–based designer has brought to L.A. her brand of fashion—trendy, cutesy, body-conscious womenswear in colorful prints and faddish fabrics. Also in Santa Monica at 2929 Main St. (☎ **310/452-7911**).

CP Shades. 2925 Main St., Santa Monica. ☎ **310/392-0949.**

CP Shades is a San Francisco ladies' clothier whose line is carried by many department stores and boutiques. Fans will love this store, devoted solely to loose, casual cotton and linen separates. CP Shades's trademark monochromatic neutrals are meticulously arranged within an airy, well-lit interior. There's also a boutique in Pasadena, 20 S. Raymond Ave. (☎ **626/564-9304**).

Polkadots & Moonbeams. 8367 and 8381 W. 3rd St. ☎ **323/651-1746.**

This is actually two stores several doors apart, one carrying (slightly overpriced) hip young fashions for women, the other a vintage store with clothing, accessories, and fabrics from the 1920s to the 1960s, all in remarkable condition.

Studio Wardrobe/Reel Clothes. 12132 Ventura Blvd., Studio City. ☎ **818/508-7762.** www.reelclothes.com.

You may recognize some of the clothes here from movies and TV shows; most of the items were worn by stars or extras before being turned over for public sale. Prices range from $10 to $1,000. New shipments arrive every few days.

Discount

Loehmann's. 333 S. La Cienega Blvd. (south of 3rd St.), Los Angeles. ☎ **310/659-0674.**

Loehmann's is huge, and packed to the rafters with clothes, shoes, and accessories. Most of its stock is name-brand and designer labels, though nothing ultratrendy is represented. The store is popular for business attire, conservative leisure wear, and bargains on fancy dresswear. Known for years as a women's enclave, Loehmann's recently opened a men's department offering the same great deals. Serious shoppers should check out the Back Room, where heavyweight designers like Donna Karan and Calvin Klein are represented alongside beaded and formal evening gowns.

Los Angeles downtown garment district. Los Angeles St. between 7th St. and Washington Blvd.

Reminiscent of the New York garment district, but not quite as frenetic, L.A.'s downtown has dozens of small shops selling designer and name-brand apparel at heavily discounted prices. A concentration of retail womenswear bargains—many by name-brand designers—can be found at the Cooper Building, 860 S. Los Angeles St. at 9th (☎ **213/622-1139**). Men should have some luck along the upper blocks of Los Angeles Street, where mostly business attire is displayed, with deep discounts on Hugo Boss, Armani, and other current suits (mainly Italian), plus similar savings on sportcoats and shirts. Ties and vests are usually less stylish.

Vintage

Aardvark's Odd Ark. 85 Market St. (corner of Pacific Ave.), Venice. ☎ **310/392-2996.**

This large storefront near the Venice Beach Walk is crammed with racks of antique and used clothes from the 1960s, 1970s, and 1980s. It stocks vintage everything, from suits and dresses to neckties, hats, handbags, and jewelry—and it manages to anticipate some of the hottest new street fashions. There's another Aardvark's at 7579 Melrose Ave. (☎ **323/655-6769**).

Golyester. 136 S. La Brea Ave., Los Angeles. ☎ **323/931-1339.**

Before she opened this ladies' boutique, the owner's friends would take one look at her collection of vintage fabrics and clothes and gasp "Golly, Esther!"—hence the whimsical name. You pay a little extra for the pristine condition of hard-to-find garments like unusual embroidered sweaters from the 1940s and 1950s, Joan Crawford–style suits from the 1940s, and vintage lingerie.

Yellowstone Clothing Co. 712 N. La Brea Ave. (at Melrose Ave.), Los Angeles. ☎ 323/931-6616.

This Santa Barbara–based vintage clothing shop provides plaid Pendleton shirts and flowered 1950s sundresses to followers of grunge style, but the best stuff here isn't for sale. The owner's collections of aloha shirts, novelty neckties, and other memorabilia are proudly displayed in cases and on walls; they're the real reason I shop here.

Wasteland. 7428 Melrose Ave., Los Angeles. ☎ **323/653-3028.** www.thewasteland.com.

An enormous steel-sculpted facade fronts this L.A. branch of the Berkeley/Haight-Ashbury hipster hangout, which sells vintage and contemporary clothes for men and women. You'll find lots of leathers and denim as well as some classic vintage, but mostly funky 1970s garb. This ultratrendy store is packed with flamboyantly colorful polyester halters and bell-bottoms from the decade we'd rather forget.

Playclothes. 11422 Moorpark St. (1 block west of Laurel Canyon Ave.), Studio City. ☎ **818/755-9559.**

Men and women alike will thrill to the pristine selection of vintage clothes housed in this boutique, tucked into a burgeoning antiques row west of Coldwater Canyon Avenue. Playclothes approaches its stock with a sense of humor and knows exactly how each item was worn and accessorized in its heyday.

MEMORABILIA

Mayhem. 1411 Third Street Promenade, Santa Monica. ☎ **310/451-7600.**

This shop sells autographed guitars and other music memorabilia from U2, Nirvana, Springsteen, Bon Jovi, Pearl Jam, and other rockers. The buyers are often collectors, including the owners of the Hard Rock Cafes.

Book City Collectibles. 6631 Hollywood Blvd., Hollywood. ☎ **323/466-0120.**

More than 70,000 color prints of past and present stars are available, along with a good selection of autographs from the likes of Lucille Ball ($175), Anthony Hopkins ($35), and Grace Kelly ($750).

Collector's Book Store. 6225 Hollywood Blvd., Hollywood. ☎ **323/467-3296.**

Recently relocated from cramped quarters nearby, this archive of film-related memorabilia, books, and photographs provides fascinating browsing for even the most jaded Angeleno. Vintage fan mags like *Photoplay* and *Screen Stars;* reproduction lobby cards; black-and-white 8x10s, including the classic Betty Grable pinup shot; and an eclectic array of collector's card series are just the beginning. Books here range from the sublime (a vintage copy of the 1943 John Barrymore bio *Good Night, Sweet Prince*) to the ridiculous (*Jen-X,* the biography of outgoing former Playmate Jenny McCarthy) and beyond (the encyclopedia-style *Full Frontal: Male Nudity Video Guide*).

Hollywood Book and Poster Company. 6349 Hollywood Blvd., Hollywood. ☎ **323/465-8764.**

Owner Eric Caidin's excellent collection of movie posters (from about $15 each) is particularly strong in horror and exploitation flicks. Photocopies of about 5,000 movie and television scripts are also sold for $10 to $15 each, and the store carries music posters and photos as well.

Moletown. 900 N. La Brea Ave. (at Willoughby), Los Angeles. ☎ **323/851-0111.** www.mole.com.

Every movie and TV buff will find something good in this amusement park of a store, where T-shirts, hats, key chains, mugs, jackets, and posters all carry logos and artwork from productions as diverse as *The X-Files* (TV and movie), *The Simpsons, Titanic,* and *Party of Five.* More traditional are goods with the logos of studios like MGM and Universal; my favorite is merchandise with artwork from classic TV series (*Bewitched, I Dream of Jeannie, Charlie's Angels,* and more). It's all officially manufactured by the studios, and available at each studio's individual gift shop—but Moletown is one-stop, crowd-free shopping.

TRAVEL GOODS

Also see Traveler's Bookcase under "Books," above.

California Map and Travel Center. 3211 Pico Blvd., Santa Monica. ☎ **310/829-6277.** www.mapper.com.

This store carries a good selection of domestic and international maps and travel accessories, including guides for hiking, biking, and touring. Globes and atlases are also sold. You can visit the store's Web site at www.mapper.com.

Distant Lands Bookstore and Outfitters. 54 and 62 S. Raymond Ave., Pasadena. ☎ **626/449-3220.** www.distantlands.com.

This duo of stores is a practical treasure trove for everyone from daring adventurers to armchair tourists. The bookstore has a terrific selection of maps, guides, and travel-related literature, while the travel outfitter two doors away offers everything from luggage and pith helmets to convenient, space-saving travel accessories.

7

Los Angeles After Dark

by Bryan Yates

The ***L.A. Weekly*** (www.laweekly.com), a free weekly paper available at sidewalk stands, shops, and restaurants, is the *best* place to find the most up-to-date news on what's happening in Los Angeles's playhouses, cinemas, museums, and live-music venues. The "Calendar" section of the ***Los Angeles Times*** (www.calendarlive.com) is also a good source of information on what's going on after dark.

TicketMaster (☎ **213/480-3232;** www.ticketmaster.com) and **Telecharge** (☎ **800/447-7400**) are the major charge-by-phone ticket agencies in the city, selling tickets to concerts, sporting events, plays, and special events.

A note on smoking: In 1998, California voted in a hotly contested law making smoking strictly forbidden inside all restaurants, bars, and clubs. That's the public mantra, at least; so far as we can tell, the smoke's still getting in our eyes at plenty of L.A. night spots that choose to risk (relatively minor) fines in order to attract patrons. If you get the urge to light up, just take a look around to see what the natives are doing first.

1 The Performing Arts

CLASSICAL MUSIC & OPERA

Beyond the pop realms (see below), music in Los Angeles generally falls short of that found in other cities. For the most part, Angelenos rely on visiting orchestras and companies to fulfill their classical-music appetites; scan the papers to find out who's performing while you're in the city.

The **Los Angeles Philharmonic** (☎ **213/850-2000;** www.laphil.org) isn't just the city's top symphony; it's the only major classical music company in Los Angeles. Finnish-born music director Esa-Pekka Salonen concentrates on contemporary compositions; despite complaints from traditionalists, he does an excellent job attracting younger audiences. Tickets can be hard to come by when celebrity players like Itzhak Perlman, Isaac Stern, Emanuel Ax, and Yo-Yo Ma are in town. In addition to regular performances at the **Dorothy Chandler Pavilion** in the all-purpose Music Center, 135 N. Grand Ave., downtown, the Philharmonic also plays a popular summer season at the **Hollywood Bowl** (see "Concerts Under the Stars," below).

Slowly but surely, the **L.A. Opera** (☎ 213/972-8001; www. laopera.org) is gaining both respect and popularity with inventive stagings of classic operas, usually with visiting divas. The Opera also calls the Music Center home.

The 120-voice **Los Angeles Master Chorale** (☎ 213/ 626-0624) sings a varied repertoire that includes classical and pop compositions. Concerts are usually held at the Music Center from October to June.

The **UCLA Center for the Performing Arts** (☎ 310/ 825-2101; www.performingarts.ucla.edu) has presented international-caliber music, dance, and theatrical performances of unparalleled quality for over 60 years, and it continues to be a major presence in the local and national cultural landscape. While the Center is composed of three venues, Royce, Schoenberg and Haines Halls, Royce is the Center's pride and stands as a pillar to the arts; it has even been compared to New York's Carnegie Hall. Recent standouts from the Center's busy calendar included a multimedia interpretation of *Moby-Dick* by performance artist Laurie Anderson and the White Oak Dance Project featuring Mikhail Baryshnikov.

CONCERTS UNDER THE STARS

Also see "The Live Music Scene," below.

✪ **Hollywood Bowl.** 2301 N. Highland Ave. (at Odin St.), Hollywood. ☎ 323/850-2000. www.hollywoodbowl.org.

Built in the early 1920s, the Hollywood Bowl is an elegant Greek-style natural outdoor amphitheater cradled in a small mountain canyon. This is the summer home of the Los Angeles Philharmonic Orchestra. Internationally known conductors and soloists often sit in on Tuesday and Thursday nights. Friday and Saturday concerts often feature orchestral swing or pops concerts. The summer season also includes a jazz series; past performers have included Natalie Cole, Mel Tormé, Dionne Warwick, and

Chick Corea. Other events, from Garrison Keillor programs and summer fireworks galas, to an annual Mariachi Festival, are often on the season's schedule.

To round out an evening at the Bowl, many concertgoers use the occasion to enjoy a picnic dinner and a bottle of wine—it's one of L.A.'s grandest traditions. You can prepare your own, or order a picnic basket with a choice of hot and cold dishes and a selection of wines and desserts from the theater's catering department. À la carte baskets run from $17 to $26 per person; appetizers and drinks are extra. Call ☎ **323/851-3588** the day before you go.

THEATER
MAJOR THEATERS & COMPANIES

Tickets for most plays usually cost $10 to $35, although big-name performances at the major theaters can fetch up to $75 for the best seats. **Theatre League Alliance** (☎ **213/688-2787;** www.TheatreLA.org), an association of live theaters and producers in Los Angeles (and the organization that puts on the yearly Ovation Awards, L.A.'s answer to Broadway's Tonys), offers same-day, half-price tickets via **Web Tix,** an internet only service at www.TheatreLA.org. Tickets are available Tuesday through Saturday from 4am to 6pm, and from 8pm to 11pm; purchase them online with a credit card, and they'll be waiting for you at the box office. The site features a frequently updated list of shows and availability, and you can also sign up for e-mail alerts. In town without your computer? You can log on at any public library, internet cafe, or office service store (like Kinko's).

The **Ahmanson Theater** and **Mark Taper Forum,** the city's top two playhouses and home to the Center Theater Group (www.taperahmanson.com), are both part of the all-purpose **Music Center,** 135 N. Grand Ave., downtown. The **Ahmanson Theater** (☎ **213/972-7401**) is active year-round, either with

---

Hollywood Bowl Tip

It's not widely known, but the Bowl's morning rehearsals are open to the public (and absolutely free). On Tuesday, Thursday, and Friday from 9:30am to 12:30pm, you can see the program scheduled for that evening. So grab some coffee and donuts (the concession stands aren't open) and enjoy the best seats in the house!

shows produced by the in-house Center Theater Group or with traveling Broadway productions. Each season has guaranteed a handful of high-profile shows, such as Andrew Lloyd Webber's *Phantom of the Opera.* The 1999 season opened with the only American run of Royal National Theatre's standout production of Ibsen's *Enemy of the People,* which starred Sir Ian McKellan. Ahmanson audiences also delighted to *Cinderella* by ballet impresario Matthew Bourne. The Ahmanson is so huge that you'll want seats in the front third or half of the theater.

The **Mark Taper Forum** (☎ 213/972-0700) is a more intimate, circular theater staging contemporary works by international and local playwrights. Neil Simon's humorous and poignant *The Dinner Party* and Tom Stoppard's witty and eclectic *Arcadia* are two recent productions, each ideally suited to this intimate setting. Ticket prices vary depending on the performance. *Insider tip:* Two hours prior to curtain time, the Mark Taper Forum offers specially priced $12 tickets, which must be purchased in person with cash.

Big-time traveling troupes and Broadway-bound musicals that don't go to the Ahmanson head instead for the **Shubert Theater,** in the ABC Entertainment Center, 2020 Avenue of the Stars, Century City (☎ 800/233-3123). This plush playhouse presents major musicals on the scale of *Cats, Sunset Boulevard,* and *Les Misérables.* The smash hit musical *Rent* reprised in Los Angeles at the Shubert in 1999.

Across town, the moderately sized **Geffen Playhouse,** 10886 Le Conte Ave., Westwood (☎ 310/208-5454; www.geffenplayhouse.com), presents dramatic and comedic productions by prominent and cutting-edge writers. UCLA purchased the theater—which was originally built as a Masonic temple in 1929, and later served as the Westwood Playhouse—back in 1995 with a little help from L.A.'s philanthropic entertainment mogul David Geffen. This charming playhouse is often the West Coast choice of many acclaimed off-Broadway shows, and it also attracts locally based TV and movie actors eager for the immediacy of stage work. One recent highlight featured Annette Bening in Ibsen's *Hedda Gabler.* Always audience friendly, the Playhouse prices tickets in the $25 to $38 range.

One of the most highly acclaimed professional theaters in L.A., the **Pasadena Playhouse,** 39 S. El Molino Ave., near Colorado

Boulevard, Pasadena (☎ **626/356-7529;** www.pasadenaplayhouse. org), is a registered historic landmark that has served as the training ground for many theatrical, film, and TV stars, including William Holden and Gene Hackman. Productions are staged on the main theater's elaborate Spanish Colonial revival.

For a current schedule at any of the above theaters, check the listings in *Los Angeles Magazine,* available at most area news-stands, or the "Calendar" section of the Sunday *Los Angeles Times,* or call the box offices directly at the numbers listed above.

SMALLER PLAYHOUSES AND COMPANIES

It's a little-known fact that on any given night there's more live theater to choose from in Los Angeles than in New York City, due, in part, to the surfeit of ready actors and writers just chomping at the bit to make it in Tinseltown. Many of today's familiar faces from film and TV spent plenty of time cutting their teeth on L.A.'s busy theater circuit, which is home to nearly 200 small- and medium-sized theaters and theater companies, ranging from the 'round-the-corner, neighborhood variety to high-profile, polished troupes of veteran actors. With so many options, navi-gating the scene, which is often a gamble, can be a monumental task. Your safest bet is to choose one of the theaters listed below, which have each established excellent reputations for their productions of consistently high quality; otherwise, consult the *L.A. Weekly,* which advertises most current productions, or call **Theatre LA** (☎ **213/614-0556**) for up-to-date performance listings.

The **Colony Studio Theater,** 1944 Riverside Dr., Silver Lake (☎ **323/665-3011;** www.colonytheatre.org), has an excellent resident company that has played in this air-conditioned, 99-seat, converted silent-movie house for over 20 years. Recent productions include the musical *Candide* and the classic American comedy *The Front Page.* Having outgrown its current digs, the venerable company intends to relocate to a 200-seater in the 'burbs some time in 2000. Plans to nest in the space formerly occupied by Burbank Natural History Museum (we didn't even know Burbank had one!) are currently afoot.

Founded in 1965, **East-West Players,** 120 N. Judge John Aiso St., Los Angeles (☎ **323/625-7000;** www.eastwestplayers.com), is now the oldest Asian-American theater company in the United States. It's been so successful that the company moved from a

99-seat venue to the 200-seat David Henry Huang theater in downtown L.A. in March 1998. To commemorate the massacre in Tiananmen square, EWP presented the musical *Beijing Spring* in 1999.

The 24-year-old **L.A. Theatre Works** (☎ 310/827-0889) is renowned for its marriage of media and theater and has performed more than 200 plays and logged over 350 hours of on-air programming. Performances are held at the delightful Skirball Cultural Center (see "More City Sights & Attractions," in chapter 5, for a full listing), nestled in the Sepulveda Pass near the Getty Center. In the past, personalities such as Richard Dreyfuss, Julia Louis-Dreyfuss, Jason Robards, Annette Bening, and John Lithgow have given award-winning performances of plays by Arthur Miller, Neil Simon, Joyce Carol Oates, and more. For 7 years now, the group has performed simultaneously for viewing and listening audiences in its radio theater series. In 1999, L.A. Theatre Works presented Tennessee Williams's *The Glass Menagerie,* which starred John Goodman and Calista Flockhart of *Ally McBeal* fame. Tickets are usually around $34; a full performance schedule can be found online at **www.skirball.org**.

Founded in 1981, **West Coast Ensemble Theater,** 522 N. La Brea Ave., between Melrose and Beverly Boulevard, Los Angeles (☎ 323/525-0022), is a nonprofit multi-ethnic assemblage of professional actors, writers, and directors. The ensemble has collected accolades from local critics, as well as many awards for its excellent production quality. Expect to see well-written, well-directed, and socially relevant plays, performed by a talented and professional cast. Ticket prices range from $15 to $22.

2 The Live Music Scene

Los Angeles's music scene is a many-headed Hydra; a daunting and dizzying beast. But, certainly, on any given night, finding something to satisfy any musical fancy is a definite possibility, because, let's face it, this city is at the center of the entertainment industry. Every day, countless national and international acts are drawn here. From acoustic rock to jazz fusion, from Judas Priest cover bands to Latin funk, from the up-and-coming to the already gone, L.A.'s got it all.

But there's a rub. The big events are easy to find, but by the time you get to town, odds are all the good tickets will be gone.

The best advice is to plan ahead. The Internet is a great source of information; both **TicketMaster** (see above) and concert business trade publication **Pollstar** (www.pollstar.com) have Web sites that include tour itineraries of acts that are on or will be going on the road. Just start your search in advance. For a listing of smaller shows closer to the date of your arrival, remember that both the *L.A. Weekly* and the *Los Angeles Times* "Calendar" section have Web sites (see above). We also recommend logging on to **www.localmusic.com**, which provides two weeks' worth of show schedules conveniently organized by neighborhood and/or style; or try **www.gigmania.com**, where you can search by date, club, or artist, and access links to music clips and online CD stores.

LARGE CONCERTS

Mostly gone are the days of the behemoth stadium shows where artists fashion themselves beyond the reach of the audience in that "gods on Mt. Olympus" way, excepting, of course, the occasional U2 or Rolling Stones tour. Still, major national and international acts tend to be attracted to some of the city's larger venues.

Amphitheaters are the staple of national rock and pop concert tours. Los Angeles's two main warriors are the outdoor **Greek Theatre,** in Griffith Park, 2700 N. Vermont Ave., Los Angeles (☎ 323/665-1927), and the indoor **Universal Amphitheatre,** Universal City Drive, Universal City (☎ 818/777-3931), each seating about 6,000. Both are among the most accommodating and comfortable facilities for big-name acts. Nearly as beautiful as the Hollywood Bowl, the Greek books a full season of national acts, from the Goo Goo Dolls and the Brian Setzer Orchestra to John Tesh and Barry Manilow. Be advised that escaping from the show afterward can be a problem, as cars are stacked in packed lots, often making exiting a slow process.

Universal Amphitheatre has one advantage over the Greek: It has a roof, so it can book year-round. Otherwise, it's not as aesthetically pleasing, but it's quite comfortable, and none of its seats are too far from the stage. For some events, the "Party in the Pit" offers a general admission section right up next to the stage. In addition to pop stars from Celine Dion to Jane's Addiction, the Universal has also booked such theater events as *The Who's Tommy.* While the neon jungle of Universal's CityWalk doesn't appeal to everyone, it does offer plenty of pre-gig dining options.

Orange County's **Irvine Meadows Amphitheatre,** 8800 Irvine Center Dr., Laguna Hills (☎ **714/855-4515**), which holds 15,000 (including a general-admission lawn *way* in the back), hosts KROQ's often-spectacular summertime "Weenie Roast" and KIIS's "Summer Jam" each year, as well as a plethora of touring rock acts, including recent shows from Marilyn Manson and Garbage. If you're going from L.A. on a weekday, get an early start, since Irvine is located at one of the most heavily traveled freeway junctions in the country.

Another popular venue is the **Arrowhead Pond of Anaheim,** 2695 E. Katella Ave. (1 mile east of I-5), Anaheim (☎ **714/704-2400;** www.arrowheadpond.com), a combination sports/event stadium that's gaining momentum as a primary concert venue. Recent highlights at the shiny new site include heavy hitters like Ricky Martin, the Judds, and Bruce Springsteen. It's about an hour from Los Angeles via the always-crowded I-5 freeway; but convenient to Disneyland-goers (about 8 min. away).

MID-SIZED CONCERTS

House of Blues. 8430 Sunset Blvd., West Hollywood. ☎ **323/848-5100.** www.hob.com.

In spite of its frequently ridiculed, cartoonish "Country Bear Jamboree" facade, there are plenty of reasons music fans and industry types keep coming back to House of Blues. Night after night, audiences are dazzled by performances from nationally and internationally acclaimed acts as diverse as Soul Coughing, Paul Westerberg, and Randy Newman. The food in the upstairs restaurant can be great (reservations are a must), and the Sunday gospel brunch, though a bit pricey, promises a rollicking time.

✪ **The Mayan Theatre.** 1038 S. Hill St., downtown. ☎ **213/746-4287.** www.mayantheatre.com.

Perhaps the strangest, yet coolest concert venue in town, with an elaborate decor in the mode of a Mayan temple (or something), this former movie house is a fine relic of L.A.'s glorious past. It holds about 1,000 for such performers as PJ Harvey, Ani DiFranco, and Depeche Mode. The place is in a part of downtown L.A. that most people don't usually visit; but there's plenty of parking, and the interior makes it seem like another dimension.

The Palace. 1735 N. Vine St., Hollywood. ☎ **323/467-4571.** www. hollywoodpalace.com.

A classic vaudeville house, the 1,200-capacity theater, just across Vine from the famed Capitol Records tower, has been the site of numerous significant alternative-rock shows in the 1990s, including noteworthy appearances by Nirvana, the Smashing Pumpkins, and Squirrel Nut Zippers. But its dominance has been challenged of late by several other venues of similar size.

Veterans' Wadsworth Theatre. Veteran's Administration Grounds, Brentwood. ☎ **310/825-2101.** www.cfpa.ucla.edu.

Operated by UCLA and just across the San Diego Freeway (I-405) from its campus, this 1,400-seat theater often mixes pop, folk, and world music into a schedule of classical, dance, and stage programs. A show by Joni Mitchell, Van Morrison, and Bob Dylan was one recent highlight.

✪ **Wiltern Theatre.** 3790 Wilshire Blvd., Los Angeles. ☎ **213/380-5005.**

Saved from the wrecking ball in the mid-1980s, this WPA-era art deco showcase is perhaps the most beautiful theater in town. Countless national and international acts, such as Radiohead, have played here. In addition, plenty of non–pop music events such as Penn & Teller and top ballet troupes complement the schedule.

THE CLUB SCENE

With more small clubs than you can swing a Gibson at, Los Angeles is *the* place for live music. Check the *L.A. Weekly* to see who's in town during your visit. Unless otherwise noted, listed clubs admit only patrons 21 and over.

MOSTLY ROCK

Doug Weston's Troubadour. 9081 Santa Monica Blvd., West Hollywood. ☎ **310/276-6168.** www.troubadour.com. All ages. Cover varies.

This famous West Hollywood mainstay radiates rock history— from the 1960s to the 1990s; the Troub really has seen 'em all. Audiences are consistently treated to memorable shows from the many already-established or young-and-promising acts that take the Troubadour's stage. But bring your earplugs—this beer- and sweat-soaked club likes it loud.

The Foothill Club. 1922 Cherry Ave., Signal Hill (near Long Beach). ☎ **562/494-5196**. 21 and over on weekends. Cover varies.

Although it's off the beaten path, this club, adjacent to Long Beach, is a special venue that deserves a special mention. It's been around since the beginning of time—country time, that is (Merle Haggard, Hank Williams, Sr., and Johnny Cash played here in their prime)—and still retains a bit of cowpoke flavor on Fridays and Saturdays. The ultimate show at this revamped punk and rockabilly venue is the Supersuckers and Reverend Horton Heat, who play here fairly regularly.

The Garage. 4519 Santa Monica Blvd., Silver Lake. ☎ **323/683-3447**. Cover none–$5.

This Silver Lake club sprang up from the underground and remains firmly planted therein. With a coat of well-placed paint and some colorful folk art, this, well, former garage is all spruced up. It also happens to book some of the finest names in local bands, both signed and unsigned. On Wednesdays, there's a hip-hop night with guest DJs.

✪ **Largo.** 432 N. Fairfax Ave., Los Angeles. ☎ **323/852-1073** or 323/852-1851. All ages. Cover $5–$15.

There's always an eclectic array of performances going on at this dinner and music venue, ranging from the plugged-in folk set to vibrant trip hoppers. Since 1997, pop-music archaeologist Jon Brion has been putting forth some amazing Friday-night shows, including regular appearances by the Eels and Grant Lee Buffalo—and some not-so-regular appearances by Fiona Apple and Colin Haye (from Men at Work).

✪ **LunaPark.** 665 N. Robertson Blvd., West Hollywood. ☎ **310/652-0611**. Cover none–$15.

This bilevel restaurant/performance space is one of the most unpredictable but reliable venues in town. The food here is better than it has to be, and the performances—from the likes of Ani DiFranco to international DJs, as well as comedy and cabaret shows—are always diverse.

McCabe's. 3101 Pico Blvd., Santa Monica. ☎ **310/828-4403**. www.mccabesguitar.com. All ages. Cover varies.

For 20-plus years, this 40-some-year-old guitar store has opened its backroom for some pretty memorable acoustic sets from the likes of Doc and Merle Watson, Wendy and Lisa, and Peter Case. McCabe's is intimate in the extreme; the gig would have to be in your living room to get any cozier. A guitar shop first and music venue second, McCabe's doesn't serve alcohol.

Roxy. 9009 Sunset Blvd. ☎ **310/276-2222.** Cover varies.

Veteran record producer/executive Lou Adler opened this Sunset Strip club in the mid-1970s with concerts by Neil Young and a lengthy run of the premovie *Rocky Horror Show.* Since then, it's remained among the top showcase venues in Hollywood—although its preeminence among cozy clubs is now challenged by the revitalized Troubadour and such new entries as the House of Blues.

Spaceland at Dreams. 1717 Silver Lake Blvd., Silver Lake. ☎ **323/413-4442.** Cover varies.

The wall-to-wall mirrors and shiny brass posts decorating the interior create the feeling that, in a past life, Spaceland must've been a seedy strip joint, but the club's current personality offers something entirely different. Having hosted countless performances by cutting-edge artists, such as Pavement, Mary Lou Lord, Grant Lee Buffalo, Elliot Smith, and the Eels, this hot spot on the fringe of east Hollywood has become one of the most important clubs on the LA circuit.

✪ **Viper Room.** 8852 Sunset Blvd., West Hollywood. ☎ **310/358-1880.** www.viperroom.com. Cover varies.

This world-famous club on the Strip has been king of the hill since it was first opened by Johnny Depp and Sal Jenco back in 1993. Although morbidly curious gawkers continue to linger at the spot where River Phoenix died, it's the intensely electric and often star-filled scene inside that's truly worth the visit. Unforgettable, late-night, surprise performances from such powerhouses as Johnny Cash, Iggy Pop, Tom Petty, Nancy Sinatra, and Everclear (to name but a few on the long and impressive list) are what separate the Viper Room from the rest of the pack.

Whisky A Go Go. 8901 Sunset Blvd., West Hollywood. ☎ **310/652-4202.** www.whiskyagogo.com. All ages. Cover varies.

This legendary bilevel venue personifies L.A. rock and roll, from Jim Morrison to X to Guns N' Roses to Beck. Every trend has passed through this club, and it continues to be the most vital venue of its kind. With the hiring of an in-house booker a few years ago, the Whisky began regularly showcasing local talent on free-admission Monday nights.

BLUES AND JAZZ

Aside from the clubs listed below, there are several casual options for evenings of free jazz in interesting settings. The **Los Angeles County Museum of Art,** 5905 Wilshire Blvd., Los Angeles (☎ **323/857-6010;** www.lacma.org), hosts free year-round concerts in its open central court every Friday night from 5:30 to 8:30pm. This is a great way to listen to good music with a glass of wine on a warm Los Angeles evening. From June through September, the **Museum of Contemporary Art,** 250 S. Grand Ave., downtown (☎ **213/663-5334;** www.moca-la.org), and its sister annex **Geffen Contemporary at MOCA,** 152 N. Central Ave., downtown (in Little Tokyo; ☎ **213/663-5334;** www. moca-la.org), take turns offering free jazz concerts from 5 to 8pm every Thursday. Both the MOCA and the Geffen Contemporary pair a new wine and microbrew beer to match the flavor of each week's performer.

B. B. King's Blues Club. CityWalk, Universal City. ☎ **818/622-5464.**

Nestled away in CityWalk's brightly lit commercial plaza, this three-level club/restaurant—the ribs alone are worth the trip—hosts plenty of great local and touring national blues acts and is a testament to the establishment's venerable namesake. There's no shortage of good seating, but if you find yourself on the top two levels, it's best to grab a table adjacent to the railing to get an ideal view of the stage.

The Baked Potato. 6266¹/₂ Sunset Blvd., Hollyv:ood. ☎ **323/461-6400.** www.bakedpotatojazz.com. Cover varies.

Like its North Hollywood parent (see below), this restaurant/night spot offers missile-sized spuds while hosting a steady roster of jazz performances by local and visiting acts. Guitarist Andy Summers, formerly of the Police and later the music director for the short-lived "Dennis Miller Show," was one recent highlight.

The valley location is a few blocks from Universal City at 3787 Cahuenga Blvd., North Hollywood (☎ **818/980-1615;** www.thebakedpotato.com).

✪ **Catalina Bar & Grill.** 1640 N. Cahuenga Blvd., Hollywood. ☎ **323/466-2210.** All ages. Cover $10–$20.

This clubby old-timer represents the very best of downtown Hollywood's golden era. Though the neighborhood has become rough around the edges, this premier supper club still manages to book some of the biggest names in contemporary jazz for multinight stints. The acoustics are great, and there really are no bad seats.

Jazz Bakery. 3233 Helms Ave., Culver City. ☎ **310/271-9039.** www. jazzqwest.com/jazzbakery. All ages. Cover $10–$30.

Ruth Price's nonprofit venue is renowned for attracting some of the most important names in jazz—and for the restored Helms bakery factory that houses the club and inspires its name. Hers is a no-frills, all-about-the-music affair, and the place is pretty much BYO in the drinks department. Drummer Jimmy Cobb, the last remaining member of Miles Davis's "Kind of Blue" band, had a 4-night stint at JB recently.

Lunaria. 10351 Santa Monica Blvd., West L.A. ☎ **310/282-8870.** All ages. Cover varies.

For a delightfully civilized evening of jazz and dining, follow local sophisticates to Lunaria, which offers dining Monday through Saturday and entertainment Tuesday through Sunday. The diverse menu of performers ranges from the up-and-coming to renowned jazz masters. If you come for dinner, there's no cover charge.

The Mint. 6010 W. Pico Blvd., Los Angeles. ☎ **323/954-9630.** www. theminthollywood.com. Cover varies.

Once a shotgun shack serving fried chicken and blues in a beer-only bar, the Mint has reemerged as a gloriously lounge-y hang-out for blues devotees. The clientele—ranging from youthful scenesters to middle-aged moms—packs the place to catch regular performances by actor-turned-singer Harry Dean Stanton (that's right, Repo Man), as well as visits from such musical luminaries as Wayne Kramer.

3 Dance Clubs

There's some good news for the city's dance scene. The momentous popularity of Latin dance and swing has resulted in the opening of new clubs dedicated to both, taking some of the pressure off the old standbys. DJ club culture is also on the rise locally, featuring some pretty noteworthy shows at some enjoyable clubs; such dance clubs, however, can come and go as quickly as you can say "jungle rave." Mere whispers of a happening thing can practically relegate a club to a been-there-done-that status. Check the *L.A. Weekly* for updates on specific club information.

The Coconut Club. 9876 Wilshire Blvd., Beverly Hills. ☎ **310/285-1358.** www.merv.com/coconut/index.html. Cover $20.

Master of entertainment Merv Griffin, remembering the legendary Coconut Grove ballroom in the now-abandoned Ambassador Hotel, has lavishly re-created its classy swank with this A-list dine-and-dance club in the Beverly Hilton. It offers some of the city's very best in Latin and swing dance on Fridays and Saturdays. This is a wonderful place to bring your guy or doll to reenact the romantic splendor of Hollywood past. Entrance to Chimps Cigar Club is also included in the steep cover charge.

✪ **The Conga Room.** 5364 Wilshire Blvd., Los Angeles. ☎ **323/938-1696.** www.congaroom.com. Cover varies.

Attracting such Latin-music luminaries as Tito Puente and Pucho & The Latin Soul Brothers, this one-time Jack LaLanne health club on the Miracle Mile has quickly become *the* night spot for live salsa and merengue. Break up the evening of heart-melting, sexy Latin dancing with a trip to the dining room, where the chef serves up savory Cuban fare in a setting that conjures the romance of pre-Castro Cuba, or indulge yourself in the Conga Room's stylish cigar lounge.

The Derby. 4500 Los Feliz Blvd., Los Feliz. ☎ **323/663-8979.** www.the-derby.com. Cover $7–$10.

This class-A east Hollywood club has been at ground zero of the swing revival since the very beginning. Located at a former Brown Derby site, the club was restored to its original luster and detailed with a heavy 1940s edge. With Big Bad Voodoo Daddy as the onetime house band and regular visits from Royal Crown Revue, hep guys and dolls knew that the Derby was money even before *Swingers* transformed it into one of the city's most happenin' hangs. But if you come on the weekends, expect a wait to get in, and once you're inside, dance space is at a premium.

Love Lounge. 657 N. Robertson Blvd., West Hollywood. ☎ **310/659-0472.** Cover $10.

DJ Mike Messex's Friday-night gig, Cherry, finds him digging deep into the 1980s for loads of glam rock, New Wave, and disco, keeping the dance floor packed all evening. Promoter Bryan Rabin knows how to keep the energy level high, with selective live performances—often with a homoerotic edge—and a sultry parade of go-go boys and girls.

The Palace. 1735 N. Vine Ave., Hollywood. ☎ **323/462-3000.** www. hollywoodpalace.com. 18 and over. Cover $10–$12.

Weekend nights this Hollywood landmark music hall turns the power of its 20,000-watt sound system on the dancing set. Fridays are hosted by local KROQ alt-rock dinosaur Richard Blade for an evening of 1980s and 1990s alterna-dance tunes. Hip-hop, house, and retro are the order of the day on Saturdays, when Klub KIIS takes control of the turntables.

Sugar. 814 Broadway, Santa Monica. ☎ **310/899-1989.** Cover $10.

From Wednesday through Saturday, clubgoers pack this popular Santa Monica spot for its great dance clubs. If you're into funky house or soul lounge, try Lollipop or Chocolate on Wednesday and Thursday, respectively; hip-hop and funk are the musical fare on Friday at In the Raw; or you can escape to the world of progressive house, trance, and Euro electronica at Pure on Saturday.

4 Bars & Cocktail Lounges

Cat N' Fiddle Pub and Restaurant. 6530 W. Sunset Blvd., Hollywood. ☎ **323/468-3800.** No cover.

Nothing to be snooty about here: No A-list crowd, no red velvet ropes, no gimmicky cocktails. This is simply Hollywood's home for lovers of the basic British pub. Sit next to the fountain in the spacious courtyard while sipping tasty pints of Boddingtons, Bass, Guinness, Harp, or Newcastle; or head inside to toss some darts and plunk those extra dollars into the jukebox.

El Carmen. 8138 W. 3rd St., Los Angeles. ☎ **323/852-1552.** No cover.

Opened by LA restaurant-and-bar impresario Sean Macpherson, the man with the mescal touch, El Carmen conjures the feel of a back-alley Mexican cantina of a bygone era. Vintage Mexican movie posters, vibrant Latin American colors, and oil paintings of masked Mexican wrestlers decorate the Quonset-hut interior, while an eclectic jukebox offers an array of tunes from Tito Puente to the Foo Fighters. The busy bar boasts a gargantuan list of more than 100 tequilas and a small menu of tacos and light fare.

Good Luck Bar. 1514 Hillhurst Ave. (between Hollywood and Sunset blvds.), Los Angeles. ☎ **323/666-3524.** No cover.

Until they installed a flashing neon sign outside, only locals and hipsters knew about this Kung Fu–themed room in the Los Feliz/Silver Lake area. The dark red windowless interior boasts

Oriental ceiling tiles, fringed Chinese paper lanterns, sweet-but-deadly drinks like the "Yee Mee Loo" (translated as "blue drink"), and a jukebox with selections ranging from Thelonius Monk to Cher's "Half Breed." The spacious sitting room, furnished with mismatched sofas, armchairs, and banquettes, provides a great atmosphere for conversation or romance. Arrive early to avoid the throngs of L.A. scenesters.

Kane. 5574 Melrose Ave., Hollywood. ☎ **323/466-6263.** No cover.

The classic spirit of American lounge is the mainstay at Kane, where sounds from recent decades—ranging from Bobby Darin to the Jackson 5—are spun by a DJ flanked by a duo of go-go dancers in hot pants. Kitsch notwithstanding, owner Ivan Kane has created a warm, friendly, inviting atmosphere reminiscent of 1960s and 1970s Vegas.

⭕ **Lola's.** 945 N. Fairfax Ave. (south of Santa Monica Blvd.), Los Angeles. ☎ **213/736-5652.** No cover.

The swimming pool–sized martinis are enough of a reason to trek over to Lola's. From the classic gin or vodka martini for the purist to the chocolate- or apple-flavored concoctions for the adventurous, Lola has a little something for everyone. Two bars, a billiard table, and plush couches hidden in dark, romantic corners make for an enjoyable setting, and plenty of celeb spotting. See chapter 4 for a full restaurant listing.

Lounge 217. 217 Broadway (between Second and Third sts.), Santa Monica. ☎ **310/281-6692.** Cover varies.

A lounge in the true sense of the word, these plush art deco surroundings just scream "martini"—and the bartenders stand ready to shake or stir up your favorite. Comfortable seating lends itself well to intimate socializing, or enjoying Monday's classical guitarist, or Thursday night's torch singer and cigar bar. Come early on the weekends, when Lounge 217 hosts a more raucous late-night crowd.

Sky Bar, at Mondrian Hotel. 8440 W. Sunset Blvd., West Hollywood. ☎ **323/848-6025.**

Since its opening in hotelier Ian Schraeger's refurbished Sunset Strip hotel, Sky Bar has been a favorite among L.A.'s most fashionable of the fashionable set. This place is so hot that even the agents to the stars need agents to get in. (Rumor has it that one agent was so desperate to get in he promised one of the servers a contract.) Nevertheless, a little image consulting—affect the right look, strike the right pose, and look properly disinterested—might get you in to rub elbows with some of the faces that regularly appear on the cover of *People*. (But please don't stare.)

3 Clubs. 1123 N. Vine St., Hollywood. ☎ **323/462-6441.** No cover.

In the tradition of Hollywood hipster hangouts trying to maintain a low profile, 3 Clubs is absent of any signage indicating where you are. (Just look for the giant BARGAIN CLOWN MART sign on the facade.) Inside this dark and cavernous lounge, though, you'll find a youthful, hoping-to-become-a-star-soon set mingling into the night. Even with two rooms, plenty of cushiony sofas, two long bars, and lots of spacious tables, this place is always loud and packed.

✪ **360.** 6290 Sunset Blvd., Hollywood. ☎ **323/871-2995.** No cover.

This 19th-story, penthouse-perched restaurant and lounge is a perfect place to romance your special someone. It's all about the view here—all 360 degrees of it. The understated and softly lit sleek interior emphasizes the scene outside the plentiful windows, including a spectacular vista of the famed HOLLYWOOD sign.

Yamashiro. 1999 N. Sycamore Ave., Hollywood. ☎ **323/466-5125.**

Enjoy the view of the city from this pagoda-and-garden perch in the Hollywood Hills. Though the place has long been considered a "special occasion" Japanese restaurant, we prefer to sit in the lounge—mai-tai in hand—and watch Hollywood's dancing searchlights dot the night sky, a scene that makes up for the overpriced and mediocre food. There's no cover, but there's also no way around the $3.50 valet parking fee.

5 Comedy & Cabaret

L.A.'s comedy clubs have launched the careers of many of the comics who are now household names. In addition to the clubs below, check out the alternative-comedy featured Monday nights at **Largo** (see "Mostly Rock," above), 432 N. Fairfax Ave., Los Angeles (☎ **323/852-1073** or 323/852-1051).

The Cinegrill. 7000 Hollywood Blvd., in the Hollywood Roosevelt Hotel, Hollywood. ☎ **323/466-7000.** Cover varies.

The Cinegrill, located in one of L.A.'s most historic hotels, draws locals with a zany cabaret show and guest chanteuses ranging from Eartha Kitt to Cybill Shepherd. Some of the country's best cabaret singers pop up here regularly.

Comedy Store. 8433 Sunset Blvd., West Hollywood. ☎ **323/656-6225.** www.comedystore.com. Cover varies.

You can't go wrong here: New comics develop their material, and established ones work out their kinks, at this landmark venue owned by Mitzi Shore (Pauly's mom).

The **Best of the Comedy Store Room,** which seats 400, features professional stand-ups continuously on Friday and Saturday nights. Several comedians are always featured, each doing about a 15-minute stint. The talent here is always first-rate and includes comics who regularly appear on the *Tonight Show* and other shows.

The **Original Room** features a dozen or so comedians back-to-back nightly. Sunday night is amateur night: Anyone with enough guts can take the stage for 3 minutes, so who knows what you'll get.

✪ **Groundling Theater.** 7307 Melrose Ave., Los Angeles. ☎ **323/934-9700.** www.groundlings.com. Cover $10–$15.

L.A.'s answer to Chicago's Second City has been around for over 20 years, yet it remains the most innovative and funny group in town. The skits change every year or so; but they take new improvisational twists every night, and the satire is often savage. The Groundlings were the springboard to fame for Pee-Wee Herman, Elvira, and former *Saturday Night Live* stars Jon Lovitz, Phil Hartman, and Julia "It's Pat" Sweeney. Trust me—you haven't laughed this hard in ages. Phone for show times and reservations.

Improv. 8162 Melrose Ave., West Hollywood. ☎ **323/651-2583.** www.improvclubs.com/hollywood. Cover varies.

A showcase for top stand-ups since 1975, the Improv offers something different each night. Although it used to have a fairly active music schedule, the place is now mostly doing what it does best—showcasing comedy. Owner Budd Freedman's buddies—like Jay Leno, Billy Crystal, and Robin Williams—hone their skills here more often than you would expect. But even if the comedians on the bill the night you go are all unknowns, they won't be for long. Shows are at 8pm Sunday and Thursday, at 8:30 and 10:30pm Friday and Saturday.

6 Coffeehouses

The L.A. coffee scene is nearly as bustling as its cocktail-lounge counterpart. So if you're looking for something beyond the usual Starbucks experience, check out one of the places listed below.

Anastasia's Asylum. 1028 Wilshire Blvd., Santa Monica. ☎ **310/394-7113.**

Stop by for a cup of joe to go or stick around and while away the hours at this top-notch coffee house. Anastasia's boasts an eclectic clientele, diverse live music ranging from jazz and folk to acoustic and plugged-in rock, vintage furniture in a classy decor, constantly changing art exhibits, and a great menu, making it a favorite draw for folks from around the city.

Bourgeois Pig. 5931 Franklin Ave., Hollywood. ☎ **323/962-6366.**

With its positively gothic aversion to natural lighting (the only street-front window is covered with a blood-red tint), this dark cavern has more of a bar atmosphere than the usual coffeehouse. In fact, Bourgeois Pig is to Starbucks what Marilyn Manson is to Celine Dion. This veteran, located on a hot business strip at the Hollywood/Los Feliz border, is a favorite among youths and showbiz drones, who enjoy losing themselves on couches tucked into shadowed corners, shooting a game of pool, or perusing something from the terrific newsstand next door.

Highland Grounds. 742 N. Highland Ave., Hollywood. ☎ **323/466-1507.**

Predating the coffeehouse explosion, this comfortable, relatively unpretentious place set the L.A. standard with a vast assortment of food and drink—not just coffee—and often first-rate live music, ranging from nationally known locals, such as Victoria Williams, to open-mike Wednesdays for all-comers. The ample patio is often used for readings and record-release parties.

7 Out & About in Los Angeles

Los Angeles has a vibrant, powerful, and active gay and lesbian community. Some of Tinseltown's most celebrated names share equal prominence as both industry and gay and lesbian community leaders and have helped the city gain an outstanding reputation for its gay and AIDS-related activism. Every year in June, this active community comes out (pardon the pun) in full force for one of the city's most widely beloved events: the gay pride parade, which all but takes over West Hollywood in the spirit of activism and fun. If you're in town, this is not to be missed (see "Los Angeles Area Calendar of Events," in chapter 1).

Although **West Hollywood,** often referred to as "Boys Town," has the densest gay population in Los Angeles, there are several other noteworthy enclaves. **Silver Lake,** in particular, has a long-standing gay community that's worked quite hard to preserve the area's beautiful homes that Hollywood names like Charlie Chaplin and Cecil B. DeMille once called their own. Now, stars like Madonna, Anthony Edwards, Nicolas Cage, and Brad Pitt have places in the 'hood. To the west of WeHo, **Santa Monica** and **Venice** also enjoy a strong gay and lesbian presence. Venice, for first-timers, can be something of a shock. With its countless tattoo and piercing joints, coupled with the active parade of joggers, surfers, and Muscle Beach beefcakes, and the usual cast of beach-bound freaks, Venice is Los Angeles's equivalent to San Francisco's Haight-Ashbury.

If you're looking for specific info on gay culture in L.A., beyond what we've included, there are several options: *4-Front Magazine* (☎ 323/650-7772), *Edge Magazine* (☎ 323/962-6994), and *Frontiers* (☎ 323/848-2222). *Edge* and *Frontiers* are the most prominent free biweekly gay mags and are readily available in coffeehouses and newsstands citywide. If you're having a difficult time locating any of these magazines, give the good people at **A Different Light Bookstore,** 8853 Santa Monica, West Hollywood (☎ 310/854-6601), a call or visit for some assistance. The *L.A. Weekly* and *New Times Los Angeles* also have lesbian and gay articles and listings.

Apache Territory. 11608 Ventura Blvd., Studio City. ☎ **818/506-0404.** Cover varies.

The small dance floor fills on weekends with Valley boys bored by the snootier WeHo scene. This is a major pickup scene. It's especially popular on Thursday nights.

Club 7969. 7969 Santa Monica Blvd., West Hollywood. ☎ **323/654-0280.** Cover varies.

Fashionable of late, Club 7969 features male and female strippers baring it all while mingling with the gay, lesbian, and straight crowd. Each night has a different theme, ranging from drag burlesques to techno parties. On Tuesdays, Michelle's CC revue—with its legion of topless female dancers—attracts a largely lesbian crowd.

Cobalt Cantina. 4326 Sunset Blvd., Silver Lake. ☎ **323/953-9991.** Also at 616 N. Robertson Blvd., West Hollywood. ☎ 310/659-8691. No cover.

For years, the "Martini Lounge" located in this Silver Lake restaurant has been one of the hottest gay cocktail bars in town. Around the long bar and zinc-colored cocktail tables, gargantuan margaritas and strong martinis are sipped by the buffed-out locals. The crowd is ethnically mixed and largely gay but definitely straight-friendly. The WeHo location's "Bluebar" is a quiet alternative to the nearby wild-party–oriented clubs.

Micky's. 8857 Santa Monica Blvd., West Hollywood. ☎ **310/657-1176.** Cover varies.

A diverse, outgoing, and mostly older crowd cruises back and forth between the front-room bar and the dance floor in back. More women—probably looking to party with the friendly crowd and enjoy the great drink specials—are drawn to Micky's than to some of the neighboring bars.

The Other Side. 2538 Hyperion Ave., Silver Lake. ☎ **323/661-4233.** No cover.

This amiable place reputedly serves the best martini in Silver Lake. It's a handsome and intimate piano bar with plenty of friendly patrons, and the ideal place to meet people if you're new in town.

Rage. 8911 Santa Monica Blvd., West Hollywood. ☎ **310/652-7055.** Cover varies.

For more than 15 years this high-energy, high-attitude disco has been the preferred mainstay on WeHo's gay dance club circuit. Between turns around the dance floor, shirtless muscle boys self-consciously strut about—like peacocks flashing their plumes—looking to exchange vital statistics.

8 Movies: Play It Again, Sam

L.A. has its share of megaplexes catering to high-budget, high-profile flicks, featuring the usual big-ticket cast of Slys, Demis, and Leonardos. But there are times when those polished Hollywood-studio stories just won't do. Below are some non-mainstream options that play movies from bygone eras, or those with an artier bent. Consult the *L.A. Weekly* to see what's playing when you're in town.

Film festivals are another great way to explore the other side of contemporary movies. Aside from AFI's yearly October fete (see the "Los Angeles Area Calendar of Events," in chapter 1), the **Los Angeles Independent Film Festival** (☎ **888/ETM-TIXS;** www.laiff.com) looks at what's new in American indies, short films, and music videos during a weeklong event in April. Each July since 1982, the **Gay and Lesbian Film Festival** (☎ **323/ 960-2394;** www.outfest.com), also known as "Outfest," has aimed to bring high-quality gay, lesbian, bi, and transgender films to a wider public awareness. In 1998, the festival became Los Angeles's largest, with 31,000 audience members.

Promoting moving pictures as this country's great art form, ✪ **The American Cinematheque** (Hollywood; ☎ **323/ 466-3456;** www.egyptiantheatre.com), presents not-readily-seen videos and films, ranging from the wildly arty to the old classics. Since relocating to the historic and beautifully refurbished 1923 **Egyptian Theater** (6712 Hollywood Blvd., Hollywood), American Cinematheque has hosted several film events, including a celebration of contemporary flicks from Spain, a tribute to the femme fatales of film noir, and a retrospective of the films of William Friedkin. Events highlighting a specific individual are usually accompanied by at least one in-theatre audience Q&A session with the honoree.

The Bing Theater at the **L.A. County Museum of Art** (5905 Wilshire Blvd., Los Angeles; ☎ **323/857-6010**) presents a specially themed film series each month. Past subjects have ranged from 1930s blond bombshell films to Cold War–propaganda flicks to contemporary British satire (complete with a 3-day Monty Python's Flying Circus marathon).

Laemmle's Sunset 5 (8000 Sunset Blvd., West Hollywood; ☎ **323/848-3500**), despite being a contemporary multiplex located in a bright outdoor mall, features films that most theaters of its ilk won't even touch. This is the place to come to see interesting independent art films with something to say. There's often a selection of gay-themed movies.

The Nuart Theater (11272 Santa Monica Blvd., Los Angeles; ☎ **310/478-6379**) digs deep into its archives for some real classics, ranging from campy to cool. One recent Nuart highlight was "Francois Truffault: A Celebration," in which new 35mm prints of the French director's works were shown during a 2-week-long retrospective.

Fans of silent-movie classics might already know about the renowned **Silent Movie Theatre,** 611 N. Fairfax Ave. ($^1/_2$ block south of Melrose), near the Miracle Mile (☎ **323/655-2520** for recorded program information, 323/655-2510 for main office; www.silentmovietheatre.com). This silent movie shrine for over 60 years was itself silent following the tragic murder, in 1996, of the longtime owner. It reopened in November of 1999 to crowds eager to step inside, where Charlie Chaplin's appeal, Clara Bow's sexuality, and Edward G. Robinson's menace are once again bigger than life. Live music accompanies the silents (classic "talkies" are shown Tues nights); the theater is open Tuesday through Sunday, and tickets are $8 ($6 for kids and seniors).

If TV's more your thing, the **Museum of Radio and Television** (465 N. Beverly Drive, Beverly Hills; ☎ **310/786-1000**) celebrates this country's long relationship with the tube. The museum often features a movie of the month, and it also shows selections from past television programs. We're still hoping for a retrospective on the wonderful women of *The Avengers.*

Index

See also Accommodations and Restaurant indexes, below.

RESTAURANTS

FROMMER'S® COMPLETE TRAVEL GUIDES

Alaska
Amsterdam
Arizona
Atlanta
Australia
Austria
Bahamas
Barcelona, Madrid &
  Seville
Beijing
Belgium, Holland &
  Luxembourg
Bermuda
Boston
British Columbia & the
  Canadian Rockies
Budapest & the Best of
  Hungary
California
Canada
Cancún, Cozumel &
  the Yucatán
Cape Cod, Nantucket &
  Martha's Vineyard
Caribbean
Caribbean Cruises & Ports
  of Call
Caribbean Ports of Call
Carolinas & Georgia
Chicago
China
Colorado
Costa Rica
Denmark
Denver, Boulder & Colorado
  Springs
England
Europe

European Cruises & Ports
  of Call
Florida
France
Germany
Greece
Greek Islands
Hawaii
Hong Kong
Honolulu, Waikiki & Oahu
Ireland
Israel
Italy
Jamaica
Japan
Las Vegas
London
Los Angeles
Maryland & Delaware
Maui
Mexico
Montana & Wyoming
Montréal & Québec City
Munich & the Bavarian
  Alps
Nashville & Memphis
Nepal
New England
New Mexico
New Orleans
New York City
New Zealand
Nova Scotia, New Brunswick
  & Prince Edward Island
Oregon
Paris
Philadelphia & the
  Amish Country

Portugal
Prague & the Best of the
  Czech Republic
Provence & the Riviera
Puerto Rico
Rome
San Antonio & Austin
San Diego
San Francisco
Santa Fe, Taos & Albuquerque
Scandinavia
Scotland
Seattle & Portland
Shanghai
Singapore & Malaysia
South Africa
Southeast Asia
South Florida
South Pacific
Spain
Sweden
Switzerland
Thailand
Tokyo
Toronto
Tuscany & Umbria
USA
Utah
Vancouver & Victoria
Vermont, New Hampshire
  & Maine
Vienna & the Danube Valley
Virgin Islands
Virginia
Walt Disney World &
  Orlando
Washington, D.C.
Washington State

FROMMER'S® DOLLAR-A-DAY GUIDES

Australia from $50 a Day
California from $60 a Day
Caribbean from $70 a Day
England from $70 a Day
Europe from $70 a Day

Florida from $70 a Day
Hawaii from $70 a Day
Ireland from $60 a Day
Italy from $70 a Day
London from $85 a Day

New York from $80 a Day
Paris from $80 a Day
San Francisco from $60 a Day
Washington, D.C.,
  from $70 a Day

FROMMER'S® PORTABLE GUIDES

Acapulco, Ixtapa &
  Zihuatanejo
Alaska Cruises & Ports of Call
Bahamas
Baja & Los Cabos
Berlin
California Wine Country
Charleston & Savannah
Chicago
Dublin

Hawaii: The Big Island
Las Vegas
London
Los Angeles
Maine Coast
Maui
Miami
New Orleans
New York City
Paris

Puerto Vallarta, Manzanillo
  & Guadalajara
San Diego
San Francisco
Sydney
Tampa & St. Petersburg
Venice
Washington, D.C.

FROMMER'S® NATIONAL PARK GUIDES

Family Vacations in the
  National Parks
Grand Canyon

National Parks of the
  American West
Rocky Mountain

Yellowstone & Grand Teton
Yosemite & Sequoia/
  Kings Canyon
Zion & Bryce Canyon

FROMMER'S® MEMORABLE WALKS

Chicago
London

New York
Paris

San Francisco
Washington, D.C.

FROMMER'S® GREAT OUTDOOR GUIDES

New England
Northern California

Southern California & Baja
Southern New England

Washington & Oregon

FROMMER'S® BORN TO SHOP GUIDES

Born to Shop: France
Born to Shop: Italy

Born to Shop: London
Born to Shop: New York

Born to Shop: Paris

FROMMER'S® IRREVERENT GUIDES

Amsterdam
Boston
Chicago
Las Vegas

London
Los Angeles
Manhattan
New Orleans

Paris
San Francisco
Seattle & Portland
Vancouver

Walt Disney World
Washington, D.C.

FROMMER'S® BEST-LOVED DRIVING TOURS

America
Britain
California

Florida
France
Germany

Ireland
Italy
New England

Scotland
Spain
Western Europe

THE UNOFFICIAL GUIDES®

Bed & Breakfasts in
  California
Bed & Breakfasts in
  New England
Bed & Breakfasts in
  the Northwest
Bed & Breakfasts in
  Southeast
Beyond Disney
Branson, Missouri

California with Kids
Chicago
Cruises
Disneyland
Florida with Kids
Golf Vacations in the
  Eastern U.S.
The Great Smoky &
  Blue Ridge
  Mountains

Inside Disney
Hawaii
Las Vegas
London
Miami & the Keys
Mini Las Vegas
Mini-Mickey
New Orleans
New York City
Paris

San Francisco
Skiing in the West
Southeast with Kids
Walt Disney World
Walt Disney World
  for Grown-ups
Walt Disney World
  for Kids
Washington, D.C.

SPECIAL-INTEREST TITLES

Frommer's Britain's Best Bed & Breakfasts and
  Country Inns
Frommer's Britain's Best Bike Rides
The Civil War Trust's Official Guide
  to the Civil War Discovery Trail
Frommer's Caribbean Hideaways
Frommer's Adventure Guide to Central America
Frommer's Adventure Guide to South America
Frommer's Adventure Guide to Southeast Asia
Frommer's Food Lover's Companion to France
Frommer's Gay & Lesbian Europe
Frommer's Exploring America by RV
Hanging Out in Europe

Israel Past & Present
Mad Monks' Guide to California
Mad Monks' Guide to New York City
Frommer's The Moon
Frommer's New York City with Kids
The New York Times' Unforgettable
  Weekends
Places Rated Almanac
Retirement Places Rated
Frommer's Road Atlas Britain
Frommer's Road Atlas Europe
Frommer's Washington, D.C., with Kids
Frommer's What the Airlines Never Tell You